Mahara ePortfolios
Beginner's Guide

Create your own ePortfolio and communities of interest
within an educational and professional organization

Richard Hand

Thomas W. Bell

Derrin Kent

open source*
community experience distilled

BIRMINGHAM - MUMBAI

Mahara ePortfolios Beginner's Guide

First published: February 2010

Second Edition: July 2012

Production Reference: 1200712

Published by Packt Publishing Ltd.
Livery Place
35 Livery Street
Birmingham B3 2PB, UK.

ISBN 978-1-84951-776-8

www.packtpub.com

Cover Image by Jarosław Blaminsky (milak6@wp.pl)

Credits

Authors

Richard Hand

Thomas W. Bell

Derrin Kent

Reviewers

Dr. Glenys Gillian Bradbury

Mary Cooch

Kristina D. C. Höppner

Heinz Krettek

Allison Miller

Pete Potter

Stacey Walker

Acquisition Editor

Kartikey Pandey

Lead Technical Editor

Pramila Balan

Technical Editor

Prasad Dalvi

Project Coordinator

Leena Purkait

Proofreader

Lydia May Morris

Indexer

Monica Ajmera Mehta

Production Coordinator

Aparna Bhagat

Cover Work

Aparna Bhagat

About the Authors

Richard Hand graduated with a first class honors degree in Computer Science from the University of Bristol in 2008 and now works full time as a frontend web developer and consultant.

Richard has worked with Mahara since joining TDM (`http://tdm/info`) in 2008, being responsible for management, configuration, hosting, and training. He has also developed on a range of open source software solutions including Drupal, Joomla!, and Moodle.

Thomas W. Bell has completed higher education in Environmental Sciences and he has a passion and enthusiasm for IT. Thomas is all about getting involved with the latest tools to improve the use of resources, communication with one another, and our role in developing our earth sustainably.

Thomas follows his Environmental education with a commitment to sustainability in all walks of life, both personal and business. He is actively thinking of ways to improve processes, procedures, software and so on, to improve efficiency and therefore, sustainability.

He is currently developing efficient use of technology in the apprenticeship delivery of the Wyre Academy, including use of cutting-edge tablets, signature capture, and fully implemented cutting-edge LMS solutions.

Thomas has been working with IT company TDM - which delivers e-Learning content, codeline development, training, and bespoke corporate branding - for over two years and is directly involved in the implementation and delivery of a new IT apprenticeships scheme through the TDM Wyre Academy. See `http://opensourcesoftwareservices.com` or `http://www.wyreacademy.com`.

Thomas has been regularly training groups in Mahara ePortfolios, TotaraLMS, Joomla!, and Moodle for over two years.

Derrin Kent (www.derr.in) loves personalized learning and open source software. Derrin has been working with Mahara since its version 0. He is MD of The Development Manager Ltd. (www.TDM.co).

www.TDM.co is a company who speaks six European languages fluently and who proudly runs a range of symbiotic business operations including:

- ◆ www.OssServices.com: Professional Codeline Development, Web/Instructional Design, and Managed Services for open source softwares including Mahara and TotaraLMS
- ◆ www.WyreAcademy.com: ICT Professional Talent Management, Short Courses, and Apprenticeships—all via Blended Learning, using TotaraLMS for Apprenticeships (specialist distro) and Mahara
- ◆ www.FolioFor.Me: An online ePortfolio built upon Mahara
- ◆ www.UK-LPI.org: The Linux Professional Institute Master Affiliate for the UK and Ireland
- ◆ www.CloudNOVA.net: High availability open source software hosting

Derrin is extremely proud of his wonderful Peruvian wife, Ely, and his two bilingual kids, Salvador and Micaela.

About the Reviewers

Dr. Glenys Gillian Bradbury originally graduated in Medicine from Cambridge, and is now back in the NHS working as a Clinical Teaching Fellow after an interesting and varied career pathway involving business management, educational project management, and e-Learning. In addition to teaching medical students, Glenys is also engaged in a variety of projects to embed technology in medical education. Current projects include using Mahara to embed portfolio based learning within clinical medicine and to facilitate inter-professional learning pathways, and also a multi media project called "Tomorrow's Clinicians" to support the teaching of clinical skills. She is also an LSIS e-guide and a PRINCE2 practitioner.

She was one of the authors for the earlier edition of this book, *Mahara 1.2 ePortfolios: Beginner's Guide*.

Mary Cooch, known online as Moodlefairy, is based at the OurLearning training centre located at Our Lady's High School, Preston Lancashire, UK. A teacher for over 25 years, Mary now spends her working days travelling Europe showing educators how best to use Moodle and Mahara. She is a regular speaker at Moodle and Mahara conferences, and is keen always to be up-to-date with the latest developments. Mary works closely with Mahara partners to help promote this excellent open source e-Portfolio, while at the same time sharing good practice in her own school with teachers and students. Mary is the author of *Moodle For Teaching 7-14 Year Olds*, *Packt Publishing* and *Moodle 2 First Look*, *Packt Publishing*. She blogs on www.moodleblog.net and can be contacted for training or consultation via OurLearning on www.ourlearning.co.uk.

Kristina D.C. Höppner is from windy Wellington in New Zealand. Kristina has been working with the Mahara Development Team at Catalyst IT, the largest independent open source technology specialist in Australasia, since June 2010. She often answers questions in the Mahara community forums and supports Mahara users. Recently, she was responsible for writing the user manuals for Mahara 1.4 and 1.5 at `http://manual.mahara.org`, which are now being translated by other community members.

She is also a project manager in the Catalyst IT e-Learning Team, Facilitator for Mahara and Moodle workshops, and frequent speaker at conferences and in webinars on Mahara.

Heinz Krettek is a German teacher at a school for vocational education. He has studied business sciences and sports. His main job is to prepare socioeconomically deprived students for lifelong learning. In 2006, he discovered the portfolio work and began to translate the German langpack for Mahara. The first translations for Mahara 0.6 were published on his own Moodle site. Soon after Nigel McNie installed a git repository, the actual files were published in the Mahara git. He has just finished the translation for the Mahara 1.4 release.

He has organized several education and training sessions for teachers and was a speaker at the German Moodle Moots. He publishes postings about ePortfolios and related topics at `http://ewiesion.com`.

He lives in the Black Forest with his wife and four kids. In his spare time, Heinz prefers the three M's—Mahara, Moodle, and marathon. He finished the New York Marathon 2000. His motto is—he who finishes a marathon will overcome all problems in school ;-)

Allison Miller has been involved in education and training for more than ten years as an Educator, Change Manager, and e-Learning Leader and Innovator.

Allison also currently leads the:

- Higher Qualification Pathways for the National VET E-learning Strategy
- ePortfolios Australia Conference Organizing Committee
- `ePortfolios Australia` **Professional Network**

Allison's previous roles include:

◆ ePortfolios Business Manager, Inclusive E-learning for Youth Project Manager, and South Australian E-Learning Innovations Coordinator for the Australian Flexible Learning Framework.

◆ E-learning Development Coordinator, E-learning Mentor, and Business Services Facilitator for TAFE SA.

◆ Allison is currently in the final year of her Master of Learning and Development (Organization Capacity Development) with the University of Southern Queensland.

Allison has a lot e-Learning and e-Assessment experience and know how, especially in the areas of:

◆ ePortfolios

◆ E-assessment

◆ **Recognition of prior learning (RPL)**/skills recognition

◆ Mobile learning/devices

◆ Open educational resources/open courseware

◆ Learning analytics

Allison's other experiences include being the:

◆ Lead author of formal reports, peer reviewed papers, and magazine/journal articles

◆ Co-author of research reports, strategic documents, position papers, and responses to discussion papers

◆ Project Manager of qualitative and action research projects

◆ Facilitator of staff development projects, workshops, seminars, and action learning activities

◆ Mentor and coach in the area of e-Learning/e-Assessment

◆ Developer of online/paper-based learning resources and content

◆ Writer of numerous online educational and e-learning journals (blogs)

◆ Convenor of national and state-based conferences and events

◆ Key note, plenary, and break-out speaker at various conferences

◆ Facilitator and presenter of many workshops and presentations

◆ Chair of and representative of numerous national and international cross sectoral reference groups

Pete Potter is a Teacher, e-learning Technologist, and Mahara Moodle Consultant. He has taught Computing in Manchester (UK) and in Timaru (NZ), and worked with teachers to enhance learning in the classroom with the use of technology. A passion for ePortfolios and specifically Mahara lead to him working on the Myportfolio.school.nz Project in NZ, sharing and consulting on the smart use of ePortfolios across the South Island.

Moodle also features prominently in Pete's work as he has worked with many institutions to introduce Moodle to build and establish their Managed Learning Environment. He has presented at conferences on using both Moodle and Mahara together in the classroom to engage and empower learners.

Moving back to the UK in 2012, he is now working with the UK and Ireland's leading Moodle partner, Synergy Learning. He is still working with Moodle and Mahara in the education sector, spending time with Techies and Educators ensuring they get the most from his experience. When not doing this, Pete is fell running, swimming, or cycling, and sometimes all three.

www.PacktPub.com

Support files, eBooks, discount offers and more

You might want to visit www.PacktPub.com for support files and downloads related to your book.

Did you know that Packt offers eBook versions of every book published, with PDF and ePub files available? You can upgrade to the eBook version at www.PacktPub.com and as a print book customer, you are entitled to a discount on the eBook copy. Get in touch with us at service@packtpub.com for more details.

At www.PacktPub.com, you can also read a collection of free technical articles, sign up for a range of free newsletters and receive exclusive discounts and offers on Packt books and eBooks.

http://PacktLib.PacktPub.com

Do you need instant solutions to your IT questions? PacktLib is Packt's online digital book library. Here, you can access, read and search across Packt's entire library of books.

Why Subscribe?

- ◆ Fully searchable across every book published by Packt
- ◆ Copy and paste, print and bookmark content
- ◆ On demand and accessible via web browser

Free Access for Packt account holders

If you have an account with Packt at www.PacktPub.com, you can use this to access PacktLib today and view nine entirely free books. Simply use your login credentials for immediate access.

Table of Contents

Preface

Mahara is an ePortfolio software that allows you to quickly set up and easily manage your own rich educational or professional digital portfolio.

This book is your step-by-step guide to getting up and running with Mahara. As a new user to the Mahara platform, you will be introduced to all of the main features in detail and you can work through all of the examples at your own pace, making use of the companion Mahara site to have a go for yourself.

You will learn about all the key Mahara features that you will need to grasp in order to develop your own impressive portfolio.

Create your own content, develop a professional profile, gather your reflections in your journal, upload your work or personal files to your storage area, and make some plans.

See how you can display all of this in easy-to-create web pages—just drag-and-drop blocks of content and rearrange them, using Mahara's innovative page framework.

When you're happy with your creations, choose who you want to share them with and when. Share with users both internal and external to your Mahara site.

Finally, connect with other members in your Mahara community and collaborate in groups by participating in forums and discussions. Exchange ideas and news with your colleagues and friends.

Add to your portfolio throughout your professional career, including all of your new experiences, reflections, and progressions. When you look back, you will have a full and thorough record of your development, a great way to see how much you have grown.

What this book covers

Chapter 1, What can Mahara do for you? discusses what ePortfolios are and why Mahara is a very good choice of ePortfolio software. You will see some practical usecases for Mahara and join up to the official Mahara Community website.

Chapter 2, Getting Started with Mahara explains how to register to join the companion Mahara site for this book. You will get to grips with some of the basics of Mahara such as finding your way around and editing your profile information. You will also have your first look at the special Profile and Dashboard pages.

Chapter 3, Create and Collect Content discusses adding your own content to your portfolio. You will write in your journal, make some plans, add some notes, and upload your files. You will finish by learning how to display these on your Dashboard page.

Chapter 4, Organize and Showcase your Portfolio explains how to make a Mahara page from scratch. You will add content to your page and choose its layout and design. You will group your pages into collections. you will see how easy it is to share your pages with others.

Chapter 5, Share and Network in Groups covers connecting with other users in Mahara. You will create and participate in groups of interest. You will learn how to share files and pages in groups. You will exchange ideas in group forums.

Chapter 6, Course Groups and Other Roles in Mahara explains what a Mahara Institution is and how you can manage one. You will work as a Mahara staff member to set up course groups, which can have pages submitted to them. You will look at a possible workflow in Mahara for the assessment of work.

Chapter 7, Mahara Extensions explores some of the extensions that are available for Mahara. You will look at a plugin that allows you to track your continuing professional development and use the embedly block to embed content from web 2.0 sites in pages and more.

Appendix A, Mahara Implementation—Pre-Planner discusses some of the important questions your organization will need to address if you want to successfully get your ePortfolio system up live and running.

Appendix B, Installing Mahara covers the installation of Mahara, along with the requirements for installation.

Appendix C, Pop Quiz Answers contains the answers to the pop quiz questions.

What you need for this book

All you will need to get started with this book is access to the Internet via a web browser. You will be able to use the demonstration Mahara to go through the examples in the book (`http://maharaforbeginners.tdm.info`), but it would be useful if you had your own Mahara website in operation too (see *Appendix B, Installing Mahara*, for installation details).

Who this book is for

This book is for learners who want to maintain online documentation of their projects and share it with a particular teacher or trainer for feedback, educators who want to set up an ePortfolio for their students in order to encourage and advance personalized and reflective learning, or professionals who want to share journals and project documents with their team, capturing and sharing their existing knowledge and creating new knowledge in communities of professional practice.

Conventions

In this book, you will find several headings appearing frequently.

To give clear instructions of how to complete a procedure or task, we use:

Time for action – heading

1. Action 1
2. Action 2
3. Action 3

Instructions often need some extra explanation so that they make sense, so they are followed with:

What just happened?

This heading explains the working of tasks or instructions that you have just completed.

You will also find some other learning aids in the book, including:

Pop quiz – heading

These are short multiple choice questions intended to help you test your own understanding.

Have a go hero – heading

These set practical challenges and give you ideas for experimenting with what you have learned.

You will also find a number of styles of text that distinguish between different kinds of information. Here are some examples of these styles, and an explanation of their meaning.

Code words in text are shown as follows: "In the example, Janet Norman uploaded a video file (.mov), but the file you upload in Mahara can be almost anything "

New terms and **important words** are shown in bold. Words that you see on the screen, in menus or dialog boxes for example, appear in the text like this: "On the resulting page, fill in your details, agree to the terms and conditions (read them first), and click on **Register** to finish."

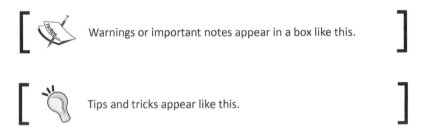

Warnings or important notes appear in a box like this.

Tips and tricks appear like this.

Reader feedback

Feedback from our readers is always welcome. Let us know what you think about this book—what you liked or may have disliked. Reader feedback is important for us to develop titles that you really get the most out of.

To send us general feedback, simply send an e-mail to feedback@packtpub.com, and mention the book title through the subject of your message.

If there is a topic that you have expertise in and you are interested in either writing or contributing to a book, see our author guide on www.packtpub.com/authors.

Customer support

Now that you are the proud owner of a Packt book, we have a number of things to help you to get the most from your purchase.

Errata

Although we have taken every care to ensure the accuracy of our content, mistakes do happen. If you find a mistake in one of our books—maybe a mistake in the text or the code—we would be grateful if you would report this to us. By doing so, you can save other readers from frustration and help us improve subsequent versions of this book. If you find any errata, please report them by visiting http://www.packtpub.com/support, selecting your book, clicking on the **errata submission form** link, and entering the details of your errata. Once your errata are verified, your submission will be accepted and the errata will be uploaded to our website, or added to any list of existing errata, under the Errata section of that title.

Piracy

Piracy of copyright material on the Internet is an ongoing problem across all media. At Packt, we take the protection of our copyright and licenses very seriously. If you come across any illegal copies of our works, in any form, on the Internet, please provide us with the location address or website name immediately so that we can pursue a remedy.

Please contact us at copyright@packtpub.com with a link to the suspected pirated material.

We appreciate your help in protecting our authors, and our ability to bring you valuable content.

Questions

You can contact us at questions@packtpub.com if you are having a problem with any aspect of the book, and we will do our best to address it.

1
What can Mahara do for you?

So you're interested in Mahara? Maybe you are already using it, but you are wondering if you are using it well. Maybe you've recently heard of Mahara and you are wondering if this is actually the ePortfolio solution you were looking for? Or, maybe you have been told to use it and you just need to get a sense of what Mahara is all about?

In subsequent chapters of this book, you will be digging into the nitty-gritty of getting your Mahara up and running, and then making it work for you as a learner or as a Mahara staff member. This particular book is not specifically pitched at helping Mahara site administrators. Before you start getting down to the basics of Mahara, you need to understand the big picture of what Mahara is about.

In this chapter you will:

- ◆ Be introduced to the concept of ePortfolios
- ◆ Learn why Mahara is almost certainly the best option out there for ePortfolio building and reflective learning
- ◆ Look at some of the different ways in which you can use Mahara
- ◆ See the four fictional case studies used as examples in this book
- ◆ Find out how to become a member of the online Mahara community at `http://mahara.org`
- ◆ Look at some other Mahara sites that are freely available on the Internet

So let's get on with it!

Portfolios go electronic

You have been learning things since the day you were born. I remember my little boy's first ever picture of a cowboy riding on a horse (it's great) that he made when he was four years old, and I will always remember the wooden toy truck that I made in my woodwork class when I was a teenager. I also proudly remember the written design paper that I had to write for my exam, which was about how I actually made that wooden truck, but now I have lost that design paper and I have no idea where it has gone. Today, I am heavily involved in online distance learning, more specifically ePortfolios, and rarely a day goes by when I don't learn something new.

Now, the thing is, all I now have are memories of my wooden truck, but if I had access back then to a digital ePortfolio, I could have kept a copy of that design paper. I could have scanned it into my computer and stored it as an image (if I hadn't created it digitally in the first place). I could have also stored a video of the 16-year old me showing off my wooden truck and I could have taken digital snapshots of the truck from all angles. If I was feeling really adventurous, I could have combined all these elements together and written about, or videoed myself speaking about how I conceived the idea and how I actually made it.

Maybe my friends would have been really impressed with my wooden truck and wanted to know how to make it, so they could have made one too. So, maybe I would have created a web page to show them. I could add all these videos, pictures, and commentaries to create a really useful and detailed resource page for my friends. Perhaps I didn't (yet) want the world to know about my new carpentry skills—especially not Barry down the road from the rival school. In this case, I could have set up a special group so only the people I selected would be able to view my wooden truck page. Maybe one of my friends would have really liked the truck, and showed his Dad, who was an engineer. Suppose they made one using my web page too, but with some tips from his Dad, they made one that went faster. He then started a forum discussing the improvements they had made. Then perhaps another couple of my friends joined in and got really excited. They shared with the group their own modifications which they had researched on the internet, uploaded a picture of an improved version to the group, and suggested we all got together once a week to work on one together and enter it in the county wooden truck championship.

And all along, without us being aware, let's imagine our teachers looking on smiling. They were watching us develop our IT skills and start off down the path of lifelong learning and collaborative working. They were watching us record our new-found learning and skills whilst developing complex social networking skills. The woodwork teacher sat back in his chair with a warm smile on his face. He knew he had taught me something of much greater worth than how to make a wooden truck.

However, this is all purely fantasy. I did not have access to an ePortfolio that had all this functionality, and the Internet back then was not much more than a concept.

Towards an ePortfolio-enabled future

I am now, however, a fully ePortfolio-enabled dad and I therefore helped my son (Salvador) to upload that picture of a cowboy on a horse. In the future, he can share it with his friends, and possibly with some other junior artistic talents, online. He is about to embark upon a lifelong learning journey, and now he (with a little help from Dad) can keep a record of his learning into posterity.

I, myself, also see the need to store and share the knowledge I am gathering about my professional life online. I want to work in a community of professionals (like yourself) using ePortfolios, who I can buzz with, share ideas with, and grow with. I want to engage with a professional community who I can give to and learn from. I want to keep my personal reflections and files to myself sometimes, to share some with my colleagues, and some to share with the rest of the world. I wish to create web pages as I see fit, not according to some predesigned fixed template. I want to use my creative skills to design web pages that I feel fit with my personal and professional style. I cannot do these things with Facebook or Bebo, I need the enhanced functionality and privacy that a socially interactive ePortfolio such as Mahara uses.

For both Salvador's needs and my own, I am going to use Mahara.

Why Mahara?

While they are not as old as the three-ring-binder and the artist's portfolio folder, digital ePortfolios have, nevertheless, actually been around for a long, long time. Have you ever stored your learning data on floppy disks, USB sticks, CDs, or DVDs? Maybe you've even created your own, personal Dreamweaver-produced or HTML/CSS website. Perhaps you've used a blogging engine such as WordPress, a content management system such as Drupal or Joomla!, or maybe a course management system such as Moodle. If you have, these are all types of ePortfolio, really.

None of these, however, were ever conceived to act as ePortfolio platforms in their own right. Mahara now gives us an ePortfolio system, which is thoughtfully and specifically designed for the job in hand. It allows us access to our own personalized learning environment. Mahara seeks to go beyond a basic ePortfolio and gives us a variety of other useful features to help us to learn reflectively and to work collaboratively.

Mahara is, therefore, a platform for personalized, reflective, and collaborative learning.

Personalized learning

Twenty-first century learning no longer needs to be delivered on somebody else's agenda. Mahara concerns itself with the personalization of the learning process:

♦ **Personalized self-presentation**: Mahara offers an easy-to-use web interface that allows you to design your own web pages, or simply pages, so that you can organize and present your own learning data precisely in the way you would like to present it. You are clearly able to demonstrate that you fully understand a subject.

What is a Mahara page?

Page is the Mahara word for a web page that you create by yourself in order to display your information, ideas, opinions, and personality. We will find out more about pages in *Chapter 2, Getting Started with Mahara* and *Chapter 4, Organize and Showcase your Portfolio.*

♦ **Privacy**: If you want somewhere to collect your thoughts and files, you probably want these to remain private until you decide that you are ready to show them to someone else. In Mahara, you now have a fairly private (only you and the administrator(s) can access your files) area on the Internet where you can keep your stuff, such as files (documents, videos, audio clips, images, and so on). You can also use this private space to write a journal as well as your ever-changing profile and résumé information.

♦ **Accessible**: You can access your private stuff whenever you like from wherever you can log into the Internet. Wow! This beats carrying your data around on a USB stick, doesn't it? No more forgotten or lost files. Access your files at work, at school, at the library, or even when you are sitting on the beach in Barbados. Mahara gives you freedom!

♦ **Transfer your data**: What about when you move schools and change companies? What happens to your data then? Many ePortfolios "lock you in" in such a way that you won't be able to transfer your data when the time comes to move. Who wants that? Mahara allows you to export your data as HTML and to create a LEAP2A object for moving your portfolio to other Mahara sites and other portfolio systems that support the format.

◆ **Access control**: In Mahara you—the user—retain the right to control who gets access over your own artefacts. You do this by setting up pages of your digital data artefacts and then deciding who gets to see them. You are also able to create groups to allow different groups of people to access different portfolio pages. Well, you wouldn't want your boss to see that picture of the office party, would you? This is another reason why Mahara is better than so many of those Web 2.0 social networking sites. You might want to work with your suppliers on a joint marketing campaign, but do you really want to share your company's sensitive financial reports with them, too? Mahara lets you satisfy all of these different needs neatly and easily. One warning though: if you pull in images, videos, and files from other web sites, it is only on these sites that you control access to those files. Mahara only has access control over content that is uploaded to your Mahara portfolio. If that photo is hosted on Flickr, for example, then the boss may still be able to see it if they can access your Flickr profile.

What is a Mahara artefact?

Artefact is the Mahara word for a bit of digital stuff, such as files, journals, plans, and profile or résumé information. You control other people's access to your stuff by deciding for yourself who can see the artefacts that you choose to display in your own pages. You won't see the term artefact used as you build your portfolio, but you might see it mentioned on the Mahara community website or in the Mahara documentation.

Reflective learning

But Mahara offers more than just being a way to store and to show off your stuff to others. Mahara encourages you to grow as a learner by reflecting on your own learning journey.

◆ **Developing your own goals and skills**: Mahara encourages you to record, reflect on and update your personal, academic, and work/career-related goals and skills. It has even created special sections just to facilitate this. Life is a journey, our dreams and objectives are in constant flux. If you've misplaced that notebook or scrap of paper with "New Year Resolutions" on it, how can you know if you've kept them? Now with Mahara you can easily check back to see that you are still on the right learning pathway. Everything is all in one place!

◆ **Keeping journals**: Ever kept a diary or a journal? Ever made notes to yourself? Keeping a journal can be a very useful way of encouraging you to stop and think about the things you have been doing, to reflect on, and to learn from your experience, and to process the things you have been studying. Taking some time out to reflect and compose thoughts is a highly useful exercise. You can now keep as many journals as you like, all in one place, stored together with your goals, skills, and files. You keep the journals for yourself, not necessarily publishing them for others to view. You can, of course, move on to put your journals into portfolio pages for others to access if you want to, or if you are asked to! You can keep a personal journal, a work journal, a project journal, and a journal to share with your friends!

What is a Mahara journal?

The Mahara journal feature is similar to a blog or online diary. You can use it to take note of things you have been doing or to reflect on your work progress. You can share these thoughts with others by publishing them in Mahara pages.

◆ **Integration with other platforms (including Web 2.0)**: Mahara is set up to allow for integrations with other online spaces. At the moment you can call in RSS feeds from your blog (outside of Mahara) or CMS. You are also able to call in content from a wide range of Web 2.0 tools including Twitter, Slideshare, YouTube, TeacherTube, and many more! Mahara can be seen as a personalized, reflective learning space where you can gather together all of your learning artefacts and store them internally within Mahara or externally within other locations on the World Wide Web.

Collaborative learning

While Mahara is a self-oriented learning platform—many call it a **Personal Learning Environment (PLE)**—it also facilitates informal learning activities amongst friends and groups:

◆ **Making friends**: Many of us learn best when we are working together with other people. For this reason, Mahara encourages social collaboration. You can present your pages with a different profile picture to different people and communities. You can find members who have similar interests to yourself and by contacting them from their profile pages, start to build a network of friends. You can then add some of your friends' pages to a watchlist that will let you know when they have been updated with new information. You are able to place feedback on other people's pages and to allow others to place feedback on yours, giving each other advice and support, and in this way, act as both teacher and learner. With Mahara's social networking features, social learning can take place—the teacher-student division is broken down and everyone can be involved in the learning process. Before long, your online learning community is born!

◆ **Working and learning in groups**: Life is more fun when shared with others! It's time to get down to some learning and working together in groups! You can join and set up for yourself different types of groups for different types of learning communities (for more detail refer to *Chapter 5, Share and Network in Groups*). In your groups you can share common files, you can share your own pages for others to see or work together on pages that you create as a group. You can also engage in group discussion forums to really get your reflective learning into gear!

What is a Mahara group?

This is Mahara's word for an online community that users can either:

- ◆ Join
- ◆ Request membership of
- ◆ Be invited to
- ◆ Or (sometimes) be selected into in a more controlled way

You can use groups in a variety of ways, but they are predominately used in Mahara to develop, stimulate, and support both social and learning activities in a social networking context.

◆ **Using groups for assessment of learning**: Mahara staff members working within the controlled Mahara groups can encourage learners to submit pages to the group for formal assessment. This is an excellent way of tracking progress on formal and evidence-based qualifications.

◆ **Integration with Moodle**: Sometimes, it is useful for a teacher to take learners through a staged sequence of learning objectives using quizzes and other formal learning activities, on which performance can be assessed and reported on in a grade book. Mahara doesn't provide this as its core functionality, although it is increasingly being used to achieve this. Mahara is a place for informal learning, not a taught Course Management System. Luckily, Mahara's "sister" program steps in here—Moodle (http://moodle.org). Where Mahara is about demonstrating learning, Moodle is about delivering it. It is a Course Management System, which can be set up to run in the background of Mahara, sharing single sign-on access.

Mahara users can set up and follow links within Mahara from which you can seamlessly migrate directly over to a course that is running on a Moodle platform (you can refer *Moodle Administration, Alex Büchner, Packt Publishing*). You are also able to submit pages for assessment from Mahara to Moodle. With Moodle 2.0, you are able to bring good work that you did in your Moodle course over to your portfolio platform. Your informal, ongoing, and never-ending reflective learning experience isn't over once your taught course is done and dusted. Viva Mahara!

Pop quiz – what is important to you in an ePortfolio?

What do you need from an ePortfolio?

Grade the following ePortfolio criteria with a number on a scale of 1-5:

- **5**: Vitally important
- **4**: Very important
- **3**: Important
- **2**: Not very important
- **1**: Not important at all

The criteria (in no particular order):

- _____ You own your own data and can control who has access to it.
- _____ You get your own file storage area (like you have on your own computer, for example, My Documents), which you can access, modify, and control via the Internet.
- _____ Your ePortfolio is portable, allowing you to migrate your data from provider to provider on your lifelong learning journey.
- _____ You have opportunities for reflective learning via blogs/journals, learning/career goal-setting, group projects, and so on.
- _____ You have the opportunity for social networking in interest groups with forum discussions.
- _____ You have creative freedom over the personalized presentation of your own learning. You can stylize your portfolio pages according to your own preferences/needs.
- _____ You get the chance to show off your stuff to other people, for example, you can show your learning achievements, résumé details, and so on to potential employers.
- _____ The ePortfolio allows you to link in your stuff from Web 2.0 social networking sites such as YouTube, Twitter, and Facebook.
- _____ Your personal ePortfolio integrates seamlessly with the learning programs you pursue on your institution or company Moodle virtual learning environment (http://moodle.org).

- ◆ _____ The ePortfolio grants you your right to know that nothing untoward is happening to your data by opening the software source code to public view and scrutiny.

- ◆ _____ The ePortfolio allows the learning provider organization to avoid locking in its own and your personal data into a proprietary data format, which belongs to a particular software company.

- ◆ _____ The ePortfolio is a community-supported open source platform, which is modular and open to modification, meaning that providers can work collaboratively to make the platform work better for their common (and also for their very particular) ePortfolio needs.

- ◆ _____ The ePortfolio can be configured to offer controlled groups a "submit for assessment" process—allowing an assessor (or external verifier) to easily verify that you have done your work—in the same way that they would do with a paper-based or USB-stick-based portfolio assessment process.

- ◆ _____ While using the ePortfolio for formal assessment via accrediting bodies, the ePortfolio can be integrated with sophisticated open source **Individual Learning Plan (ILP)** and assessment manager tools (such as The ULCC Personalisation of Learning Framework at `http://moodle.ulcc.ac.uk/course/view.php?id=139`).

As you have probably already guessed, Mahara is capable of satisfying all of the preceding criteria.

Ways of using Mahara

Mahara can be used in lots of different ways towards lots of different ends. Here are just a few different examples:

- ◆ A recruitment agency might use Mahara to forge links between jobseekers and employers, employers with other employers, and jobseekers with other jobseekers.

◆ A university or college might use Mahara as a reflective learning platform for all of their students, following all different types of learning programs. You can refer to the following example of a Mahara ePortfolio, created by Joanne DeMarco at Pace University:

◆ A students' union might use Mahara as a vehicle for members of its clubs and societies to share their knowledge and their passions. For example, football, canoeing, the darts team, political groups, and so on.

◆ A school teacher might use Mahara to get his/her small group of students to work together on a curriculum-related topic.

◆ A professional body may wish to set up Mahara for communicating with members and for the continuous professional development of its members.

◆ A private training provider might use Mahara as a way for learners to collate and submit their work for assessment as part of their qualification.

◆ A group of friends may wish to use Mahara to communicate and collaborate in a much more controlled way than Facebook.

◆ A group of professionals from different organizations/locations may wish to work together on sharing best practice ideas, and to support each other through a variety of challenging situations, for example, a group of social workers. See the following screenshot of a Mahara page example, **Web 2.0 Tools & Video Gaming in Physical Therapy**:

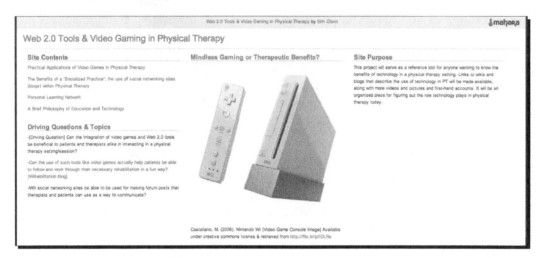

◆ A large organization or corporation could use Mahara for their informal knowledge management processes, encouraging people in similar roles in different branches to work together in online communities of practice.

The list goes on...

The example screenshots in the previous section can be found by visiting `http://groups.diigo.com/group/everything-mahara` and filtering by the `mahara_portfolio_example` tag. There are plenty of other examples to look at there.

In this book, we want you to look at the many ways in which you can use Mahara to fit your own specific situation. To help you to do this, we will often be illustrating the different things that you can do with Mahara by using any of the following four imaginary case studies.

Case study one: Punam from Pennytown Primary

Punam is a teacher at Pennytown Primary and she is taking her nine-year old students through a project on the Tudors. She is working with an institutional-themed Mahara, which is set up on "Schools Online", a large, county-wide Mahara implementation for school teachers who are working in an English county called Rurishire:

Punam will be helping her students to work as a class group in order to gather files and discuss their learning. She doesn't just want them to upload a whole load of files, she wants them to organize files and data in a meaningful way, just like a paper-based project. This will mean that she wants her students to create pages in smaller working groups for their class project. She likes the idea of smaller working groups as this will allow her students to start working collaboratively. She likes the fact that Mahara facilitates this by allowing you to set up different groups and to create a collaboratively created group page.

Some of her students' parents have come up to her and expressed concerns about online safety; one of their children has been the victim of cyber-bullying. However, Punam is satisfied that Mahara addresses this concern as, unlike Facebook, the only people that have access to the site are those that have been given permission by the school. The local education authority has set a policy that any adult that has access to this site must have passed a police check. If there are any concerns regarding cyber-bullying of the children, she can request that the administrator accesses all the pages and forum posts so that she can find out who was responsible, and request suspension of the user if appropriate. She can happily reassure the parents that this is a walled garden site where their children are safe. There is even a facility for the learners to report objectionable material to the administrators, should they stumble upon any.

Finally, Punam has heard that there are a few Google Android mobile phone applications and an iPhone application available for Mahara. Now her students will be able to capture video and images from school field trips and upload them instantly to their personal portfolios saving the time taken in putting them onto a USB stick and uploading them to the Internet.

Case study two: Janet Norman from Pharmaceuticals International Inc. (PI Inc.)

Janet is a learning technologist who holds overarching responsibility for PI Inc.'s International Corporate University. Each country, indeed, each and every branch that she represents, has its own local learning agenda:

As a learning technologist she wants to encourage informal, personalized, and reflective learning. She knows that spending time in encouraging reflection and **Continuous Professional Development (CPD)** helps to:

◆ Develop staff skills - creating a better workforce.

◆ Increase staff morale.

◆ Encourage the development of professionalism.

◆ Increase staff retention as staff feel more valued.

◆ Encourage innovation, which will help give PI Inc. an edge over their competitors.

◆ Give out a strong corporate message about investment in people.

However, Janet's main focus is on implementing Mahara to facilitate informal international knowledge transfer processes. She wants to spend some time setting up different types of groups. She can see the benefit of setting up groups to work on a variety of research projects being carried out throughout the organization. She is hopeful that the group members are going to make use of Mahara's journaling features to keep everyone up-to-date with their particular projects.

There are currently three pilot studies being carried out in England, Peru, and Spain for a new cancer drug, and she wants these three research groups to collaborate and discuss early findings. She also wants to set up some international groups of practice and collaborate in the hope that this will lead to some useful organizational innovations. Finally, she wants to set up some groups that a few selected individuals can access from outside the company to bring in some fresh ideas and perspectives, whilst also contributing to the wider pharmaceutical community.

PI Inc. is, therefore, running their own large international Mahara implementation with a range of their own institutions. Janet's people will be sharing their knowledge. PI Inc. will be capturing their knowledge before they leave. And, by engaging in this process, Janet's staff members will be creating new and innovative knowledge, which PI Inc. can make use of as they move into the future.

What is a Mahara institution?

An institution in Mahara is a subdivision of the site, which can have its own theme, users, and administrators. There is more on Mahara institutions in *Chapter 6, Course Groups and Other Roles in Mahara*.

Case study three: Neil from Training for Work

Neil trains and assesses learners who are taking national vocational qualifications with a private training provider called Training for Work. He is helping sixteen to nineteen-year olds to gain their vocational qualifications in Electrical Engineering. Although Training for Work only has about fifteen people on its staff, they have installed their own organizational Mahara because they like to have control over their own site:

Neil is keen to use the Résumé Builder feature of Mahara. He has a number of links with local businesses for work placements, and he prides himself on the high percentage of learners who go on to full time positions. He knows if he can get all his learners to input all of their information into the résumé builder and create an online résumé, not only will this make matching his learners to work placements easier, but also really impress prospective employers.

Neil knows that at the moment his learners' files and evidences are stored all over the place in a variety of locations. Some of the homework is currently handed in as paper assignments. Some assessors have video and audio evidences stored in their video cameras, smart phones, or on their laptops, with handwritten notes. Some other parts of the work that his learners have done are stored on the Training for Work desktops up in the computer room. His inbox is always full of e-mails from students sending him files with huge attachments to check. New students want to submit evidence in an ePortfolio as they did at Uppertown Secondary School. Finally, when he makes on-site visits he finds that his students have often forgotten to bring their evidence with them, leading to yet another wasted trip! Assessing has become a complete nightmare! He spends more time actually trying to find the evidence than he does teaching and supporting his students.

Neil says he will make extensive use of Mahara's artefacts feature. This will allow him to get the students to organize their digital stuff (artefacts) into one central location where they can then share them with him, verifiers, and also other students easily, using pages. As it will be accessible anywhere, anytime there is Internet access, students can no longer forget or lose their work. He has also been set up as a Mahara staff member (more on this in *Chapter 6, Course Groups and Other Roles in Mahara*), which will allow him to assign his learners to a controlled group—it is into this that the learners will submit pages evidencing their learning, enabling their formal assessment. Neil will, of course, set up a template page for learners to copy and build their evidence upon. The learners will not be able to edit their submitted pages again until Neil releases them with his feedback. Neil needs this sort of control because his accrediting body and external verifiers require him to have it.

Neil is also excited by the fact that his learners are able to make plans.

What is a Mahara plan?

Plans in Mahara allow you to create task lists. These can be used to organize your time and to help you to meet important deadlines.

Neil can't wait to start using Mahara! It will make his life so much easier. He can give online coaching as and when needed, there will be no more forgotten files and wasted trips, and most importantly his students will learn more—and learn to reflect more—as this will help them not only to gain their all important qualifications, but also to become more valuable employees.

Case study four: Christophe from Silverworks University

Silverworks University has recently decided that they would like to offer an online ePortfolio building system for their fine arts students alongside the traditional artist's portfolio. They can see the benefit of having a single location where students can access all their videos, images, and inspirations from anywhere, as opposed to the traditional carry-folder approach. The system they have chosen to work with is Mahara.

Christophe is a tutor of fine arts at the Silverworks University and is responsible for mentoring 10 students.

He is the person in the department with the most interest in technology and has excitedly offered himself and his tutor group as the test bed for the new system. He's really interested in the potential of Mahara to allow his students to quickly add their work, sketches, and developments to their online portfolios. No longer will work that is being developed at the students' home be inaccessible for tutorials.

He likes that with Mahara, students are able to control exactly who can see their work. In the run up to their degree show, Christophe is encouraging his students to use Mahara pages to show off their portfolios to the web. He really likes the collections feature, which enables his students to link sections of their portfolios together into a coherent story.

What is a Mahara collection?

A collection in Mahara is simply a group of pages. If you think of a page like a web page, a collection is like a web site. A collection can be navigated via its menu bar, which has links to the different pages it contains.

He has even started to look into a few extensions that are available for Mahara, which will allow his tutor group to pull a wide range of content from external websites and to integrate with social media.

Not only that, but Christophe is himself a graphic artist. He will be using Mahara for his own personal use. He is keen on the journal feature, and has decided to keep a log of each day that he spends on a new comic. He is glad that he will no longer have to keep track of all those scraps of paper with ideas scribbled down in cafes—he can add them to his Mahara portfolio!

Join the Mahara community

There is already a vibrant and active international Mahara community working together over at `http://mahara.org`. Mahara is all about collaborative learning and it's a great idea for you to come and join in. Not only is it exciting to become part of this active community, but you can also receive help and support, and as you become more confident, start giving your own suggestions to the Mahara team and complete the circle, fully engaging in the collaborative spirit!

The community site is itself based on the Mahara platform, that's to say, it has some of the same features as a standard Mahara instance (profiles, friends, forums, and so on). This is great because just by using the community site you get a feel of many of the Mahara features! It's important to note though, you should not use this site to try and build your own free ePortfolio; in fact, the Mahara terms and conditions prevent it. Luckily there are many other sites out there that serve this purpose; you will look at this later in the chapter:

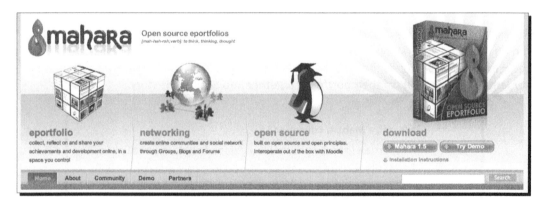

Have you ever seen a Maharan?

Some members of the Mahara community have started calling themselves Maharans.

Let's find out how to register as a user at `mahara.org` and explore the features available there.

Time for action – join mahara.org and explore

Let's register to `mahara.org`:

1. Head on over to `http://mahara.org` and click on the option to register, a small link that you will find near the login box in the top right-hand part of the screen. On the resulting page, fill in your details, agree to the terms and conditions (read them first), and click on **Register** to finish:

Register ⓘ

Welcome! To use this site you must first register. You must also agree to the terms and conditions. The data we collect here will be stored according to our privacy statement.

Email address *	[ ]
First name *	[ ]
Last name *	[ ]
I agree to the Terms and Conditions *	○ Yes ● No
	Register

---

2. You will need to confirm your registration by clicking on the link that has been sent to your e-mail address. You must do this within 24 hours, otherwise you will have to register again. Once you have done that, you will find yourself logged in to `http://mahara.org`.

3. Lets look around! Click on the **Community** tab. This is the group where all the community members gather and, by default, you are a member now that you have signed up. Can you see all the latest forum posts listed on the group page? This is useful for keeping up-to-date with latest discussions related to the Mahara project:

4. Now let's find another Maharan: click on the **Members** tab. Let's see if you can find one of the authors! Can you see the query box? Type in the name of one of the authors, Derrin, and see if you can find him:

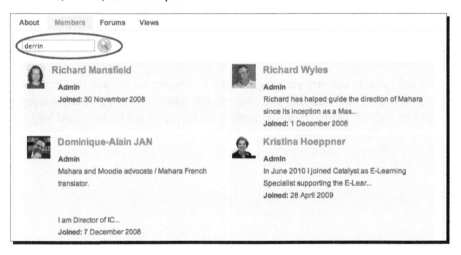

5. Let's look at some pages. Now you've found Derrin, click on his name to view his profile page. Once you're there, click on a few of his pages listed there to see what he has been up to:

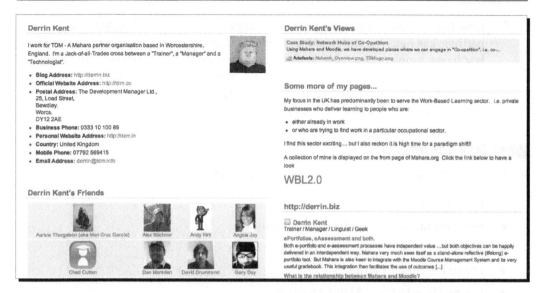

6. Now, let's join a forum. Click on the **Community** tab again, and now on the **Forums** tab. Can you see the **Support** forum? Its description is **Need help using or installing Mahara? Ask your questions here**. That's going to be useful to you I bet! Why not subscribe to this forum by clicking on the **Subscribe** button. You will now be e-mailed with all the updates to this forum. Maybe there are other forums you want to subscribe to. If you only want to browse the forum, just click on the name of the forum and you will be taken to a list of the posts:

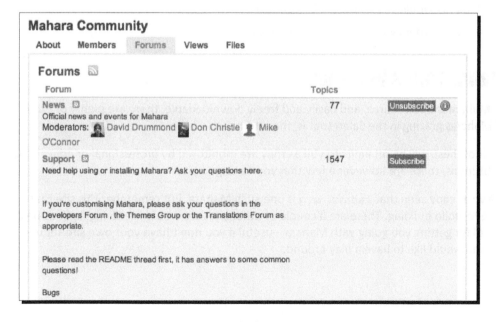

7. Now, have a look at the Mahara partners. Click on the **Partners** tab. Mahara partners can help you with hosting, theming, training, coding, tweaking, extending, bug-fixing, problem-resolving, implementation consultancies and, well, just about anything to do with Mahara, if you ask them nicely enough. All Mahara partners are excellent support agencies and, if you are really keen on using Mahara, you really should give one of the partners a shout.

What just happened?

You have just become a Maharan! Does it feel strange? You have:

◆ Registered on `http://mahara.org`

◆ Been introduced to the Mahara Community

◆ Found Derrin and his Mahara pages at `mahara.org`

◆ Joined the support forum

◆ Learned how to find a Mahara partner

Pop quiz – learning about http://mahara.org

The following questions will test what you have learned about `mahara.org`:

1. What's the value of registering at `mahara.org`?

2. How would you find another `mahara.org` member?

3. Why would you want to join a forum?

4. How would you find a Mahara partner?

Mahara sites in the wild

As Mahara is open source, and easily and freely downloadable, there are plenty of examples of Maharas grazing in the Safari that is, the Internet.

Most of these will be off limits to you as they are monitored by professional or educational institutions, there are however a few that you can sign up to.

We've already seen that `mahara.org` is one such Mahara, but remember this site isn't for ePortfolio building. There are a couple of other sites we would like to highlight as being useful for getting you going with Mahara—useful if you don't have your own site set up yet and would like to have a play around.

Time for action – looking at some real-life Maharas

Let's get going and have a look at a couple of real-life Maharas:

1. Visit `http://demo.mahara.org`. This is Mahara's demo site. You can register and have a play around with Mahara safely in here. The site gets reset every 24 hours, so your data isn't retained there.

2. Visit `http://foliofor.me` to have a look at a Mahara site in action. This is a Mahara site, which allows you to set up your own free ePortfolio. You can just go there and register by clicking on the link in the right-hand panel.

What just happened?

You just had a very quick look at a couple of Mahara sites that are out there on the web.

You saw the Mahara demonstration site. This is a great place to familiarize yourself with Mahara generally, as well as to explore the latest up-to date version of Mahara - which may be more advanced than your own instance. As with mahara.org, it isn't a place where you can create your own portfolio as it is reset every 24 hours.

You also registered yourself at `foliofor.me`. This is an example of a free ePortfolio solution that can be used by individuals who don't belong to any particular institution or who simply want their portfolio in its own space. This isn't the only example of one such solution, you could also have a look at:

♦ **FolioSpaces**: `http://foliospaces.com`

♦ **icampus21.com**: `http://icampus21.com`

♦ **Portfoliocommunities**: `http://portfoliocommunities.com`

Your decision about where you ultimately decide to create your portfolio is up to you. Is it going to be within an educational or professional institution where it may be obligatory for you to do so? Or, perhaps you would like to host your own Mahara site in the cloud or on a local machine for your individual use (if you have the technical know-how). If neither of those are an option, the above free solutions offer a very useful alternative.

And remember, with Mahara's export facility, you don't have to worry about making that decision as you will be able to move your portfolio around easily.

Lookin' good...

One of the beauties of Mahara is that it is easy for a web designer to make some pretty significant changes to the theme. Notice that the `http://mahara.org` site looks really quite different to the `foliofor.me` site and different again to the default Mahara theme, which we will be working on throughout the rest of this book.

Have a go hero – pressing the buttons till it hurts

Some of us are inchworms who like information to be presented to us logically and sequentially. Inchworms like to be taken through a new process step-by-step. Others amongst us are grasshoppers who like to hop around bits of information wherever we find it and then gradually start piecing together the big picture of our understanding.

Inchworms are no better or worse than grasshoppers. We are just different.

This book is structured for inchworms, but we know you grasshoppers will easily be able to hop around our book and pick up on the useful bits.

Right now, though, be you an inchworm or a grasshopper, we want you to behave in grasshoppery sort-of-a-way as you engage in this task (take a deep breath, inchworms, you may just enjoy it!).

Once again, visit `http://demo.mahara.org` and log in. If it has been a day since you registered your account, it won't be there any more. If you don't feel like registering again you could just use one of the default accounts on offer. The details are all on the home page.

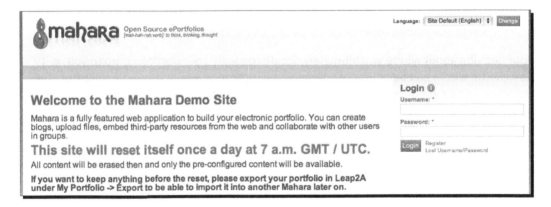

Remember, this is a test-bed site where you should feel free to go around and bang all of the buttons until it hurts. You really can't do any damage in there so just go in, explore, and experiment. Click the links and buttons, and follow wherever your mouse leads you. This will stand you in very good stead for when we walk you through Mahara's functionalities later on in this book.

Summary

We learned a lot in this chapter about why Mahara ePortfolios are useful.

Specifically, we understood what an ePortfolio is and looked at possible uses of Mahara. We discussed the importance of personalized, reflective, and collaborative learning and learned what is so special about the Mahara ePortfolio.

We also looked at some real-life Mahara sites. Hopefully, you became a member of the Mahara community by joining yourself up at `http://mahara.org`. If you did, you would have had a browse around `mahara.org` and looked at some of the useful features. Finally, some of you would have gotten an initial feel for Mahara by clicking around in the demo area `http://demo.mahara.org` and also in `http://foliofor.me` or one of the other free ePortfolio sites mentioned.

Now that we've seen the big picture as to why Mahara matters, you're probably keen to start working in your live Mahara environment. First of all, it's a good idea to get started by adding some of your information to your portfolio, and have a go at organizing your own profile page—which is the topic of the next chapter.

Getting Started with Mahara

2

Now that you have understood some of the potential of Mahara, it's time to get started. The very first thing you are going to do is to register for a Mahara site, log in, and set up your own personal profile and dashboard pages. You will also have your first look at how you receive notifications and manage your Mahara settings.

In this chapter you will:

- ◆ Register to join the demonstration Mahara site that accompanies this book
- ◆ Explore the Mahara user interface
- ◆ Learn how to enter your personal information
- ◆ Begin to configure your personal profile page
- ◆ Have a brief introduction to the Mahara text editor
- ◆ Have a look at the dashboard page
- ◆ Understand how you can manage your settings and receive notifications

By the end of this chapter, you will have started to set up your own profile page. You will have also had a look at your dashboard page in Mahara and be ready to start adding your stuff.

Registering with a Mahara site

I'm sure you can't wait to get inside a Mahara site and have a look around. Luckily, for this book we have created a demonstration site, so you can do just that.

Usually, a Mahara site administrator will provide you with your own username and password, so that you can log in straight away. Sometimes though, to join a Mahara site, you will have to register.

Let's have a look at some of the Mahara sites available on the Internet that you can register to join:

- `http://maharaforbeginners.tdm.info`: This is the demonstration site for this book. Register here to work through the examples in each chapter.
- `http://foliofor.me`: This is a freely available Mahara platform in the cloud. Anyone can register here to set up their own portfolio. A fairly large international community is already using this site.
- `http://demo.mahara.org`: This is a default Mahara installation that always runs on the latest version of Mahara. It is a demonstration site that can be explored by the users who are interested in Mahara but don't have the resources to set up their own test installations. Be aware though, all the content of this site is removed every day.
- `http://mahara.org`: This is Mahara's own website, which is a highly stylized version of a Mahara site. This is where the international Mahara community interacts and you really should register here to follow and take part in discussions about all things related to Mahara. The site is just for community discussions. You shouldn't keep your portfolio here.

If you have login details for your own Mahara site, you might want to skip the following *Time for action – registering to the Mahara for Beginner's demo site* section and get straight into logging in. However, we recommend that you register to join the demonstration site accompanying this book. The demo site will allow you to work through the examples.

Time for action – registering to the Mahara for Beginners' demo site

So, let's practice registering for a Mahara site:

1. Enter `http://maharaforbeginners.tdm.info` into your browser's address bar.

2. Click on the **Register** link found at the bottom of the **Login** block:

3. Fill in the registration form. Enter your **Email address**, **First name**, and **Last name**.

4. Agree to the terms and conditions if there is a button asking you to do so. Make sure you read them first:

5. Then, click on the **Register** button at the bottom of the page.

6. On the following page you will see an input box inviting you to give a reason for joining the site. Write a quick description and click on **Complete Registration**. Hopefully, you will now get an on-screen message telling you that you have successfully registered and to check your e-mail inbox for instructions on activating your account. If not, don't worry, you will get a message on the screen letting you know what went wrong. Then, correct the problem and try again.

7. Now that your details have been accepted, you will receive an e-mail from the Mahara site. In the e-mail, click on the link provided to register:

Thank you for registering an account on Mahara. Please follow this link to complete the signup process:

http://maharaforbeginners.tdm.info/register.php?key=5XJzjctbR4TPp0h8

The link will expire in 24 hours.

--
Regards,
The Mahara Team

8. A new page will open in your browser inviting you to choose a **New username** and **New password** for your account. Your username (as with your e-mail) must be unique on the system and Mahara will complain if it isn't. When you're happy, click on the **Submit** button:

You need a username and password to log in to Mahara. Please choose them now.

New username	The username you use to log into Mahara. Usernames are 3-30 characters long, and may contain letters, numbers, and most common symbols excluding spaces.
New password: *	Your new password. Passwords must be at least six characters long. Passwords are case-sensitive and must be different to your username. For good security, consider using a passphrase. A passphrase is a sentence rather than a single word. Consider using a favourite quote or listing two (or more!) of your favourite things separated by spaces.
Confirm password: *	Your new password again
	Submit

What just happened?

You have just registered yourself to the Mahara demo site for this book by entering some valid details and responding to an automated e-mail.

While registering for some Mahara sites, you might find that there is an extra drop-down option inviting you to select an institution. You can read about institutions in *Chapter 6, Course Groups and Other Roles in Mahara*.

Logging in for the first time

If you just registered for the demo site, you will be logged in to Mahara. In the future though, you will need to know how to log in by yourself. By now you should have a username and password, either for the demonstration site or those that have been provided by your Mahara admin in your own Mahara page. We're going to use those details to log in.

Time for action – logging in

Let's find out how to log in to Mahara for the first time with your username and password:

1. Once your account has been registered, you can log in to the site whenever you visit by using the **Login** block on the home page. Type your **Username** and **Password**, and click on **Login**.

2. If this is the first time you are logging in and your account was created for you by your site administrator, it is likely that you will be asked to change your password. If this is the case, enter your **New password** twice and click on **Submit**:

You are required to change your password before you can proceed.

New password: *	••••••••••••
	Your new password. Passwords must be at least six characters long. Passwords are case-sensitive and must be different to your username. For good security, consider using a passphrase. A passphrase is a sentence rather than a single word. Consider using a favourite quote or listing two (or more!) of your favourite things separated by spaces.
Confirm password: *	••••••••••••
	Your new password again
	Submit

3. That's all there is to it! You have just logged in to Mahara for the first time.

What just happened?

You have just learned how to log in to Mahara.

Logging in is easy, if you can remember your login details. If you are a bit forgetful like me, then don't worry, Mahara provides a useful way of retrieving your username and password. All you need is your e-mail address (let's hope you don't forget that!).

To retrieve your details, just click on the **Lost Username/Password** link at the bottom of the **Login** box. You will then see the page shown in the following screenshot:

If you have forgotten your username or password, enter the email address listed in your profile and we will send you a message you can use to give yourself a new password.

If you know your username and have forgotten your password, you can also enter your username instead.

Email address or username *	pr@email.com
	Send request

Enter your e-mail address and click on **Send request**. You will get your login details in an e-mail at the address you just entered.

I'm sure at this point you can't wait to start pressing a few buttons to try out Mahara's functionality. But first, let's have a look at some of the important features of Mahara's layout, which is the topic of the next section.

Mahara's user interface—finding your way around

One of the beauties of Mahara is that the menu options are laid out very simply. After clicking through the menu options a few times you will find that you instinctively know where the option that you are looking for is located.

A word on Mahara themes

It is important to realize that Mahara is an Open Source software and can be easily personalized and themed. This means you are able to change the visual layout of Mahara—the header section can be configured to have a different logo, layout can be altered, and font size/color can be adjusted (among other things). Theming doesn't affect Mahara content, it affects only the way it looks. For example, the theme for the site `http://maharaforbeginners.tdm.info` is an adaptation of the Default theme, which is the theme you will begin with:

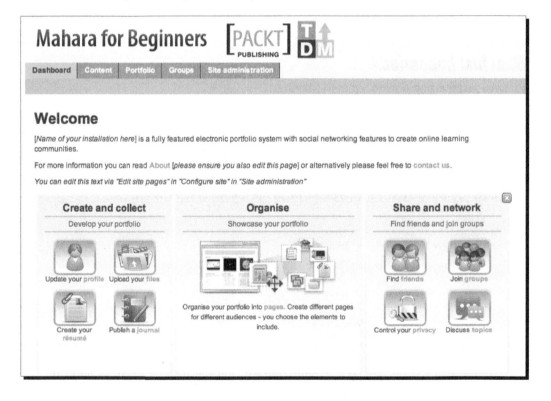

Let's now explore the Mahara user interface so that you can get used to finding your way around.

The main menu and submenus

The main menu is the first place to look when navigating around your Mahara. That is because it appears on every page that you visit and contains options for linking to all the important sections of your portfolio. You should see it towards the top of the page in your Mahara and it will look a bit like this:

As you can see, this menu is very simple. It only has four options, each one representing a different area of your portfolio. You will be looking at each of the sections of the main menu in detail, as you go through this book. Let's get a quick idea of where each button takes you:

◆ **Dashboard**: Clicking here takes you to your dashboard page—a customizable home page for your portfolio.

◆ **Content**: This is where you can create and collect the content for your portfolio including files, journals, and profile information. This is essentially your own private storage space (or closed cupboard/locker).

◆ **Portfolio**: This is where you put your content together into pages and collections of pages, which you might later choose to showcase to others. Pages are essentially web pages and collections are essentially websites. In this section, you are also able to share and export your portfolio.

◆ **Groups**: This area contains all the social aspects of Mahara. You can join groups, access forums, and get in contact with other Mahara users in this section.

Each of the menu items discussed in the preceding list, with the exception of the **Dashboard**, has its own menu associated with it. These are what we call **submenus**. Submenus are found below the main menu. The following screenshot shows the submenu for the **Content** section:

Drop-down menus

Mahara has introduced a drop-down menu feature, which shows the submenus as drop-down menus when you hover over a main menu item. It may be that your version of Mahara has this feature enabled, so don't be put off if yours doesn't act as we've described here. If drop-down menus aren't enabled for you, why not talk to the Mahara admin and ask them to allow it!

Side blocks

Side blocks are another important navigational tools. In a standard theme, they appear on the right-hand side of the screen. Side blocks contain quick links to sections of your portfolio, offering you rapid access to certain areas of your portfolio such as groups. In the side blocks, there are some links to areas that can't be accessed through the main navigation menus, such as tags. You can use the main side block to link to your personal profile (by clicking on your profile picture):

There are side blocks that display useful information such as the **Online users** block, which shows the users of the site who have been online within a certain time period. By default, this is 10 minutes:

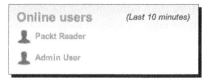

The footer

The footer is located at the bottom of the Mahara site and contains links to **Privacy Statement**, the **About** page (which tells you a bit about Mahara), and the **Contact Us** page (which allows you to get in contact with the site administrator). Mahara provides templates for some of these pages, but your site administrator should have adapted them to your own organizational requirements. There will also be an image linking to www.mahara.org. There may also be a **Terms and Conditions** link, if they have been set. Here is what the footer could look like:

A workflow for building your portfolio

You may have already noticed that on your dashboard page (the home page you see when you first log in), there is a three column information block that contains links to different parts of your portfolio. Here is what it looks like:

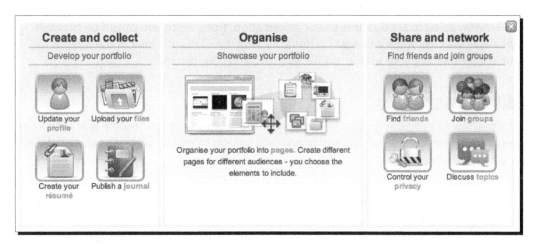

This dashboard information block is not only useful for navigating but it is also structured to give you some clues about the process that you should go through when building your portfolio.

In this book, you will be first encouraged to create and collect content, then to organize it, and finally to share and create networks.

This book is structured to walk you through each of these stages one by one. We're therefore going to start by adding your first piece of content—your profile information.

Setting up your own profile

One of the first things you will want to do is to add your own information to your portfolio and to make it feel like you own it. In this section, you will see how to do just that. For the following examples, we will be working with Janet Norman of PI Inc., showing you how she has configured her own profile. Why not set up your own profile in the demonstration site as you work through the examples? Let's start by looking at profile information.

Profile information

Later you will set up your own profile page—showing yourself and your knowledge off to others in an attractively personalized way. However, before you do that, you need to add some profile information. Your profile information is the first example that you will see of an artefact (piece of content or stuff, if you remember?) that you can add to Mahara.

You are now going to set up some profile information, from which you can go on to select repeatedly, and use again and again within your ePortfolio. You will look at three types of profile information—your profile, profile pictures, and your résumé.

Editing your profile

Let's see how to edit your profile. Any information you enter into your profile is private from everyone (except for the site administrators). You will get to choose who can view what, later on in the Mahara process.

Site administrators can masquerade

Site administrators are the only other members of a Mahara site who are able to access your private profile information without you deciding to share it. That is because they have the power to masquerade, whereby they are able to log in as your user and see your whole portfolio the same as you can when you are logged in.

Time for action – editing your profile

So let's get going and add some details to your profile:

1. Click on the **Content** button on the main menu.

2. You will notice that Mahara has opened the **Content** submenu. The **Profile** tab is selected when you first enter your content space. Let's take a quick look at Janet's profile. You will notice that the **About me** tab is selected. Janet has already entered her name:

3. Say something about yourself! Scroll down to the **Introduction** section of the **About me** page and enter some text. Here is what Janet typed in:

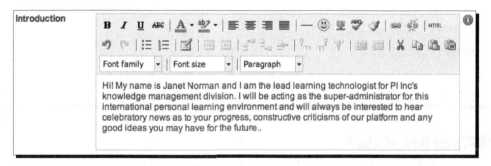

4. Whenever you make any changes, click on the **Save Profile** button at the bottom of the page. If you don't, you may find yourself losing all your hard work! This can happen sometimes if there is a period of inactivity and you get logged out.

5. Next, click on the **Contact information** tab to the right of the **About me** tab.

6. You will see that you are expected to fill out some telephone numbers and addresses. The first thing you should notice is that you can have more than one e-mail address in a Mahara site. These different e-mail addresses can be displayed via your profile page. To add another e-mail address, click on the link **Add email address**. You then need to click on the **Save Profile** button at the bottom of the page to action the new e-mail addition. The e-mail address will receive a confirmation e-mail from the Mahara site, and you will have to go to your e-mail account and follow the link to confirm that it is genuine.

7. You can now use radio buttons to toggle which e-mail address you would like to be the primary one for your account. This selection is important because at this address you will receive system messages. You will also notice that you can delete an e-mail address by clicking the small, red-colored cross to the right of the e-mail address.

8. Fill in your contact information on this page. Remember, you don't have to complete all the fields if you don't want to, but even if you add them, they aren't seen by anybody else until you decide what to share.

9. Click on the **Messaging** tab. Mahara will bring together the types of people you are likely to engage within live text, audio, and video conversations. People can display these contact details to each other in their profile page and other portfolio pages. Enter your contact details for the services you use on this page.

10. Finally, click on the **General** tab. On this page, enter your **Occupation** and **Industry** (remember to click on the **Save Profile** button when you have finished). The following screenshot shows what Janet Norman typed for these fields:

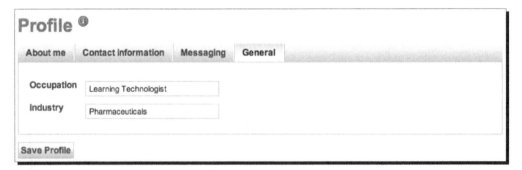

What just happened?

You have just completed your profile by entering some information about yourself, including your personal information, what messaging tools you use, and your industry background.

You were hopefully able to add your first name, last name, and other personal information in the **About me** section. Sometimes, though, the modification of the input fields you see in this section may be restricted depending on what has been allowed by the administrator; you may not be able to edit your name, for example.

Both the contact information and messaging information are private and will only be seen if you add them to a page. This is because you don't necessarily want anybody in the Mahara site to be able to see your telephone number and address for security reasons.

Help!

If you have found so far that you wish you had a bit more information about what certain options do, then don't worry! Mahara is very well documented software. On most pages, you will see little help icons, that look something like this:

If ever in doubt, click on these and you will be given very useful and specific help relating to your area of doubt.

You can also access a very complete Mahara user manual by visiting `http://bit.ly/mahara15manual`.

Let's now continue to add some more stuff into your profile with profile pictures.

Profile pictures

Profile pictures bring your profile to life! They are the first thing that people see about you when they are interacting with you in different areas of the site.

Mahara allows you to upload up to five different profile pictures. This becomes very useful (as you will see in *Chapter 4*, *Organize and showcase your portfolio*) when you are making pages out of your stuff.

Out of the five pictures that you add, one must always be the default. Your default picture is the main picture that will be shown throughout the site, for example in the **Online users** side block or in a group you are a member of.

After that, you can use any of your five profile pictures when presenting your profile block within a Mahara page. This is great because you can present yourself to different audiences in different ways, simply by altering your profile picture. For example, you can display a serious passport photo to your professional work colleagues, a more informal photo to your closest work colleagues, perhaps an avatar for public groups where you would like to be a bit more anonymous, and a picture of you having fun at a party for some of your more social interactions.

Time for action – uploading your profile pictures

Let's get a few different profile pictures uploaded to your portfolio:

1. Click on the **Profile pictures** submenu button under **Content**.

2. You will notice that to begin with there are no images found—that's because you haven't added any yet. Click on **Choose file** to find the profile picture you want to upload from your computer or external hard drive (or wherever). Mahara asks that your image is between 16x16 and 1024x1204 pixels, so make sure it is!

3. When you're happy with the image that you have selected, don't forget to add an **Image Title** for your profile picture before you click on the **Upload** button.

4. You are allowed to upload up to five profile pictures and you can delete any picture at any point. You have the option to set a default picture—if you do, you should probably choose a fairly sensible one. If you click on **Use no default**, the default Mahara profile shadow will be shown instead. Janet Norman has uploaded two profile pictures:

What just happened?

You have just uploaded a profile picture to represent yourself in your Mahara site. As you saw in the *Time for action – uploading your profile pictures* section, Janet has uploaded two pictures. One of these is an avatar of herself and the other is the company logo. She plans to use the company logo in pages where she would like to appear more professional, whereas the avatar will be used more generally.

If your Mahara site has been set up to allow the display of avatars from remote sites (if you are using such a service), your remote avatar will be displayed if the **Use no default** button has been clicked. One such remote service you could use is Gravatar (http://gravatar.com/).

Make yourself an avatar!

An **avatar** is simply a character or cartoon representation of yourself. If you don't want a passport photograph as your profile picture, an avatar is a very good alternative. There are many websites that help you create your own. A few of the most fun include the Simpsons Avatar Maker (http://www.simpsonsmovie.com), DoppelMe (http://www.doppelme.com), and Mr Picassohead (http://www.mrpicassohead.com).

Editing your résumé

No longer will you need to trawl through ancient hard drives trying to find the résumé you last wrote five years ago. Instead, you can keep your résumé information within your Mahara system and update it when you make changes. How impressive will it look when you show your résumé to your prospective employer as a portfolio page rather than on a piece of paper?

ePortfolios help you get a job!

Charlotte Brammer from the Department of Communication Studies, Samford University, Birmingham, Alabama, USA found that job applicants who use an ePortfolio alongside or instead of a pdf or printed résumé have a greater chance of securing employment. For more information, download Brammer's research paper as a pdf at http://link.tdm.info/ep-resume-paper.pdf.

There are six parts to complete in your résumé:

♦ **Introduction**: This is where you get to introduce yourself as a potential employer. It is essentially the equivalent of a cover letter.

♦ **Education and Employment**: List all of your previous educational successes at schools, universities, and colleges as well as your previous employment history.

♦ **Achievements**: Have you ever written a book, won an award, or belonged to a professional organization? This is the section to list them if you have.

♦ **Goals**: What do you want to do in the future? Here you can make personal, academic, and career goals.

♦ **Skills**: What are you specifically good at? Here you can describe your personal, academic, and work skill sets.

♦ **Interests**: Here you can informally list what you do in your spare time and why you enjoy doing it.

Punam from Pennytown Primary thinks:

It might be too early to get my children writing up their résumé, but the goals, skills, and interests sections will certainly be a useful process for me. I would like to enter my goals and skills now and look back at them again in a few months' time to check that I am achieving the goals I set for myself and that I am continuously expanding upon and consolidating my skills.

Janet Norman from PI Inc. thinks:

PI Inc. needs our staff to get into the habit of adding their résumé information within our system. Before Mahara we never had such a neat way of keeping résumés together.

Neil from Training for Work thinks:

I didn't like the word "résumé" so, as I have administrative access to the site code, I looked through the Mahara forums and found out how to change it to "CV". Some of the learners we take on at Training for Work already have work, but others are looking for jobs. I will be able to get learners to compile their CV, goals, and skills information into Mahara pages. Links to these can then be e-mailed to their potential employers. I will also encourage my learners to show video clips of themselves doing engineering work and to put up audio clips of me talking about how they have progressed during their time with us. They might even post up a journal on their job search progress, there are many possibilities.

Christophe from Silverworks University thinks:

I see the Mahara résumé-building process as an educational one for my students. I not only need to teach my learners to express themselves artistically (the ePortfolio pages serve as great spaces where my learners can display and describe their work) but also need them to celebrate their successes. An artist may produce beautiful art in their bedroom, but to make a living, the artist need to build a résumé of achievements and public-facing experiences.

Time for action – editing your résumé, goals, and skills

Let's see how to edit your résumé, goals, and skills.

1. Click on the **Résumé** tab under the **Content** submenu.

2. The **Introduction** section asks you to type in a cover letter and some personal information. Type in some information about yourself in this section. What is it that you do? This is about your writing style and how you want to represent yourself—do you want to write formally or informally? Don't forget to click on the **Save** button immediately after you have entered your information.

3. Now, click on the **Education & Employment** tab. Use this section to fill in all your past education qualifications. Just click on **Add** to start filling out a new listing. You should see that you can add details such as the dates of the education placement, its name and address, and details of the qualification you gained there. Here is a listing that Janet entered for her own Master's degree:

4. Do the same for your previous employments.

5. Click into the **Achievements** tab and list any of your certifications, accreditations, awards, books and publications, or professional memberships.

6. Click into the **Goals** tab and write up your three different types of goals.

7. Click into the **Skills** tab and write up your three different types of skills.

8. Finally, click into the **Interests** tab and fill out all the things you like doing in your spare time.

What just happened?

You just completed your first online résumé! Now, that probably seemed like a lot to do all in one go, but don't forget that your résumé will evolve over time; as such, don't feel like you need to get everything perfect first time. You could even write in a few unfinished ideas to start with. Don't forget, this information is now stored in Mahara. The beauty of this, of course, is that you need to go through this process only once, then in the future you will only need to make updates depending on changes in career or skill sets. This is much better than having to update a word-processed document!

We encourage you to use Mahara to become a reflective learner. It can be a useful self-developmental process:

- **Set yourself to concrete, academic, educational, and career-related goals that you then strive to achieve**: It is all too easy to just roll on from one year to the next. Some people have twenty years' worth of experience, other people have one year's worth of experience twenty times. Mahara is encouraging you to be a bit more proactive with your life than this. Why not push yourself? Set yourself some forward-looking targets and then strive to achieve them.

- **Honestly, openly, and critically self-evaluate your skills**: It is just as important that you are able to identify what you *can* do as it is for you to be able to identify what you *want* to be able to do or achieve. Use the Mahara skills section to see if you can be honest and open with yourself about where your own skills and strengths actually lie. Are you intellectually and emotionally mature enough to actually be able to identify what you are good at? Many people find this difficult. Using Mahara can help you to get better at doing this.

Pop quiz – understanding your profile information

1. How many profile pictures can you upload to your profile?

2. Where can you see your default profile picture?

3. In which section of your portfolio should you be adding career related targets?

   a. **Goals**

   b. **Skills**

   c. **Contact information**

   d. **Résumé**

Have a go hero – doing more with your profile information

In the preceding section, you saw that you can add links to your messaging nicknames in your profile information. Mahara is encouraging you to play with some live messenger and audio/video conferencing clients such as Skype and Jabber. If you are not using these already, visit www.skype.com or www.jabber.org, and sign up. You could also add your MSN, AIM, or Yahoo! accounts. You can now share this information with other users on your profile page as we'll see in the next section, so that people will have a different way of getting in touch with you.

Your profile page

Now for the exciting bit, your profile page.

One of the most important pages you create in Mahara will be your profile page. Whichever of your other pages other people look at, they are likely, at some point, to come back to your profile page to find out exactly who it is writing and recording all the fascinating stuff they are reading, listening to, and watching. All they have to do is to click on your name or your profile picture wherever they see it and they will be taken straight to your profile page.

Time for action – viewing and investigating your profile page

Let's have a first look at your profile page:

1. Start by clicking on the **Portfolio** tab in the main menu. By default you will be in the page's section of your portfolio. You will be looking at this section in more detail in *Chapter 4, Organize and Showcase Your Portfolio*. For now, you will notice that there are already two pages—your **Dashboard** page and **Profile** page.

2. Click on the link for your **Profile** page.

3. Scroll down the page and look at the different sections. Can you see the section for **My Pages**? This is probably empty at the moment, but as you start adding pages, they will appear here. Similarly, it is unlikely that the **My Groups** section has any information in it yet. The **About Me** block in the top left is also looking empty. Here is what Janet's profile page looks like at the moment:

4. Have a look at your wall. Try typing a message directly into the box in the **Wall** section and click on the **Post** button. If you are just playing around with it at the moment, it might be best to tick the little box **Make your post private?**, so no one else can see it.

5. Go and have a look at Derrin's `mahara.org` profile page at `https://mahara.org/user/view.php?id=106`. This will allow you to see what a more populated profile page can look like (you won't need to sign in because Derrin's Mahara page is accessible to anyone):

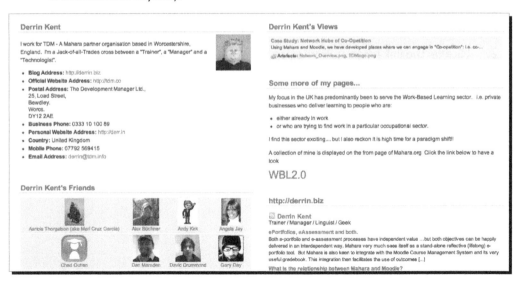

What just happened?

You just viewed your profile page for the first time ever and learned a bit about how it is organized initially.

When you add your personal information, Mahara remembers it all and uses it to automatically enter details to save you time. Information from your profile is autoloaded into different sections of your profile page depending on whether you have chosen to display it or not.

At the moment, your profile page will be looking quite empty. You would have probably noticed that there are sections for groups, friends, and pages, but no information is shown in these sections. This is because you haven't added any groups, friends, or pages yet!

The profile page wall

You just found out how to post on the wall on your profile page, but what is it and what is it used for?

The wall gets used as a place where people post messages, which are directly and publicly aimed at you (as opposed to messages in forums that are aimed at closed groups of people and system messages, which are privately sent to you). Anybody who visits your profile page will see what has been written about you on your wall. This means you have to think carefully before writing on someone else's wall, as it is open to other Mahara site users and maybe even to the Internet, if shared publicly.

We also touched on the idea of making your own post private. This essentially turns your wall post into a message as it can't be seen by everyone. A private wall post will be viewable only by the user to whom that wall belongs.

To see a good example of a Mahara wall being used, visit a former Mahara core developer, Nigel McNie's wall at `https://mahara.org/blocktype/wall/wall.php?id=12`.

Some more profile page examples

Having a look at some other's profile pages can give you ideas on content and construction. If you go back to `https://mahara.org/user/view.php?id=106` and click on some of Derrin's friends, you can see some more profile pages. Many of them have made their Mahara profile pages open to be viewed by the public in just the same way as Derrin has. Other people require you to sign in to Mahara before you view their profile pages.

Punam from Pennytown Primary thinks:

All logged-in users can see my profile page, so my own learners and also learners and teachers from other schools are going to be able to visit it. I will be able to show off some of the things that interest me, but I don't want to put up too many contact details. I don't want calls from my learners at 11:30 at night.

Janet Norman from PI Inc. thinks:

I am going to suggest that all PI Inc. users leave their pages available for logged-in users only, but I am not going to enforce this because some branch directors may wish their staff to make their profile pages public for some reason or other. I will definitely be encouraging staff to put up contact details such as their addresses, phone numbers, blog pages, messaging usernames, and so on. It will be a useful way of quickly finding out someone's details within Mahara rather than accessing our separate employee database.

As for my own personal profile page, I need to use it to show both who I am and why I am excited about using Mahara as a personalized learning platform, using it to cross international boundaries and bring all of our staff closer together in our working practices.

Neil from Training for Work thinks:

My profile page will only be seen by students and by other staff members, although some of the clients we provide training for may come and look at it. I am not going to let people view my profile page unless they are logged-in. It is there for the learners to find out how to contact me, really. I think I will populate my own page with contact information for myself and I might include some of my basic CV details.

Christophe from Silverworks University thinks:

 My profile page is not only there to give people my contact details but also I am using it to draw in my Twitter tweets as an RSS feed. It displays images and videos of a representative sample of my professional work. It also shows people many of my career successes, drawn from my résumé, a YouTube video where I introduce myself, my work, and my social and leisure interests. I have added some styled text box entries in which I give even more information about my work and leisure interests. I want my profile page to give people a rich sense of who I am.

You can do lots of different things with your profile page. Let's start by looking at something that you can add.

Adding a text box to your profile page

One useful thing you can add to your profile page, or any page that you create in Mahara, is a text box. These are extremely useful for giving meaning to your page. You can include far more than text in the text box. You will use it to put in descriptions or snippets of information that help you to structure your page in a more logical way.

In the following *Time for action – creating a text box for your profile page* section, you will look at how you add a text box to your profile page. Along the way, for the first time, you will encounter Mahara's drag-and-drop user interface for adding blocks to pages—this is very exciting! One of the things that makes Mahara stand out is its flexible framework for creating pages. It is extremely intuitive as you will see, and reflects in some ways how you would create a poster display—taking bits of information such as text and pictures, moving them around until you are happy with their location, and then sticking them in place. Of course, the advantage is that, with Mahara, they aren't stuck down forever with glue and can be repositioned whenever or wherever you like.

Time for action – creating a text box for your profile page

Let's add a text box to your profile page:

1. In the **Pages** section of the **Portfolio** area, click on the button to the right of your **Profile** page to begin editing it:

2. You will now see your profile page in edit view. It will look something like this:

3. You will notice that you are being encouraged to select different blocks from within a set of six tabs at the top of the screen and drag them down onto your page. Later you will be looking at these blocks and learning how to position them on your page. Right now though, you will be focusing on how to work with the text box. Click into the **General** tab. You should see this:

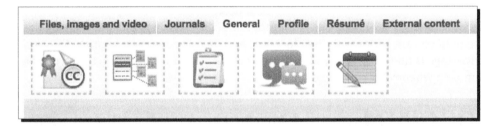

4. Click on the text box icon and drag it somewhere onto the space below in the page, to position it amongst the other blocks already present on your page layout. You will see the other blocks moving as you are dragging to make space for the text box. You will also see a dotted gray line showing you where the new block will appear. Here is a diagram showing the drag-and-drop action:

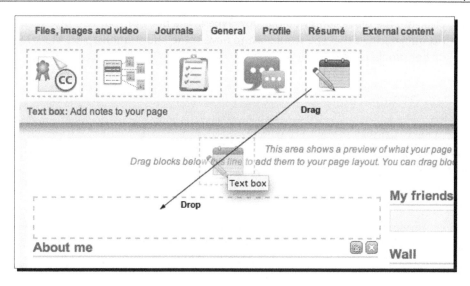

Can't drag-and-drop in Internet Explorer 6

The functionality allowing you to drag blocks around the page, when you are editing, is enabled by JavaScript. All modern browsers support JavaScript as default, including Chrome, Firefox, Safari, and Internet Explorer 7, 8, and 9. Unfortunately, for Internet Explorer 6 users, Mahara's drag-and-drop facility won't work in this browser because of problems (or bugs) it has with layout that newer browsers don't have. Tablet computers with touch-input also have this issue. You can still use IE 6 without the drag-and-drop feature, and use the radio buttons instead, but it is recommended that you upgrade your Internet Explorer browser or (even better) upgrade to an Open Source browser, such as Mozilla's Firefox (www.mozilla.com/firefox/).

5. A box will open. Click into the **Block title** field and add your title. If you don't want a title, just leave this blank.

6. Click into the **Block content** input box. Type in the body of your text box. Janet Norman decided that she would like to have some information about Mahara on her profile page:

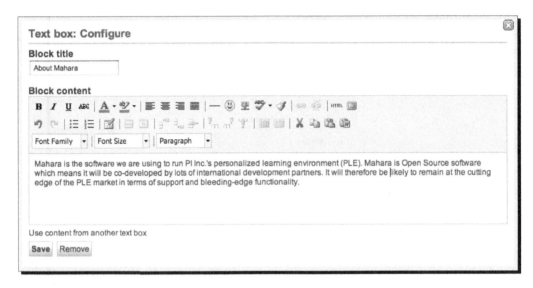

7. Click on **Save** to finish, and that's it, you've added your first text box.

What just happened?

You just added a text box to your profile page.

A section on your page is called a **block**, and you've just learned how to add a new text box by clicking and dragging it onto your profile page. Blocks are what Mahara uses to personalize your profile page and your other pages. You can add and delete blocks, and move them around. There are actually quite a variety of blocks, and the Mahara developers are keen to keep adding to the list. You have started here with a basic text box, as it's probably the one you will use most frequently. In *Chapter 4, Organize and Showcase Your Portfolio*, you will be exploring what you can do with the other blocks that are already available.

You may have noticed that in the text box there is a link to **Use content from another text box**. This is linked to the Mahara notes feature that we will discuss in detail later. It allows you to re-use information that you have typed into different text boxes rather than writing it all out again each time.

One of the other things you would have probably noticed when adding text to your text box is that you have a number of editing options available. Janet would like to make her text look more interesting, so let's revisit your text box and look at what these options do.

Options in the text editor

You will probably find that you have already used most of the options in the text editor when working in word processing applications. Let's have a quick look at some of the most commonly used options:

Icons	Function
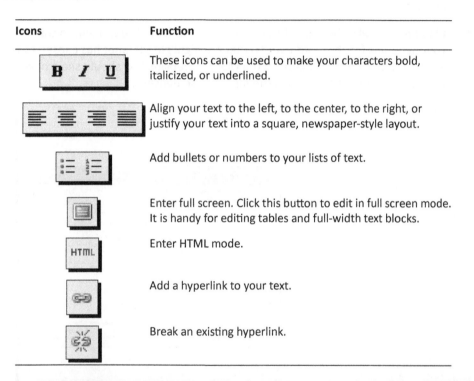	These icons can be used to make your characters bold, italicized, or underlined.
	Align your text to the left, to the center, to the right, or justify your text into a square, newspaper-style layout.
	Add bullets or numbers to your lists of text.
	Enter full screen. Click this button to edit in full screen mode. It is handy for editing tables and full-width text blocks.
	Enter HTML mode.
	Add a hyperlink to your text.
	Break an existing hyperlink.

Time for action – editing a text box by adding a hyperlink

Now let's try formatting some of the text that you have just entered:

1. Open up the text block that you created earlier for editing. You can do this by clicking on the icon that looks a little bit like a cog at the top of the block:

About Mahara

Mahara is the software we are using to run PI Inc.'s personalized learning environment (PLE). Mahara is Open Source software, which means it will be co-developed by lots of international development partners. It will therefore be likely to remain at the edge of the PLE market in terms of support and bleeding-edge functionality.

2. You are going to add a hyperlink to the text. Did you notice that the two link icons are grayed out and unclickable? This is because you can't hyperlink to something before you have highlighted it. Do this by clicking and dragging your mouse over the text that you want to hyperlink. Now you should see the two hyperlink buttons in color.

3. Click on the **Make Hyperlink** button (the one that looks like a chain) to start creating your hyperlink for the word (words) that are highlighted. Janet has chosen to make a link from the word "Mahara" to the Mahara website. You should see a new dialog box similar to the one shown in the following screenshot:

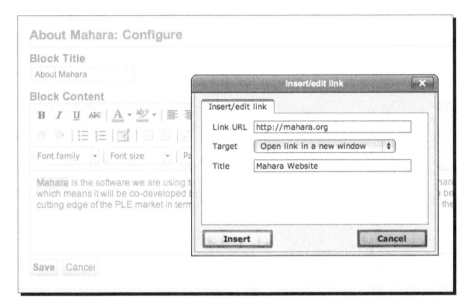

4. You now get the chance to enter your link. Janet therefore has entered a link to the Mahara website `http://mahara.org`. You can then choose a **Target** for your link. This determines if the link is opened in a new tab/window when it is clicked. Janet has also added a **Title** to her link. This title is displayed when the user hovers over the link. It may also be read by screen readers for the visually impaired.

5. Click on **Insert** and your link will be created.

6. To finish, remember to click on **Save**, otherwise you will lose the work you have just done. You should see the link highlighted in a different color:

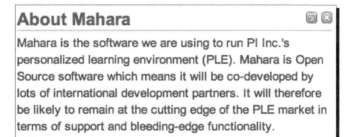

What just happened?

You just edited a text box by adding a hyperlink.

In the preceding section, you saw that HTML editing is one of the options in the text editor. Web developers have traditionally used HTML code to write their web pages. It will be useful for regular Mahara users to learn a bit of basic HTML in order to gain more control over their Mahara pages.

The World Wide Web Consortium offers free, beginner-level HTML tutorials at http://www.w3schools.com/html/.

Taking the formatting and editing one step further

Now, let's have a look at some of the more advanced options available to you in the text editor:

Icons	Function
	This allows you to change the font color. The drop-down box shows you a set of default colors to choose from and also allows you to choose more colors from a color picker, from a palette, or even by naming your color with a hexadecimal value.
	This drop-down box allows you to set a background color for your text entry. This can be useful for highlighting text or for making header titles, for example.
	This allows you to add a horizontal ruler to your text box. This can be a really useful way of splitting your text box up into separate sections.

Icons	Function
	This allows you to add emoticons (more commonly known as "smileys") to your text area. You might be familiar with them from text messages or if you use an instant messenger. Click the button to view the sixteen different emoticons you have to choose from. If you hover your finger pointer over each icon you will be told in words what feeling the individual emoticons express.
	Use this to add a table to your text box. You will see that the buttons to the right of this one become colorful once the table is selected. Use these to edit the table as you would in a standard word processor.
	This button allows you to display online images in your text box.

Janet has decided upon seeing these extra options that her text box needs an image to brighten it up.

Time for action – adding an image to your text box

Let's see how you can add an image to a text box in Mahara:

1. Find an image on the Internet that you would like to add to your text box. Janet went straight away to a free images site that she knows—Stock xchng at `http://www.sxc.hu`. She entered the word e-portfolio into the search box and found some suitable images. She has chosen an image of a man jumping in the air with his portfolio in hand:

Image by Asif Akbar (`http://www.sxc.hu/photo/991217`)

2. Copy the link of the image. You can usually do this by right-clicking on the image and clicking on **Copy image location**.

3. Reopen the text box on your profile page that you created earlier and click on the **Insert/edit image** button.

4. You will see a dialog box pop up. In the **Image URL** field, paste the location of the image that you copied in step 2.

5. Give your image a relevant **Image description**. This shows when you hover over the image with your mouse.

6. Select the **Alignment**, **Dimensions**, **Border**, and **Vertical space/Horizontal space** for your image.

7. When you have finished, click on **Insert**. This is how Janet configured her image:

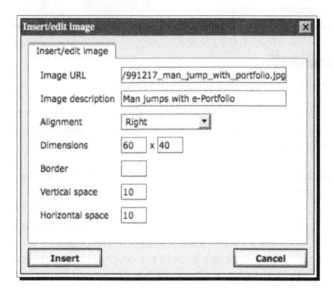

8. You may find that you have chosen the wrong dimensions for your image. Rather than going back into the image editor by clicking on the image itself and then clicking on the **Insert/edit image** button again, you can resize the image in the text editor itself by clicking and dragging the corners to stretch it. Seeing her image on the page, Janet decided that she wanted it to be bigger:

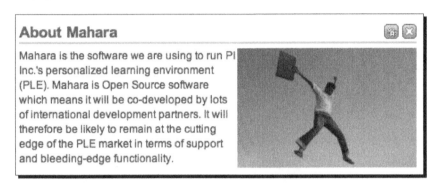

About Mahara

Mahara is the software we are using to run PI Inc.'s personalized learning environment (PLE). Mahara is Open Source software which means it will be co-developed by lots of international development partners. It will therefore be likely to remain at the cutting edge of the PLE market in terms of support and bleeding-edge functionality.

What just happened?

You just saw how to add an image to a text box in Mahara.

Why don't you play around yourself with a few text boxes on your profile page? Have a go at inserting an image into the text box. When you feel you are finished editing, don't forget to click on the button to save your changes.

When using images that aren't your own, it's important to ensure that the person who took the image has given permission for it to be used. Some people choose to use a Creative Commons license (http://creativecommons.org/licenses/) as a simple way for making it clear when their images can and can't be used. Some, for example, allow their images to be used as long as it's for a strictly noncommercial purpose. Whatever license is present it's always good to provide a link back to the original source and credit them.

Your dashboard page

Do you remember, while looking at your profile page, that there was also a **Dashboard** page available in your pages listing? This dashboard is the second type of special page in your Mahara portfolio.

It is special because it is the page that appears as your home page when you first enter your portfolio—the one related to the **Dashboard** link on the main menu.

Just as you were able to configure your profile page, you have flexibility and control over your dashboard too. This is great! You can make your dashboard page contain all the links, journals, RSS feeds, and information you want to view when you first enter the site, making your Mahara portfolio feel more personal to you.

You will be looking in more detail at how to configure this very special page and what you might want to put into it, in *Chapter 3, Create and Collect Content*. For now, let's open up your dashboard and see what it contains.

Time for action – viewing and investigating your dashboard page

It's time to have a look at your dashboard page. Here it goes:

1. Click on the **Portfolio** tab in the main menu. This time, click on the link to the **Dashboard** page. This will open up your current dashboard page. The screen should look something like the following screenshot. As you can see, it's quite empty, but already has a welcome message, an information section, and some blocks to show latest pages, forum topics, and activities:

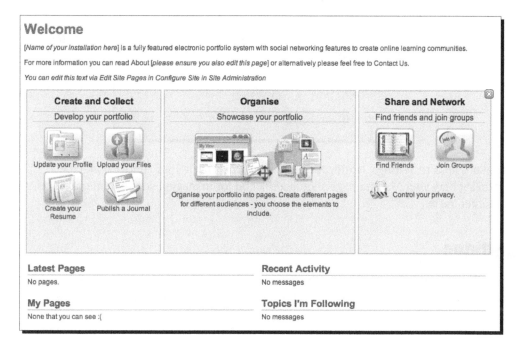

2. Now return to the pages listing by clicking on Portfolio once again or clicking on the back button in your web browser.

3. Click on the page editing button next to the dashboard page listing to start up the page editing view.

4. One thing you'll notice is that you don't have access to the welcome message or the information section to edit them. This is because these are controlled by the site administrator—they have the power to choose what the welcome message says. If you don't want the information section to be displayed on the dashboard, you can just click on the cross in its top right-hand corner to hide it from the dashboard page. The welcome message cannot be hidden in the same way.

5. That's all for now.

What just happened?

You just took a very brief peek at your Mahara dashboard page, you will be coming back to this page later in the book.

The final sections you are going to see in this chapter relate to your site settings and notifications.

You may have noticed a small menu hiding in the top right hand corner of your screen that we haven't touched on yet. It looks like this:

It contains links to **Settings**, **Notifications**, and **Logout**. This is your control panel for controlling how your Mahara page should work and for managing your communications with other users.

Settings

This is the place in your portfolio where you can go to fine-tune and personalize your system settings. You can control things such as your password, username, and other options.

Time for action – changing your settings

Let's discuss changing your settings:

1. Click on the **Settings** button in the control panel menu on the top right of the screen:

2. You will now be on a page called **Settings**. On this page, you have a number of options available, the first is to change your password. You may feel like you can't remember your old password very well and want to switch to a more memorable one. If you need to, try entering a new password for yourself. Enter your current password along with the new password and a confirmation of your new password.

3. Next, you have the option to change username. Perhaps your current username is too long and you would like to shorten it. Type in a new username for yourself. Ensure that you remember your new username. The username you choose must be available and should not be already taken by another user. Some users might not have this option available depending on how the site administrator has set things up. Janet decided to change her username from **Janet** to **Jan**:

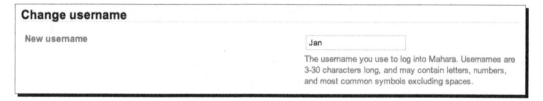

4. You will then see a group of General account options. The first is to allow you to control who is your friend in the site. You will find out more about friends and authentication later, so leave this as it is for now.

5. Leave the HTML editor option set to **On** because you will be needing it.

6. If you choose to tick the **Disable e-mail** field, then Mahara won't send you any messages to your e-mail inbox. As a site administrator, Janet definitely wants to keep this unselected. You should never really tick this as you are able to control where you would like to receive mail more specifically via the notification settings. There, you can ask to only receive mail to the Mahara inbox if you wish.

7. Messages from other users are set to **Allow anyone to send me messages**, which is fine for now because you want others to contact you, but you could restrict this if you want to make things more private.

8. If you are interested, have a look through the next three options and decide whether you want to change them or not. We will discuss these features later in the book.

9. Finally, the **Homepage information** option refers to the dashboard page information section, which we discussed earlier. I think it's a good idea to include it, but you may decide not to—it's up to you.

What just happened?

You have just learned about the settings that are available to you in your Mahara portfolio. You found out how to change your username and password and about a few of the more general options. If you change your username and password, and find that you have made the wrong choice, you can set them back to what they originally were by revisiting your settings.

Mobile upload token

You may have seen a setting related to a mobile upload token when you were looking through your settings. This allows you to send files straight from your Smartphone to your Mahara files area when used with the MaharaDroid Google Android application. This feature must be enabled by an adminstrator and requires some configuration on your Smartphone.

Now, let's look in more detail at a couple of the settings that you saw in the preceding *Time for action – changing your settings* section, thinking about why and when you would change your settings.

Changing username and password

Before changing your username or password, you should be certain that you will remember the new details. You may need to change your password if you feel that you find it difficult to remember, perhaps you have a standard password for lots of online activities (for example, instant messaging/e-mail) and would like to use this for your Mahara too. Another good reason to change your password is because you have accidentally revealed it to someone else and now want to protect your own privacy.

Very rarely will you want to change your username. More often than not your username will have been set by your administrator and they are likely to have a naming system for all usernames in the site. It is best to check with your administrator before changing your username.

HTML editor

You can choose to use a **WYSIWYG (What You See Is What You Get)** editor in Mahara, which makes your experience of typing into Mahara similar to that of using a basic word processor. It also gives you the ability to edit HTML code, if you know how to do this. This gives you more flexibility while creating content in your portfolio. Some people switch this option off because they prefer to enter plain text. It's your choice.

Notifications

Notifications are Mahara's way of letting you know about lots of different events that may occur, and are related to you or your portfolio. You can receive notifications for all sorts of different reasons. It could be that one of your friends has created a new group on the site and wants you to join, or that a journal in a page you've been following has been updated.

To start with, you will receive notifications for actions that take place in all groups, forums, pages, and friend activities. This means you can receive a lot of notifications! If the site is busy, most users opt to use a daily digest.

Of course, you will see how journals and friends work on in Mahara later in this book, but for now let's get used to opening up the notifications page and seeing what's in there.

Time for action – open up your notifications inbox

Let's open up your notifications inbox and have a look around:

1. Click on the button on the control panel menu, which is represented by a letter with a number next to it in the top right of the screen. The number in this link represents the number of unread notifications you have. At the moment Janet doesn't have any notifications and so a zero is displayed:

2. Now, you will be on a page called **Inbox**. This is the place where you will see all of your messages, just as you would see in a normal e-mail inbox. You can mark messages as read or delete them, as well as filtering them by activity type.

What just happened?

You just found out where all your Mahara notifications can be found and had a look at your inbox for the first time. If you see that icon change from zero to one at any point, you will know you have something to read!

Summary

You have learned a lot in this chapter and really got going with the basics of Mahara. Hopefully, you will now feel like you have a good understanding of some basic concepts in Mahara, including your profile information and profile page. You specifically looked at registering on a Mahara demo site, logging in, navigating, entering profile information, and creating your own profile page. You also looked at notifications and settings.

Now that you've learned about profile pages, let's put some more of your stuff online using files and journals, which is the topic of the next chapter.

3
Create and Collect Content

In the last chapter, you got started with Mahara, learning how to register and log in, as well as looking at some of the basics. You also learned how to set up your own profile. Now you are going to start putting information into your portfolio and seeing how to add some of this to your dashboard page.

In this chapter you will:

- ◆ Learn how to upload files to your portfolio
- ◆ Organize your files using folders and tags
- ◆ Start writing in your Journal!
- ◆ Make a plan and set some tasks
- ◆ Learn how to manage your notes
- ◆ Show off content on your dashboard page

Putting your files online

Before we go into the detail of how you can put your files into Mahara, let's think over why you would want to do this.

Mahara replaces the USB stick

You can log on to Mahara from anywhere, if you have access to the Internet, using an Internet browser. This is great, because it means that you are able to upload and review your files, folders, journals, and pages whenever you need to! Some have described Mahara as an online USB stick, although you have already seen that Mahara offers so much more than this, when you started creating your profile page.

Mahara is a full-fledged ePortfolio and social networking system. It facilitates reflective learning both for individuals and for groups (communities). Mahara is not just another file storage area.

However, it remains true that Mahara is a central resource space, which allows you to share the stuff you put into it. No longer will you need to store all your important files in one place. Soon enough, you are going to be presenting your work to others while you are sunning yourself on the beach!

Mahara prides itself on its extremely quick file upload facility. You should give it a whirl and see just how fast it is to upload a file into Mahara. So, this is the feature you are going to look at first.

Time for action – adding some folders and files to your portfolio

Let's upload your files into your own private space:

1. Click on the **Content** option on the main menu. By default, the **Profile** tab will be selected, click on the **Files** tab.

2. We recommend that you start by creating a structure of folders just like you would do on your laptop or desktop computer. Don't worry about getting them perfect because you will be able to edit this structure later. Enter the name for your first folder and click on **Create folder**. In the following example, Janet Norman has created a folder in her portfolio called **Social**:

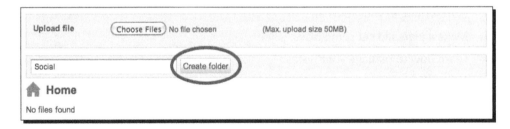

3. You should now see the folder that you have just created. By the side of it, you have the option to edit or delete it. Let's add some more detail to your new folder by giving it a description. Click on the edit button, which is represented by a pencil in Mahara:

4. You will now see a new section appear as shown in the following screenshot. Write in your description for your folder. This will appear in the information next to the folder under the heading **Description**. Don't worry about the tags, you'll see more about those later. When you have finished, click on **Save changes**:

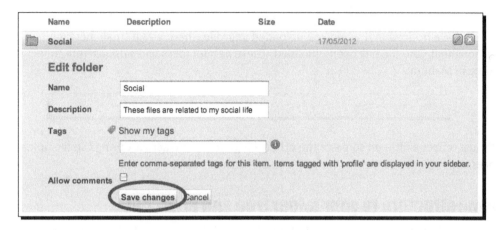

5. Go ahead and make as many folders as you like. You can make folders within folders too.

6. You're ready to start adding files. Click into one of the folders you just made. You will notice that there is a section called **Upload file** at the top of the page; click on **Choose Files**, and search for a file on your own computer that you would like to add to your portfolio. You may also have to tick a box to say that you have permission to reproduce and distribute the file. Choose the file you want and click on **Open**. You will see a spinning progress wheel that is telling you that your file is uploading. Be patient and let Mahara do its work—the larger the file, the longer it takes to upload. When the file has uploaded, the spinning progress wheel will turn into a confident check mark and you will see that your file has appeared in your files area. In the following screenshot, you can see that Janet has uploaded a video, called **myHobbies.mov,** of herself talking about her hobbies:

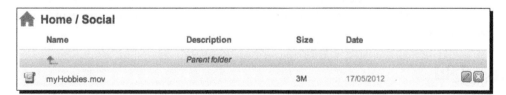

What just happened?

You have just used the files area of your Mahara site. You have learned how to set up a folder structure and uploaded your first file. In the example, Janet Norman uploaded a video file (.mov), but the file you upload in Mahara can be almost anything—a word-processed document, a spreadsheet, an audio clip, a PDF, and so on.

You may have noticed that when you uploaded your file, there was a small message indicating that your file has been uploaded. These helpful messages appear from time to time in Mahara:

Let's just reflect a little on some of the other things you came across during the file upload process.

Giving structure to your folder tree and branches

Although it is possible to make modifications to your folder structure at any time you wish, it is a good idea to work out how you want to organize your folders right from the very beginning. Here are some options for you to think about:

- You could set up folders by file type. For example, video (mp4, avi, and ogv), audio (mp3), doc (odt, odp, ppt, ods, and xls), images (png, gif, and jpg), and so on.

- You could set up folders by audience. For example, friends, colleagues, finance, sales team, and so on.

- You could set up folders by content or topic. For example, electrics, lathe, cutting, and so on.

- You could set up folders according to commonly known in-house reference codes. For example, Class3A, Topic7a(ii), and so on.

- Or any way you wish.

The key point is that you should try to keep things organized as this will help you later when you come to create Mahara pages. Later in this chapter you will see how you can use tags to be even more organized.

Copyright

When you uploaded a file in the preceding *Time for action – adding some folders and files to your portfolio* **section**, you may have been required to tick a box (if your administrator has set up the site in this way) to say that you have the permission to reproduce and distribute the file you are uploading:

Upload file	☑ Yes: The file I am attempting to upload is my own or I have express permission to reproduce and/or distribute this item. My use of this file does not breach any local copyright legislation. This file also adheres to the terms and conditions outlined on this site.

It's important that before you use any files in your portfolio, you have legal ownership over them. Anything you publish will be your personal responsibility, so please do not upload material that you are not allowed to upload. You can always link out to existing material published by other people on the web, if you need to, and you will see how to do that in the next chapter. But, just to remind you again, you will have legal responsibility for anything that you upload into your files area. By uploading a file here you are either saying that it belongs to you or that you have the expressed permission to use it as if it was your own.

Upload limit

You may have noticed the **Quota** block appearing on the right-hand side of the screen that looked a bit like this:

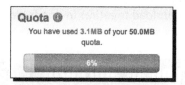

This useful information tells you how much storage space you have in your site's quota. On the demonstration site, by default, this value is **50.0MB** although it may be different on your own site. You can see in the preceding screenshot that Janet has used **3.1MB** of her quota, which is **6%** of what she is allowed, according to the progress bar. As you upload more files you will notice the progress bar moving across to indicate what percentage of your allocated space you have left. If you feel that you need to have a larger quota, get in touch with your Mahara tutor or administrator. If you are likely to be uploading lots of large files, for example audio or video recordings, you will very quickly run out of storage space, but you can always nudge an administrator to see if they allow you some more.

Now, let's have a look at how you can edit, delete, and move your files, as well as tag them.

Moving and deleting files

Mahara's filesystem is intuitive and easy to get to grips with. Wherever you see a folder named **Parent folder**, click on its small arrow icon on the left to jump up to the parent folder:

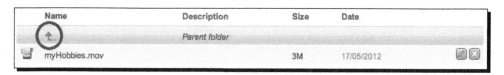

To move files around different folders, just click on their icon and drag them onto the icon of the folder where you want them to be. Simple, isn't it?

To delete a file, simply click on the small cross button to the right of the edit button.

Uploading more than one file

In Mahara, there are a couple of simple ways to upload more than one file to your portfolio at a time. This is a great time saver, especially if you have lots of files to add to your portfolio in one go.

The first approach is one that some of you may be familiar with. When you come to browse your computer's filesystem, simply hold down *Ctrl* (or *Command* for Mac users) and click on all of the individual files that you would like to upload. You should see them all highlighted. When you are happy with your selection, you can go ahead and upload them.

You can also use a compressed file (zip, tar) to upload more than one file at once. You can put all the files you want to upload together in one folder, zip it up and then upload it to Mahara.

Time for action – zip, upload, and unzip

The following steps will help you to upload and unzip a compressed file:

1. Start by putting all the files, which you want to upload to Mahara, into one folder on your local machine.

2. Then compress or zip the folder. The resulting zipped folder will end with .zip, .tar, or .tar.gz. How you zip a folder will depend on which operating system you are using, but there is plenty of online help to show you how to do this.

3. Upload your newly created zipped folder to a relevant place in your Mahara portolio, as you would with any other file. You should now see it in your files area.

4. You will see that an unzip button has appeared. Click on it to begin unzipping the folder:

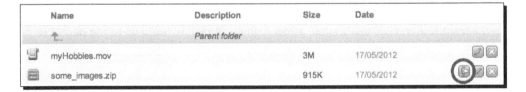

	Name	Description	Size	Date	
	🔼	*Parent folder*			
	myHobbies.mov		3M	17/05/2012	
	some_images.zip		915K	17/05/2012	

5. The next page will show you the details of your zipped folder, including where the new files will appear in your portfolio and which files are included in the zipped folder. Click on **Unzip** again:

6. The final page shows the unzipping in progress. When it's finished you will see how many files/folders have been created. Click on **Continue** to finish:

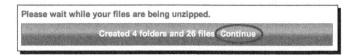

7. You will now see that the new folder (folders) and files have been added to your portfolio:

What just happened?

You just learned how to add more than one file at a time to your Mahara portfolio.

Now, let's look at how you can add tags to your files.

Using tags to organize your files and search for them

Tag is a really useful feature, which is being increasingly used in modern web technologies. When you tag something, you are giving it a label, which describes something about it. Each tag is a single descriptive keyword. Tags become useful later on when it comes to searching for items. All files tagged with a certain keyword are grouped together, so they become much easier to locate. Also, you may not want to locate a single file, but to find a file within a certain topic area.

As an example, you may know that you have some images of cars in your files area and would like to find any of them without knowing their file name or location. Since you have tagged all the files with the keyword `car`, you can search on that keyword and will have a selection of car images to choose from.

Janet chose to tag her video upload with three different tags:

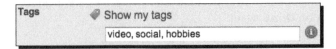

The next time Janet uploads a file, she chooses to click on **Show my tags**. She will then see:

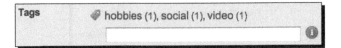

She can now see that **hobbies**, **social**, and **video** have been already used as tags and she can also see how many times that has happened. As an example, you may know that you have some images of cars in your files area and would like to find any of them without knowing their file name or location. Before long, Janet is going to have a really useful tagsonomy or classification system for her files.

Tagsonomy

Tagsonomy is a word we have just invented. The word **taxonomy** refers to the classification of things. You have a famous taxonomy of the different evolutionary lines and eras prehistoric dinosaurs, for example. Also note that the word **folksonomy** (at `http://en.wikipedia.org/wiki/Folksonomy`) is used for the Web 2.0 habit of getting the social community (the folks) to create a user-driven taxonomy. The main problem with a folksonomy as a bottom up process, of course, is the problem that arises from the existence of similar words, for example, movie, movies, film, films, cinema, and so on.

But do you know what's best of all? When Janet puts up a lot of files in her Mahara site, she will be able to quickly search for her files. She can do this by using the very useful **Tags** side block, which comes with Mahara. This block shows you all the most popular tags in your Mahara site. Currently Janet just has three tags entered:

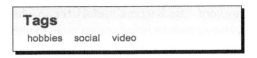

As a certain tag becomes more popular (because you have tagged more files with the same tag), you will see that the size of the text in your **Tags** block will change to reflect this. The bigger the text, the more popular the tag. Janet has tagged another file as being a **video**, but it is neither a **hobby**, nor **social**. The **video** tag text has changed to show that it is more popular than the other tags:

If you click on any of the individual tags listed in the tags block, you will see a screen where you can manage your tags:

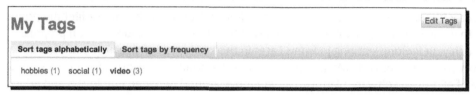

When you have a lot of tags in your Mahara, have a play using this section to search through your tags. You get the choice of doing this both alphabetically and by frequency. You can also edit your tags here.

It might be a good idea to use tags to complement, not replicate, your folder structure. For example, if you organize your folders into file types, it might be a good idea to use your tags to describe subject matter.

Punam from Pennytown Primary thinks:

I will use my folder structure to first of all distinguish between who the files are for —pupils, teachers, or friends. I am then going to split my pupils folder into the names of all the different class groups I teach. I am going to use the tagging system to group things up according to their content or topics, for example, tudor-clothes, tudor-food, tudor-pastimes, and so on.

Pop quiz – files, folders, and tagging

1. Which feature of Mahara is being described as "a single keyword that describes something about an item such as a folder or file in your portfolio and useful for helping you to search for items in your portfolio"?

    a. Tags

    b. Profile information

    c. Journals

    d. Files

2. Think of three different ways with which to organize your Mahara folder structure.

3. When uploading a file to Mahara, are you legally responsible for that file?

4. If you are running out of quota space in Mahara, who should you contact to look at getting some more?

Have a go hero – start setting up your files, folders, and tags

It goes without saying that your Mahara ePortfolio will probably become a lifetime project and that you will be making pretty big changes to your files and folders as you progress through your lifelong learning journey. Later in this book you will see how you can import/ export your data from one Mahara platform to other Mahara platforms (or, indeed, another type of ePortfolio software platform) as you move around between employers and education institutions.

However, we hope that we have helped you to understand that it is a good idea to organize your files, folders, and tags systematically and logically.

Now, please spend some time uploading some of your most precious and useful files, and then start organizing those files into some sort of sensible structure using folders, file descriptions, and tags.

Writing in your journal

Have you ever kept a handwritten diary or created a blog? In this section, you are going to learn how to do something similar by creating a journal in Mahara and by writing journal entries. You are not going to publish these journal entries yet, that will come later.

What is a journal in Mahara?

In the past, the journals in Mahara were referred to as blogs, which I am sure many of you are familiar with as a term. It seemed like a good match given that blogs are widely considered to be a form of online diary.

In fact, the word **blog** derives from the combined words web and log , for example:

web + log = weblog

Think of a log as in:

"Captain's Log, Stardate 43198.7. The Enterprise remains in standard orbit ....".

Whilst this is essentially exactly what the Mahara journal feature is—an online log of your thoughts over time, the term blog has also come to be associated with self-promotion, marketing, and communication.

The term journal fits much better within the world of ePortfolios—it conveys more a sense of thoughtful, reflective self-analysis. Compare the Mahara journal with either a lined-page notepad or a hardback blank-page diary, which you can buy from a stationery store. What you write inside is something you may or may not decide to share with others. That's not to say you wouldn't still want to share journal content with others. You are very much encouraged to do that if you want to.

In Mahara you create either one or a variety of journals (if you have multiple journals enabled in your site settings) and then you use this/these journals as a way of collecting your reflective thought processes on different topics. Actually writing things down is a useful process for helping you to understand your thoughts more clearly than you would understand them otherwise. It obviously helps to use different topics, which can organize your thoughts and learning in a neat and ordered way.

Some people then choose to share these written reflections with others, and Mahara will actually allow you to go public with your journals, if you choose to. Once you have got the hang of it, Mahara actually offers a really easy way of setting up really attractive public journals.

Though, if you are really serious about public blogging, we would still probably advise you to go for a dedicated blogging tool such as WordPress. You could also then go on to use the RSS Feed tool to display WordPress entries in your Mahara pages.

So now that you know that you should be writing in your journal, let's find out how you can do that in Mahara.

Time for action – creating your first Mahara journal

Let's get started and see how you can create a Mahara journal:

1. Click into **Content** in the main menu and then into **Journals** in the submenu bar of your Mahara. You only have one journal ready for you to use. It will be named according to your own name. For example, Neil from Training for Work's journal is called **Neil Martin's Journal**:

2. You will notice that there is an option to create multiple journals. Rather than making entries in the default journal, let's start by looking at how to enable multiple journals and make a brand new one. Click on the button to link to your **account settings.**

3. Do you remember that we discussed your account settings in Chapter 2, *Getting Started with Mahara*? This is where you now find yourself. Scroll down the page to the option called **Enable multiple journals**, check the box to the right of this option, and click on **Save**.

4. Now that you have told Mahara that you want more than one journal, return to the **Journals** screen. You will notice that the user interface is slightly different now—you can see your default journal listed. Click on the button labeled as **Create journal** in the top right-hand corner.

5. On the next screen, you will have to enter a title and description for your journal. Mahara handily gives you some examples of the kind of titles and descriptions that could be used. You can also add some tags for your journal in just the same way as you added tags for your files earlier on. Go ahead and fill in the information, and when you have finished click on **Create Journal**.

6. You will see your new journal displayed on your **Journals** page. Neil has already started making a few journals in his Mahara:

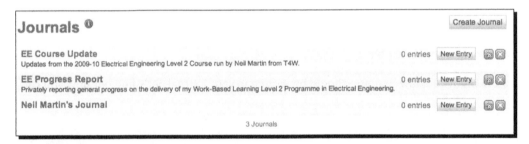

7. Now that you have created your first journal, let's see how you can add entries to it. You can add an entry directly from the journals listing page. On the right, click on the button labeled as **New Entry**:

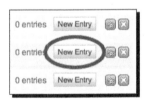

8. You will see the familiar options to add title, body, and tags again. Remember this time that you are adding a single journal entry. Neil is currently entering an entry called **May Report** into his **EE Progress Reports** journal, which he is sharing with his boss:

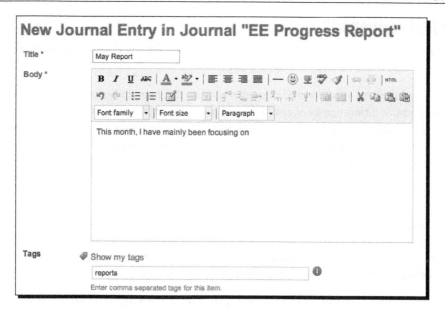

9. Scroll down the page. You will see that you have some more options available here. Click on **Add a file** to add a file to your journal from either your hard drive or your Mahara filesystem.

10. You also have the option to toggle this entry as a draft by placing the check mark in the check box. This means that if you choose to allow access to a page containing your journal in the future, this particular entry will remain private until you take away that check mark. In this set up, Neil, for example, can work on his monthly report journal entries as and when he wants to but can release them for his boss's viewing only when he feels they are ready to go. Click on **Save entry** to finish.

11. After your journal entry is published, you will see the date of entry, and you will have the options to edit and delete them later:

12. As you add entries to your journal, your journal will display the most recent entry first:

What just happened?

You just learned how to use journals within Mahara. Later in this chapter, you will be seeing how you can add these to your dashboard page.

You saw how to create a journal and add entries to it. You have to be careful in Mahara to understand the difference between the two. A journal should be given a more general name, and should contain journal entries related to the subject area. Compare the journal with the front cover of a paper-based diary and the journal entries with the page titles. For example, a journal may be entitled "My fitness regime". The journal entries are the individual articles of the journal. A journal entry within the "My fitness regime" journal may be called "Day 1 - Gym session".

You revisited your settings page and learned how to allow multiple journals. It is recommended that you do this if you want to start writing on multiple topics or for different audiences. Otherwise, if you are happy with keeping a simple, private, and reflective log of your thoughts, the default personal journal will be fine for you.

Now, you should have started to think about the kinds of journals that you would like to write. Perhaps you want to write an end-of-week report, that you will want to share with your boss, or with your students. Perhaps you would like to write a funny weekend diary to share with a few of your friends. Perhaps you have a passion, a topic that you want to engage a Mahara group with so that you can share your rants and ramblings with the world. Don't be scared to have a go—nobody needs to look at what you write if you don't want them to. Remember this is for you and it doesn't have to be perfect.

Neil from Training for Work thinks:

I mustn't confuse my journals with my journal entries. A journal contains many entries. Therefore, I should not create a journal entitled "May Report"—I should call my journal "EE Progress Reports" and write various entries in that journal called "May Report", "June Report", and so on.

I also need to remember who the intended audience is for my journals. "EE Progress Reports" is going to be for my boss—so I can write some fairly personal stuff about individual students. "Neil's Notes" is going to be a private space for me, I am never going to publish this in a page, so I can write what I like in here. "EE Course Update" is a journal that I am going to publish for my learners to view. I will need to keep what I write in here depersonalized, and always upbeat and positive.

Embedding an image in your journal entry

In the last *Time for action – creating your first Mahara journal* section, you saw that Neil made a very simple textual journal entry. One great feature of Mahara is that you are able to add audio, video, and images to your journal entries. You saw that to do this, when creating your journal entry, you should click on the **Add a file** button at the bottom of the journal entry creation screen. Select the file to add it to your journal:

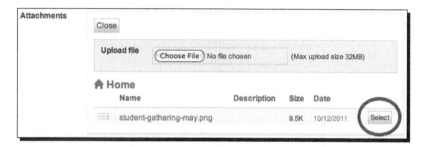

Now that the file has been added to your entry, you can use the image upload icon in the body of your entry to include the file you just added. You will see a drop-down called **Attached image** that lists all the attached images for you to include. Once you have added the image to your entry you are able to align it and resize it as you wish.

Pop quiz – writing a journal in Mahara

1. What can a journal be used for?

    a. Reflecting on your own experiences

    b. Showing other people what you are thinking about

    c. Both of the above and more

2. Apart from using simple text journals what can you do to make your Mahara journals more attractive?

Punam from Pennytown Primary thinks:

I don't think my nine-year old pupils are really cognitively ready to use journals as a reflective learning tool. They could use journals as a way of telling me what work they have done during the week, though. This will encourage them to think more carefully about what they do in their project time in class. It is also a way for me to see whether they are doing their homework activities or not.

Janet Norman from PI Inc. thinks:

Journals will be central to PI Inc.'s work. Not only do we need PI Inc. staff to grow from their reflection as they write their journals, but we also need to encourage knowledge transfer between people working in similar roles in different branches and in different countries. We will, therefore, need to get people producing interesting journals, which they will be publishing for others to read within their different interest groups. We will benefit as an organization if we can encourage our staff to think creatively and to exchange their knowledge! Journals will facilitate this.

Neil from Training for Work thinks:

I am writing journals by myself for different audiences within my Mahara site. I am going to use Mahara to write a journal on electrical engineering topics, which I am going to make public on the World Wide Web and advertise at conferences and in trade journals. I am also going to get my learners writing individual journals on a weekly basis for me to read in their WBL evidence pages. This way, I can track their individual progress on the course and open up an online channel of communication between me and each and every one of them.

Have a go hero – go on... get reflecting...

As a personalized learning environment, Mahara is very keen to get you reflecting on your learning. Journals are a key tool for you to use to do that. If you take time to sit down and express what you understand about something in writing, you will generally find you come out of the experience knowing and understanding more about your topic area than you did before you started.

If you are blogging or keeping a diary already, try writing a journal in Mahara, we think you will like it. If you have never written a journal before, get started now, you really won't regret it!

Reflecting is one of the most important parts of the portfolio process. Helen Barrett and Jonathon Richter have developed a good set of resources on the subject—it's worth a look (https://sites.google.com/site/reflection4learning/Home).

Make a plan and set some tasks

If you are building your ePortfolio within an educational or professional setting, it's likely that you are doing so to meet particular course or business objectives. A lot of these objectives will be timely and therefore, it's important to be organized to ensure you meet your deadlines!

Mahara plans are there to help you. You can make a plan, which consists of a number of tasks, each with their own completion date. When you've finished a task you can just check it off to mark it done.

It's probably unreasonable to suggest that you will log in to Mahara to use this feature in organizing your daily life tasks such as doing the shopping or going to see Auntie Flo (it's more likely that you would keep an online diary or perhaps even better a checklist application on your mobile Smartphone). However, it is still a very useful addition because it enables you to set learning-related schedules for yourself. These could be over the course of a year; for example, an allotment gardener who celebrates their work within their Mahara ePortfolio might want to use the Mahara planning facility to set seasonal task lists for seeding, hoeing, planting, and harvesting.

Somebody assessing a cohort of learners on a portfolio-building project might want to use this planning tool within the portfolio itself to manage their schedule of monthly activities. Alternatively, as a portfolio-building learner, you might want to track your completion of tasks directly related to your portfolio and work schedule such as "Finish the journal entry about my visit to Edinburgh Castle" ... and that's why we really like this feature!

Neil from Training for Work thinks:

It was a nice surprise to see that Mahara has a simple plans feature included out of the box. From a tracking point of view, it gives me a simple mechanism for seeing that the learners are setting realistic goals related to work competencies. I can sit with my learners and they can explain to me how they are progressing.

Because this is built into the Mahara system, it also means that plans can be included in pages of evidence and shared with me, which is great.

I like that whilst this has enabled me to see whether or not the students are doing the things they should be, it also gives them the flexibility to set themselves their own deadlines and work schedules—taking ownership of their progress.

I will not only encourage the students to use this feature, but also use it for myself to set targets for checking student progress. I've had an idea to display my plans on my dashboard page, to remind me of the important things I have left to do.

Time for action – make a plan and set some tasks

Let's see how you can make a plan and set some tasks for yourself:

1. Click into **Content** in the main menu and then into **Plans** in the submenu.

2. To begin with, you don't have any plans at all, so let's make one! Click on the **Add one!** link to get started.

3. On the screen that follows, you will see a really simple form where you can enter a **Title** and **Description** for your plan. When you have finished, click on **Save plan**. Neil has decided to make a plan related to a block of assessments that are due for his level 2 learners. Here is what he entered:

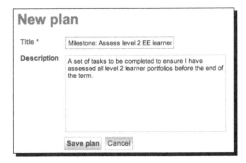

4. On the resulting page, you will see that the plan you just created is open, with its title displayed across the top. This is where you can now begin to add individual tasks that need to be completed. Start by clicking on the **New task** button on the top right.

5. On the task creation screen, you will see a form that allows you to create your task. Give it a **Title**, choose a **Completion date**, and put in a description for the task in the **Description** field. To finish, click on **Save task**. Neil has added a task to his plan:

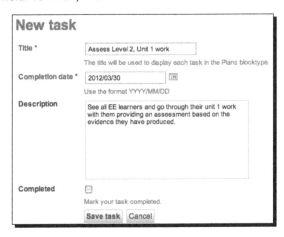

6. You will see your new task appearing in the listing for the plan:

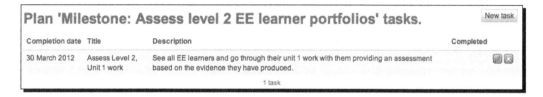

7. When you've decided that you have completed your task, click on the pencil icon to see the task once more in the editing view. Check the box labeled as **Completed** and save the task.

8. Now, when you revisit the task listing for the plan, you will see a little tick showing you that the task has been finished.

9. Finally, if you forget to do a task before its completion date, Mahara lets you know by turning the text for that task to red:

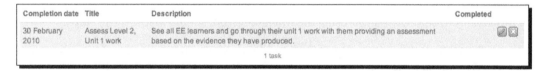

10. Try adding a few more tasks for things that you need to achieve, by setting deadlines for each one.

11. And that's all there is to it, you have created a plan and some tasks in Mahara!

What just happened?

You have just created your first plan and set some tasks for yourself.

You can create plans in Mahara to remind you of your goals/objectives or to show others how you are planning and managing your time. If you are using Mahara for work, you could use Mahara plans to set out a list of **Continual Professional Development** (**CPD**) activities for your forthcoming year (there is also a CPD plugin for Mahara that you will learn more about in Chapter 7, *Mahara Extensions*). By doing this you can put the CPD plan on a portfolio page to share and agree activities with your boss. Planning and self development have never been so professional looking and so easy to do.

Planning is a core and crucial element of any reflective learning journey. Perhaps the best thinking in this area has been done by David A. Kolb who has deeply explored the idea of a cyclical learning process.

For more information visit the following sites:

◆ `http://www.brainboxx.co.uk/a3_aspects/pages/kolbcycle.htm`

◆ `http://www.learningandteaching.info/learning/experience.htm`

For now though, let's look briefly at the simpler model, from which Kolb took inspiration to underpin his own thinking. This simple idea was a four-stage model of experiential learning coined by Kurt Lewin:

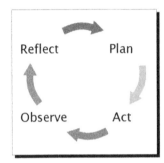

In this idea from Lewin, a learner using the Mahara system should follow these steps:

◆ **Plan**: Think about and systematically write up what you are going to do by using the Mahara planning tool.

◆ **Act**: Do whatever it is that you do (whilst capturing evidence of your work using digital media such as image, audio, video, and so on).

◆ **Observe**: Organize and showcase the media you have gathered in your Mahara pages and collections. You should also use the other tools that Mahara puts at your disposal (general text boxes, RSS feeds, and so on).

◆ **Reflect**: Use Mahara pages, their feedback sections, Mahara journals, and Mahara groups as tools for reflecting on how well you are learning. You can then start thinking about your next learning steps, which you can go on to plan.

Don't get us wrong, we are not suggesting that Mahara needs to be used with a strong formulaic approach to the learning process such as this (we actually think that it would be a mistake to insist on too formulaic an approach with Mahara), but we are showing you this experiential learning principle as a means of helping you to understand how you can utilize planning as an important part of the learning process.

Notes

Mahara notes are simply snippets of text that can be re-used between the various portfolio pages that you create. They become useful when using the text box block within pages.

I think you can probably see how this would be a huge time saver! Rather than having to copy and paste the same text into each page, you can simply define that block of text once, and select it over and over again.

When you change the snippet, you will be changing all of the instances of that text, meaning you don't have to go through all the pages and add it again.

You can also choose to make a copy of a note. This means that if the note ever gets changed as described above, your text box isn't affected.

Let's see just how easy it is to use notes.

Time for action – exploring notes

In this section you will see how to view and edit existing notes as well as how to re-use notes in your pages:

1. Click into **Content** on the main menu and then into **Notes** in the submenu.

2. Now, you will be on the **My Notes** screen. This is where you can manage notes that you have created. You aren't able to create notes here, they are created via the text box block in pages. Have a look at the notes listing. You are likely to see a few notes already listed that you added to your profile page in Chapter 2, *Getting Started with Mahara*. Janet has created one note so far—the **About Mahara** information that she added to her profile page:

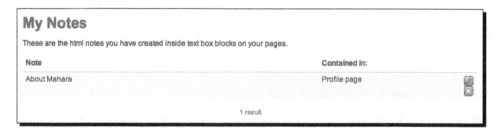

3. You will see that the **Note** column shows you the name of the note, which is the title of the text box where they are first defined. The **Contained in** column shows you the pages to which this note has been added. Janet's note is shown only on the **Profile** page at the moment.

4. Let's add an existing note to another page. Janet decides she would like to include the **About Mahara** note on her dashboard page. Click on **Portfolio** and then click on the pencil edit icon next to the page to which you would like to add the note.

5. Drag the **Text box** block onto your page.

6. Click on the link below the input box labeled **Use content from another text box**.

7. You will see a section displaying all the notes available to use. Click on the one you want to add. Janet clicked on her **About Mahara** block:

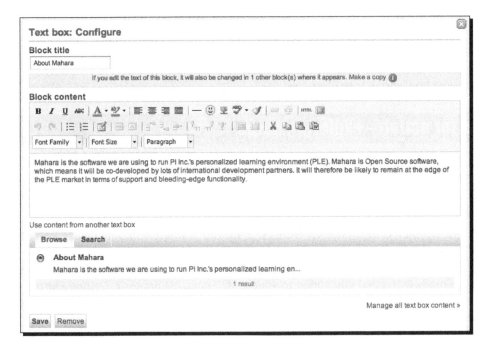

8. Notice that the content of the note is now displayed in the input box. You should also see a message informing you that if you change the content, it will be changed in all other pages that display this note.

9. Click on **Save** to add the block to your page.

10. Revisit the **My Notes** page. You will now see that the block you added is displayed on more than one page:

11. You are able to edit and delete notes. Click on the pencil edit button. Janet decided that she would like to change her **About Mahara** note slightly, so she edited the text. You will also notice that you can allow comments on your note: decide whether you would like to do that or not, and click on **Save**. Remember, when you edit a note, it will change on every page in which it is contained.

12. That's all there is. When you revisit the pages in which the note is contained, you will see that its content has changed.

What just happened?

You just re-used an existing note in a page and edited the note from the **My Notes** screen.

This is so useful! No longer will you have to type out commonly useful blocks of text every time you need them.

Here are some ideas for the kind of notes you could re-use:

- A project introduction text box on every page in a collection
- A list of links to your social media or web profiles
- Interesting quotes and thoughts from experts in your field

It's important to remember that you can't use the **My Notes** screen for creating notes. That happens when you create a text box in a page—it automatically gets turned into a note.

You can use the **My Notes** screen for managing, editing, and deleting your notes. You saw that editing a note here edits that note wherever it has been included in your portfolio. You can also edit a note globally from any page that it is included on via the text box block.

Be careful before deleting a note, because that will remove it from all of the pages in which it is included.

You may have noticed when re-using the note on a new page that there was also the option to make a copy of it:

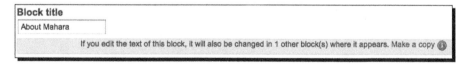

This is a way of using the same note and being able to make changes to it without affecting all other instances—that may be useful in some cases.

You are going to finish this chapter by revisiting your dashboard page.

Linking to files, folders, plans, and journals on your dashboard page

In the last chapter and in the preceding section, you learnt how you can add text boxes to your profile page to convey useful information and to add structure. Now let's see how you can add some of the different artefacts that you have looked at in this chapter to your dashboard page.

It will be really useful to add some links to your files, plans, and journals on your dashboard. When you log in, you will be reminded of what you have been writing about recently and what tasks you have set for yourself.

Time for action – linking to files, folders, plans, and journals on your dashboard pages

So let's see how you can add your stuff to your dashboard page:

1. Click on the **Pages** tab, which is under the main menu's **Portfolio** tab. Click on the link to open up your **Dashboard** page.

2. Click on the tab on the right-hand side to edit this page.

3. Let's start by adding a file that you can download. Click on the **Files, images and video** tab and drag the **File(s) to Download** block into your dashboard page.

4. You will see a dialog box open. Here you can add a file from your portfolio, or quite handily, Mahara allows you to upload a new file into your profile from this block's interface. Choose the file to add and give your block a title so that it's clear what the file is. To finish, click on **Select**. You will see your file has now moved to the top spot under the **Files** label.

5. Continue selecting all the files that you would like to add until you are happy.

6. To finish, click on **Save**. Janet Norman adds her myHobbies movie to her dashboard page:

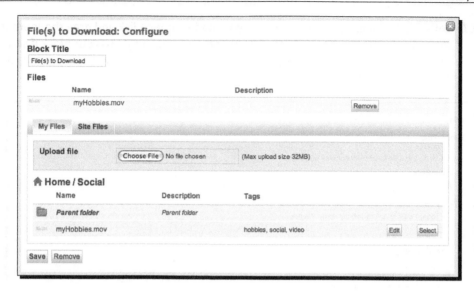

7. You can now see your file available as a download on your dashboard page:

8. Now, click and drag in the **Folder** block. You can make a folder from your files area available on any one of your pages, including your dashboard page. This will make it possible for you to download any of the files that are available in that folder. If you have several files, this will be much faster than using the **File(s) to Download** block several times. Try selecting a folder and adding it to your dashboard page.

9. Click on the tab called **Journals**. Do you remember those journals you started creating earlier? You will now insert them into your dashboard page.

10. You will see that you have four options. You can add an entire journal with all its entries, a single journal entry, a list of the most recent journal entries, or a list of journals with a particular tag:

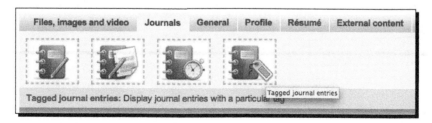

11. Let's add the single journal entry that you made earlier. Click and drag the Journal entry block onto your page. In the box that opens, add a title to your block if you wish to. Then, click on the radio button next to the journal entry you want to select, and then click on **Save**:

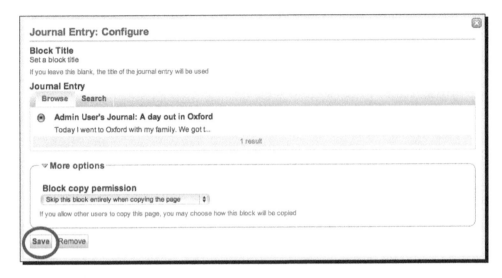

12. Hey presto—your journal entry has now been placed in your dashboard page automatically! Try doing the same with the other journal block types.

13. Finally, click into the block tab called **General**. Drag and drop the **Plans** block into your dashboard page. You will see a list of all the plans available for you to add. Tick the radio button of the plans that you want to add and click on **Save**. Neil decides to add his **Milestone: Assess level 2 EE learner portfolios** to his dashboard page:

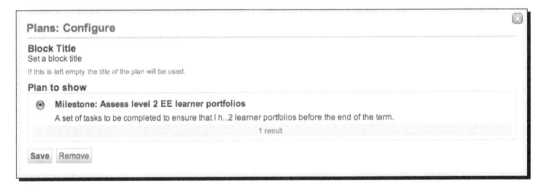

What just happened?

You just learned how to add files to download in your dashboard page. Adding a file to a page is a quick way of giving you, or other people, access to that file. Obviously, the person opening the file needs to have the computer program to open the attachment at the other end. This is sometimes why it is better to embed an image or video in your site so that it can be viewed in Mahara without the need for the person to download it and then find a program to open it with.

You also added a journal entry to your dashboard page. You are allowed to display an entire journal, a single journal entry, the last ten entries (or however many you choose) and a set of journals related to a tag. Mahara gives you these options, as it is often preferable to display the most recent, or last entry, rather than displaying an entire journal, some of which could contain scores or even hundreds of journal entries.

You will notice that in the recent journal entries and tagged journal entries blocks, you are given a drop-down list asking you to determine if other people can copy this element of your page (if it were placed on a standard page and not your dashboard). Remember, if you have checked any of your recent journal entries as being "draft only", these journal entries will not be displayed here.

Think about whether you want people to copy your journal or not. As you can link to other journals and feeds outside Mahara, maybe you would like the world to do the same, or maybe you want to keep this journal as an internal one. The choice is yours. We will talk all about page copying and templating in the next chapter.

Finally you also saw how to add a plan to your dashboard page. Now, whenever you update that plan with new or completed items, it will be reflected on the page when you log in for the first time. This is a very useful way of reminding yourself what needs to be done and what your priorities are.

Punam from Pennytown Primary thinks:

I am going to make a folder viewable later for my students—not in my dashboard or profile pages but in another page that I will set up as an introduction to our course. In this folder, I am going to make all the worksheets available that my students have to fill in by hand. They can then download these worksheets onto their own computers and either edit them in their word processors or print them out and write onto them before handing their work back to me. I can see this working very well.

Janet Norman from PI Inc. thinks:

It will be a great idea for me to display the last ten entries from my "PLE Developments" journal on my profile page. Members of the international PI Inc. Mahara community are going to be keen to keep up to date with the developments surrounding our new online Mahara space. If my journal is there for all registered users to see on my profile page it will be the easiest thing in the world for people to pop by and catch up with important changes and events.

Neil from Training for Work thinks:

My job-seeking learners can make a PDF version of their CVs available for download from application-specific portfolio pages for potential employers. I am looking forward to learning how to set up some specialist group pages in Chapter 5, because I can then put all of the important course documentation into one of the pages ready for the learners to access and download. There are no files I want to make downloadable from my dashboard or profile pages, though. Not at the moment, anyway...

Christophe from Silverworks University thinks:

I want my art students to grow through thinking about their artwork, not just to improve their technical skills. I also want them to have a broad artistic range, not to entrench themselves in a single style. I therefore engage with my students in order to systematically stretch their performance in areas they may or may not be naturally comfortable with. I often ask them to parody other artists' styles or often just to try something new. This is not something they are always comfortable with. But, I find that broadening the artist's mind in this way helps to accelerate his/her own maturing process. You don't become a Picasso by only painting in one style! The Mahara planning tool helps me do this. It helps me to work with my learners to set an agenda where they are clearly challenged and clearly time-restricted in order to do things they may not naturally choose to do if I leave them to their own initiative.

Summary

You learned a lot in this chapter about how you can add files, folders, and journals to your portfolio. You also learned about how to tag things in your portfolio.

We discussed how you might use these different tools in the different learning contexts represented by the four fictional case studies. Hopefully, you now appreciate some of the values of journals, goal-setting, and skills-appreciation as useful reflective learning tools.

You also saw how to make plans and set yourselves realistic targets and goals in Mahara.

You had a look at how to use the notes feature in combination with the text box block.

Finally, you added some of your stuff (files/folders and journals) to your dashboard page. You are now ready to learn more about pages and start adding some stuff to your pages, which you can show to other people. That is the topic of the next chapter.

4
Organize and Showcase your Portfolio

In the last few chapters, you learned about your profile page, dashboard page, files, journals, plans, and notes. You saw how you can add your profile information, files, and folders to your dashboard page, using some of the blocks provided. You learned that your profile page and dashboard pages are special types of page in Mahara. In this chapter, you are going to find out more about how to showcase your content by using pages. You will see how standard pages differ from your profile page and dashboard page, including which extra blocks you have to choose from. You will also see how to control who has access to your pages as well as how to group your pages together into collections. Finally, you will learn how to export your portfolio.

In this chapter you will:

- Create a new page from scratch
- Share your page with others
- Limit the length of time for which you allow access to your page
- Learn how to copy pages
- Create a collection of pages
- Look at a guide for assessing the quality of your pages
- Export your portfolio

What are pages in Mahara?

In Chapter 2, *Getting Started with Mahara*, you were introduced to the concept of being able to create web pages in Mahara, which are called **pages**. You also got a glimpse of how easy it is to use the drag-and-drop facility to add blocks to a page when tailoring your profile page and dashboard page.

Pages are great! They are one of the stand-out features of Mahara and we think you are really going to enjoy learning to use them. Pages, like journals, are an excellent tool for reflection. The difference between the two is that a journal is very text orientated with a user reflecting on a topic in writing (usually with an image or video to supplement the text), and pages are more flexible, allowing you to pull in content from a wide range of sources (both from your own portfolio or freely available on the web) by using the blocks feature.

Janet Norman from PI Inc. thinks:

I often compare pages to photocopied handouts. They are representations of content for colleagues to refer to. The beauty of them is that they are so easy for anyone to make!

You can include a variety of items in your page such as text, images, external media, profile information, and journals. When you have done that, you can rearrange them how you wish by changing the page layout.

Pages are not only for personal reflection on a topic, but they are also great for presenting information to others in a beautifully simple web display.

You can control access to your pages, meaning you get to decide who sees your pages and when.

Let's look at some of the things that you can do with pages in Mahara:

You could present all of your ideas related to one of the topics in a course you are taking. This could be for your own reference only or you may choose to share access to this page with your tutor or classmates:

- ◆ You could use a page to explore and express your thoughts on a particular aspect of your social or family life, such as a family holiday. This is likely to be private, and something you would only share with other members of your family.

- ◆ You could use a page as a tutor to present all of the important materials that your learners need to read, watch, listen to, and think about in preparation for a particular topic that they are going to study with you. Lots of lecturers prefer to use Mahara to present their work instead of doing so in a virtual learning environment such as Moodle. This may be partly because the lecturer's name (and avatar) will continue to be associated with the work presented in the Mahara page even after they retire or move on to another academic institution if their account is still available.

- ◆ You could use a page to present an ongoing progress report on a project you are doing at work. You might make a journal on an element of this page as well as making important files related to your project available for sharing.

- ◆ You could use a page to take notes on all of the thoughts, ideas, links, and so on, that you gather while you are attending a conference (if you have a wireless connection). You can then share the page with your colleagues after the event to show them what you have learned.

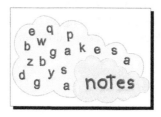

These are just a few examples, but of course there are potentially hundreds of different things that you could use a Mahara page to achieve.

Time for action – create a page and edit the content

1. Let's get started and make your first page:

2. Click on the **Portfolio** tab on the main menu bar.

3. You will see that you are in the **Pages** area. You can see that your profile and dashboard pages are already listed there, but this time, we're going to make a brand new page. You will see a screen similar to Punam's page as shown in the following screenshot. She has decided that she is now going to create a page about the Tudors. So let's get going, click on the **Create page** button:

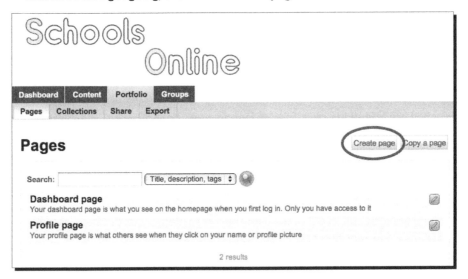

4. Now, the screen you will see is almost identical to the one that you saw while editing your profile page, apart from that you will see one more tab on the top tab bar—**Edit title and description**. In this *Time for action – create the page and edit the content* section, you will be concentrating on the **Edit content** tab, so click on that. You will notice that no blocks have been added automatically for you, and your page is currently empty:

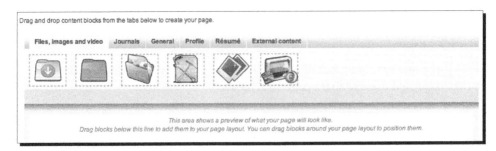

5. Decide what you would like your page to be about. Start by adding a text box to your page. Click on the **General** blocks tab. Drag a text box onto your page. Punam has written a page about "The Tudors" and used the text box to write an introduction:

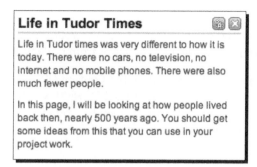

6. Next, add an image to your page, click on the **Files, images and video** blocks tab.

7. Drag the **Image** block into the position on the page and fill in the settings to link to an image stored in your files area or upload a new image. Punam has added an image and this is what her page now looks like:

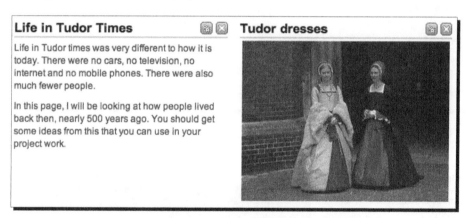

8. Finally, add a video to your page. You will find the **External media** block under the **External content** tab. You are going to add a video from the popular video sharing website, YouTube (`http://youtube.com`). Start by dragging the **External media** block into your page.

9. You will then see the **Options** pop-up box for this block. Before you enter your settings here, you will need to navigate to the external video site and choose a video that you like. You can embed more than just video by using this block and can select from a range of services that include TeacherTube (`http://teachertube.com`), SciVee (`http://scivee.tv`), and SlideShare (`http://www.slideshare.net/`). Search for a video that you would like to add to your page. When you have found it, copy the URL from either the address bar or from the link provided with the video.

10. On the **Settings** page, enter the URL in the **Content URL** section. Then choose a **Width** and **Height** for your video in pixels. 250 width x 250 height is usually fine. When you've finished, click on **Save**. Punam has found a video from the "Horrible Histories" series on YouTube:

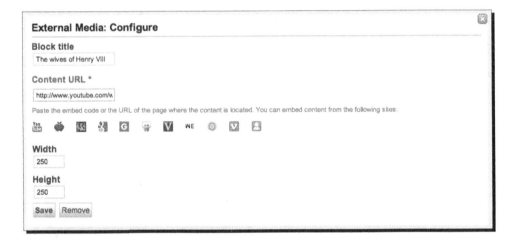

11. Her page now looks like this:

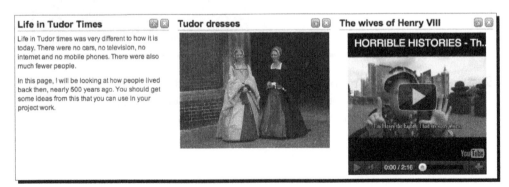

12. Let's now rearrange the blocks on your page. You can move blocks around the page by using the same drag-and-drop method that you used to add them. Click on the title of any block and try dragging it around the page. You will see how the other blocks move to make space and a dotted box appears to show you where it will be positioned. Punam has decided that she would like the video to be in the middle column and the image to be in the right-hand side column:

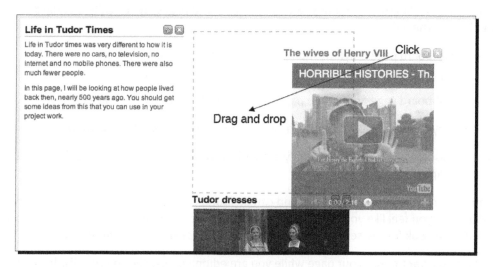

13. Release your mouse click when you are happy with the new positioning and everything will drop into place. Punam has dragged her blocks into the correct position and her page now looks like this:

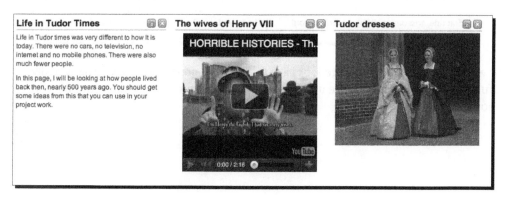

14. That's all for creating a new page, adding blocks, and rearranging them.

What just happened?

You just saw where you can go to make pages in your Mahara. You had a go at adding some blocks (text box, image, and external media) and learned how to rearrange the blocks on the page.

You may have noticed that some of the blocks that are available to you on the special pages (profile and dashboard) are not available on the standard pages. Specifically, standard pages don't include the following:

◆ Dashboard page only: My inbox, Latest pages, My watched pages.

◆ Profile page only: Wall.

◆ Dashboard page and profile page: My friends, My groups, My pages.

This is mainly to protect your security (as is the case with My inbox) and privacy.

There are also some blocks that are only available in group pages, which you will look at in the next chapter.

All other blocks are generically useful and can be found on any standard page that you create in Mahara. If you feel like you would get to know a bit more about the blocks available to add to your page, look for the section called *Blocks*, which appears later in this chapter.

Any time you want to see your page while you are editing it, just click on the **Display page >>** button on the top tab row:

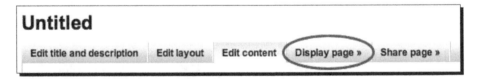

This will show you what your page looks like to a user (in nonediting view). This is really useful for stripping away all those unnecessary editing features and seeing your page in its normal viewing form.

As you are the owner, you will still have a handy button displayed to the top right labeled as **Edit this page**, so that you can pop back into editing view really quickly:

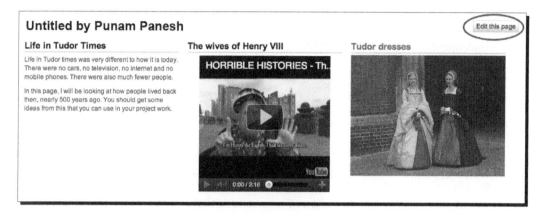

A word on small page headers

In Mahara, there are two possible ways that you may see your page. These depend on how the site has been set up by the administrator.

Without small page headers

The default page view shows the page within the context of the Mahara site and its theme. That means that the logo and menu bars (if you are logged in) will be on display to the viewer as well as the contents of your page. See the following screenshot for what this page view looks like. Notice the logo and menu are still on show:

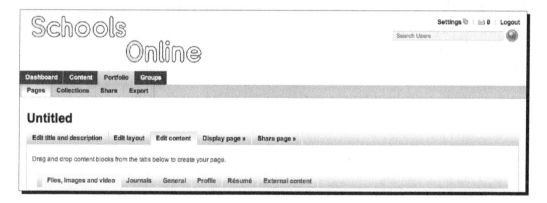

With small page headers

These are displayed when the administrator has allowed small page headers in the admin settings. In this format, the logo and menu bars, at the top of the page, are replaced by a much slimmer header. See the following screenshot for what this page view looks like. Notice that the menu is now much smaller:

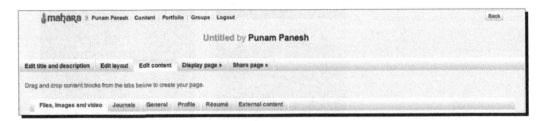

When you have small page headers allowed, you will see that the mini menu at the top can be shown by hovering over the Mahara logo on the top left. You can click on the **Back** button on the top right to return to the **Pages** section of the site.

Throughout the tutorials in this chapter, you will be working without small headers as it's the default option and more likely to be the one you experience.

Right, now you know that your page might look different depending on whether small headers have been enabled or not, let's get back to creating your page. You've already looked at adding content, but so far, that's been in a rather rigid three column layout. How about if you want a different setup, maybe four columns, or columns with different widths? That is the topic of the next section.

Adding/removing columns from your page

Punam is happy that she has managed to add some blocks to her page, but this has also made her think that she would like to give it more structure. She would like to have four columns so that she can associate each column with the following topics:

- **Column 1**: Introduction and general information such as homework assignments/quiz questions
- **Column 2**: Politics of Tudor Britain
- **Column 3**: Culture
- **Column 4**: Welfare

So, let's go ahead and show you how to change your page layout.

Time for action – editing your page layout

You can follow these next steps for editing your page layout:

1. To add/remove columns from your page, click on the top tab **Edit layout**:

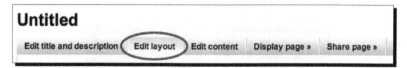

2. You will now see a screen that shows you a visual representation of all the options that you have for editing your page. You will notice that you can select between **1 column** to **5 columns**. Scroll down the page and decide how many columns you would like to use. Then, each column has a number of possible layouts controlling the size of the columns. These typically involve a choice between equal widths or larger left, right, and central columns. Choose the layout that suits you. On looking at the options for **4 columns**, Punam decided she would like to have **Equal widths** and so ticked the appropriate option:

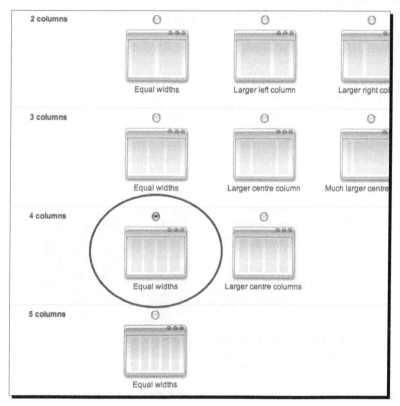

3. And that's all there is to it—once you've selected your layout, click on the **Save** button at the bottom of the page.

4. Punam's page now adjusts to look like the following screenshot, with one extra column to the right:

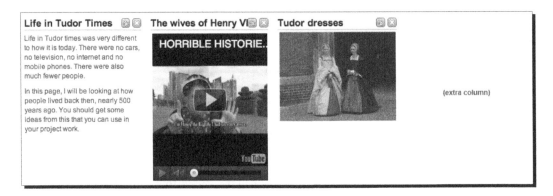

What just happened?

You have just changed the layout of your page by adding an extra column.

How many columns you add to your page depends on the content you want to add—with there being a maximum of five to choose from. Punam has a clear idea about the kind of information she wants to put in each column. You may decide that you want your page to be simpler and choose only two columns. This may be important if you are just showing images, for example, and you want them to be as big as possible.

You also saw in the *Time for action – editing your page layout* section that you may choose to have large center columns in your page. This is what Punam's page would have looked like with larger center columns:

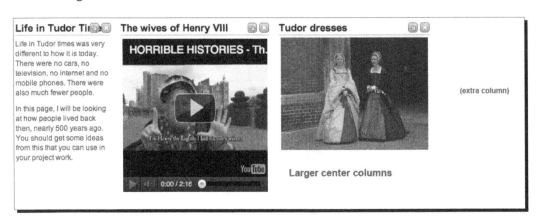

Notice how the left-hand column is now squashed to be smaller than the two center ones. This could be useful, for example, if you would like the main information in the center with small images or web links in the side columns.

Now that you've added some content and learned how to rearrange it the way you want to, it's time to give your page some details. You might have noticed earlier when you viewed your page that by default it is called **Untitled**, which isn't very descriptive of anything, so let's change that...

Time for action – adding page details

Let's give your page some details...

1. Start by clicking on the top tab called **Edit title and description** in page editing view.

2. You will see a form appear asking you to give your page some details. Start by giving your page a title under the **Page title** option.

3. Next, give your page a page description and add some tags. These tags work in the same way as those you added to your files in Chapter 3, *Create and Collect Content*. Remember they make it easier for you to search for your page later on, so it is worthwhile taking the time to fill them in.

4. Finally, choose the format of the name to be displayed in the **Name display format** field. You can decide whether or not to show your first name, last name, full name, or display name. This name appears at the top of your page. Punam has decided to choose her full name:

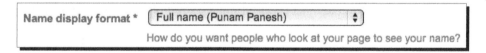

5. Click on **Save** to finish.

What just happened?

You have just added some details to your page, including the title, description, tags, and display name. The description section is a really useful way of saying something important about your page before someone has even clicked on it.

Make your page description attractive

Users can get a brief impression of what your page is about by reading the description. It is a good idea to make this as attractive and descriptive as possible. Give an introduction to what you will be discussing in the page. Imagine your description to be a snippet from the front page of a newspaper; you not only want to summarize the most important facts from your page, but also want to make it interesting so that people want to read on. It's also a good way for you to remember what your own pages are about! Including an image in the description is one way of making the page more attractive.

Once the page has been saved, the title and description will appear in the page's listing in your portfolio. Here is how Punam's Tudors page is displayed in the listing:

The tudors
This page is all about tudor Britain. You can use the resources on this page as inspiration for your group ...

Page access

So you have made your page and given it some details, but there is still one very important thing to do—deciding who gets to see it!

One of the beauties of Mahara is just how much flexibility it gives you over controlling access to your information. You can specify who gets to see what and when.

If you don't do anything, then the page by default is only ever private to you (and an administrator). If you want to share it, follow the instructions given in the following section. You may choose not to give access to other people if you are still drafting the page, for example.

But, for now, let's assume you want to go on straight away to share your page with others...

Time for action – editing your page access

Let's see how to edit your page access:

1. When editing your page, click on the **Share page >>** option. Sharing of all your pages is controlled at one central place in Mahara and you may notice that you are now in the **Share** section of your portfolio as shown by the highlighted submenu item in the following screenshot:

2. You should be on a page titled **Edit access**. Click on the help button next to the title to get an idea about what you can do on this page. At the top of the page you will see all of the pages that you have created. You can choose one or more pages to edit access for. For now, let's edit the access for one page, the one you just created. Punam noticed that her Tudor's page is already selected:

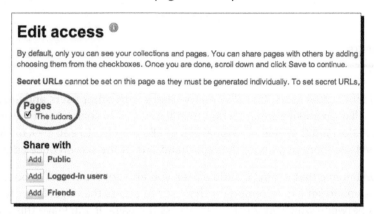

3. Now, let's decide with whom you want to share your page. To the left of this page, there are all the people or groups of people you can allow access to and to the right, there are those people/groups who can already access your page. Currently you will see that there are no people/groups on the right-hand side:

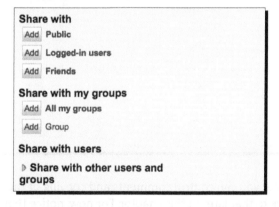

4. To add a group of users, click on the **Add** button next to that set of users:

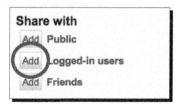

5. You will now see that the user group you selected has moved to the right-hand side under the **Added** label. Punam has decided that she doesn't want to allow access to all logged in users, just to limit it to those who are in her class. Click on the small cross to the right to remove access for the user group:

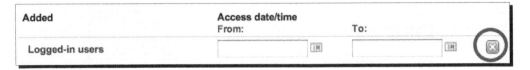

6. To add individual users, first click on the **Share with other users and groups** option. That will drop down a small section that allows you to search for the user you would like to add. Find the user you would like to allow access to and click on **Add**. Again, you will see them pop up on the right-hand side of the screen once added.

7. You will notice that when you add a user, you also get **From** and **To** boxes. This allows you to set a date period for that user to access the page. Enter from and to dates between which your users can access the page. If you leave this blank, it means that there is open access.

8. Finally, at the bottom of the page, you will see the **Advanced options** section; click on the link to drop down the available options:

9. You will see that you can control comments and copying of the page here, but we will come back to that later in this chapter. For now, notice that you have the ability to add an overriding start/stop date. This allows you to set a start and stop date for individuals and groups accessing your page. It will supersede any from or to dates that you have set.

Use the calendar!

Whenever you can add a date of any description in Mahara, you will see that there is a small calendar to the right of the input box. Usually, this is a quicker way of adding a date than typing it manually because it will enter the date in the correct format for you. You can also see ahead visually to the dates available in the future. This can help in deciding which dates you need to choose by seeing on which day of the week they fall.

10. When you are happy with who you have allowed access to and when they can see your page, click on **Save** at the bottom.

What just happened?

You have just learned about how to allow different groups or individuals to access your page, and setting when those people can access your page.

Be careful when sharing your page with all logged-in users. When you do this, all users will receive an e-mail notification (if they have their notifications set up this way) to let them know that the page has been shared with them. Only share with all logged-in users if you really need to, so as to help prevent this spamming issue.

That was quite a lot to get to grips with. So, let's have a look at those stages in more detail now.

Deciding who can access your page

Another of the beauties of Mahara is just how much flexibility it gives you with regards to controlling access to your information. You can specify who gets to see what and when.

There are four standard global settings (five, if your site has additional institutions), and you can also allow access to individual users:

◆ **Public**: Choosing this option will allow your page to be seen by everyone whether the user has logged in or not, very much like a public-facing website. Sometimes your administrator may have switched off this option.

◆ **Logged-in users**: This will allow your page to be seen by everyone who is a member of your Mahara site and logged-in.

◆ **Friends**: This option will allow access to everyone you have as a friend. You will learn about friends in the next chapter. This is a useful option if you would like to share a page that is only relevant to people who know you within the Mahara site.

- **My groups**: You can choose to share your page with one, several, or all the groups you belong to as well as with individual groups you aren't part of yet. You will also be looking at groups in the next chapter.

- **Institutions** (if enabled): You can allow access to all users in an institution if there are any institutions available in your site. You will find out more about institutions in Chapter 6. *Course Groups and Other Roles in Mahara*.

You also saw that you can choose people individually.

If you have lots of users or groups, it might be easier to type their name or part of the name into the **Search** box and get Mahara to search for you. Another thing you will notice is that you can limit access for a group to different roles, including the **Admin** and **Member** roles. Also, if the group is a course group, you can give access directly to your tutor. Don't worry too much about that now, you will be finding out what all that means in Chapter 6, *Course Groups and Other Roles in Mahara*.

Here is an example of Janet Norman searching for the **allergy** research group:

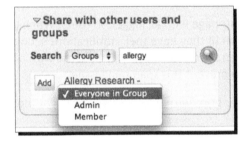

Time limiting access

You saw how you can date-restrict access to certain users, but you may have also noticed that when you add a date from the calendar, a 24-hour time period also appears. Use this to set the access time to a specific minute of the day that you have chosen:

A student may use this feature to seek feedback on a job application. The student may ask a tutor, mentor, or friend (or all three) if they could provide some feedback on an application that they have put together for an internship at an employer they're interested in applying to. The student could give a week's worth of access to the application so that the reviewer can provide feedback. After that period the access is removed.

Another great feature is that you can add a user or group more than once and give them both different access slots. This may be useful if there are two parts of a course and you would like a break in between for you to rearrange a page for a second part of a course. Perhaps you would like to add answers to a page that posed some questions to a learner.

Using the calendar more efficiently

Rather than using your mouse to scroll through the months of the calendar to select an appropriate day, you can use the directional arrow buttons on your keyboard. When you are positioned over the correct day, press the *Enter* key and that day will be set as the to or from access date.

Finally, you also saw how you can give an overriding time. Remember, this takes priority over the access times set for individuals or groups.

Punam from Pennytown Primary thinks:

I am going to give the student teacher I am helping, Lizzie, access to my page for a week. I want her to be able to see it and get some ideas about how she may make her own page later on. Once she has some ideas for the kind of content she should add, she can start making her own pages from what she has seen.

I also want to limit the dates between which my group of learners are going to be able to access the page. Once I know how to make groups, I will revisit my page, and set the access and time limits for my group.

Neil from Training for Work thinks:

I really see this idea working for our learners. We have some people outside of our institution who need to verify a selection of learner work. I don't really want these "verifiers" to have long term access to the pages. Also, if you have restricted access to just before and after the visit, they won't get confused by seeing lots of pages that they don't need to see in later visits.

Making a page copyable

You saw that Mahara has a tick box, which enables you to allow your page to be copied by those who can view it. This function can be useful in a variety of settings. You might want your colleagues to be able to copy your page. Suppose you wanted to create several similar pages, on different topics, but to keep a similar presentational theme for all of them. Rather than checking back constantly to see how you set up the first one, by ticking this box, you will be allowed to copy the first page (and as you will see later) rename it and edit it—much quicker than setting up several pages from scratch. This is great for teachers who want to create templates for learners.

Punam from Pennytown Primary thinks:

I really like this copying facility. All the teachers in our school are really good at working together and collaborating on ideas. Stewart has expressed an interest in our Tudors project, but thinks the content might not be suitable for his year 6 as it is aimed at younger students. I'm going to permit copying so he can copy my page and edit it so that he can put links with handouts that are more relevant for his year 6 group.

Naming copyable pages

It is sometimes a good idea to make it obvious in the title of a page that it is copyable. This way, both you and other users will know that the page is copyable. One way you could do this is by calling your page a Template. For example, Punam may call her Tudors page "Template: The Tudors".

When somebody copies your page he/she takes over some of the artefacts (files and journals) that you have created, but this doesn't have to be the case. You may notice that if you have made your page copyable, you will have some more options for some of the blocks that you add:

You can decide whether or not a block gets skipped when somebody copies the page. For example, you may not want the copier to copy your journal. The extra options available for you are as follows:

- **Skip this block entirely when copying the page**: The block won't be copied.
- **Others may display your Journal Entry in their page**: The journal will be displayed, but you will not receive a copy in your journal area.
- **Others will get their own copy of your Journal Entry**: The whole journal entry will be copied to the journal area of the person who makes the copy.

Secret URLs

There is one other way of sharing your page that you haven't seen yet and that's via secret URLs.

Secret URLs are a quick and easy way of giving access to your page to people who aren't already members of the Mahara site. The URL is simply a link to the page, which you can set up as a hyperlink and send via e-mail for others to open. The URL that is created is difficult to guess so that the general public can't easily find your page. Don't share this secret link via standard web pages otherwise it is likely to be found by Google and other search engines, and then it won't be so secret!

Instead of your Mahara page URL looking like this:

- `http://foliofor.me/view/view.php?id=2`

It will look like this:

- `http://foliofor.me/view/view.php?t=18pzcMLlGK4Yq5TyDkbN`

This complexity in the URL adds a little bit of privacy/secrecy to your content. It's highly unlikely that somebody will guess a link like that.

Let's see how to create a secret URL for the page that you created earlier.

Time for action – create a secret URL

You are going to make a secret URL for the page that you created earlier:

1. Go back to the page/collection sharing control area by clicking on **Portfolio** on the main menu and **Share** on the submenu.

2. You will see a list of all the pages that you have created. You can use the key button to the right to edit access again, instead click on the pencil icon to create a new secret URL:

Pages	Access list	Edit Access	Secret URLs
The tudors	Public		

3. On the resulting screen, click on **Add** next to the **New Secret URL** label:

4. You will see a new secret URL pop into place above the **Add** option. It should be quite long.

5. You can even control access for your secret URL by clicking on the pencil to the right and setting a start and end date.

6. That's all there is to it! You can add as many secret URLs as you like and manage existing ones by deleting them with the cross on the right-hand side.

What just happened?

You've just learned how to create a secret URL for sharing your page:

Neil from Training for Work thinks:

The secret URL will be useful to our learners. I can see them using it to give potential employers and work placements the access to pages containing their CVs and assessed work, without it being available to the public in general. I know that if they present digital (online) CVs, it really improves their chances of success in getting a job as it makes them stand out from the crowd. They could not only put up their résumé information but also display video clips of themselves in action in the workplace, audio clips of their tutors talking about the good progress they have made and recommending them as employees, still images showing some of the work they have completed, and so on. Who wants to present an old-fashioned paper-based CV when you could go digital?

Pop quiz – creating a page

1. Which block is available in your profile page but not in a standard page?

2. Which has greater priority, the access times you set to an individual or the overriding time?

3. What is a secret URL?

4. Can you give access to more than one person or group?

5. Can you remove access once it has been granted?

Editing your page once you have created it

The page that you created will now have appeared in the **Pages** area of your portfolio. In this screen you will notice a couple of icons on the right-hand side, which allow you to either jump back into editing mode or to delete your page.

Have a go hero – edit your page

Now that you know how to go back and change things, try to:

◆   Change the title

◆   Add a new block

◆   Change access rights

You can use the block descriptions in the next section to make a choice about which new block you would like to add. Try adding one that you haven't used before to see what you can achieve.

Blocks

So far, you have seen a few of the blocks that are available for you to add to your page, including the text box, profile information, and image blocks. Here is a breakdown of all the blocks that are available in Mahara and what you might use them for:

Category	Name	Image	Description
Files, images and video	File(s) to Download		This allows you to add files to your page that can be downloaded by other people. You can allow people to download files from your own files area as well as group files and site files.
			You may have lots of files you want to share with others. Why not turn your page into a file sharing space where you can allow other people to download files such as pdf files, documents, or images.
	A Folder		Use this to display a single folder. People will be able to see all the files or folders that are contained in this folder.
			By adding a folder you can allow other people to download lots of files rather than using the file block.
	Image Gallery		You can use this lovely image gallery to display pictures you've added to your portfolio and even external galleries you have created, using, for example, Flickr or Picasa.
			You can choose between two views—thumbnail and slideshow—and choose exactly which images to add. If you have all the images in one folder, you can simply select that folder and all the images will be displayed.
			This is a good way to add an element of interaction to your page.
	Some HTML		You can add an HTML file to your page from your files area. If you know the basics of HTML coding, this allows you to add something more bespoke to your page that you wouldn't get by using the other blocks. See http://www.htmlcodetutorial.com/ for an introduction to HTML coding.

Category	Name	Image	Description
	An Image		Use this block to display a single image from your Mahara files area. You can set a width for your image and decide whether or not to show its description. You can also choose group or site images to put in your page.
			An image makes a page more appealing.
	Embedded Media		Using this, you can directly display your own media files (video/audio) in your page. Simply choose the file that you would like to embed and give it a width and height.
			Record your own audio podcast and add it to your files area, you can then add a short snippet of you discussing topics relating to your page. This can often get a message across much better than using a text box.
Journals	Journal		Use this block to display your entire journal. All the entries from the journal are shown in the block.
			If you are writing a journal on a certain subject, you may want to use Mahara to show other people your reflections. You could display your whole journal in a page and make it publicly available. People will then be able to give you feedback on what you are saying.
	Journal Entry		This shows a single entry from a journal. In the block options, you can choose the entry you would like to display.
			If you are making pages on a specific topic, you may remember that one of your entries is relevant. Include the entry to show your own reflections on the subject.
	Recent Journal Entries		Rather than displaying the whole journal, you can use this block to display the 10 most recent entries.
			You may feel that you want to show updates from your journal, but not the whole thing because previous entries are a bit outdated. If so, this is the block you should use.

Category	Name	Image	Description
	Tagged Journal Entries		You are able to show journal entries that have a particular tag. This is really useful if you would like to see updates in content related to a specific keyword.
General	Creative Commons License		You can use this to add a Creative Commons License to your page. The license displays as a small image. With this, you can indicate if you want to allow commercial uses of your work or you want to allow modifications of your work. If you would like to know more about Creative Commons licensing, visit `http://creativecommons.org/`.
	My Inbox (Dashboard page only)		Used on your dashboard, this block allows you to see your inbox messages when you first log in. This is great for keeping you up-to-date with recent activity in the site, without having to go into the messages area. You can filter the block to choose which message types to display as well as how many messages you would like to see (between 1 and 100).
	Navigation (Can only be used in collections)		This is used specifically in collections. It displays a neat navigation tabbed menu across the top of the pages in the collection. This is recommended if you are presenting a series of pages and would like to make them easily navigable.
	Latest Pages (Dashboard page only)		Gives a list of all the recent pages created in the site. This will give you some quick links on the log in page. So you can get to pages that have been created recently. You can choose how many pages you would like to show.

Category	Name	Image	Description
	Your Plans		Use this to display your plans in your page.
			This is very useful in a reminder page that collects all your tasks and work schedules together.
			You can select individual plans to show and they will be displayed neatly in the page with each task listed along with its completion status.
	Recent Forum Posts		You can use this block to show recent forum posts from any groups that you belong to.
			This would be useful for your dashboard page as it would keep you updated with the latest goings-on from your areas of interest.
	Text Box/ Notes		With this, you can add a block of text to your page. You can format the text how you wish— changing layout and color, and so on.
			This block also allows you to pick from text boxes that you have written before. These are called **notes**. Notes are stored in your content area but can be selected using this block.
	My Watched Pages (Dashboard page only)		This block allows you to display a list of the pages that you have selected to keep track of.
			This is useful for a teacher trying to keep track of student pages.
			Watched pages send notifications to you when they are changed, so you can see a list of the most recent changes.
Profile	Contact Information		Use this to display contact information that you entered into your profile. You are able to choose exactly what information to display and have the option to hide your e-mail address if you would like to.
	My Friends (Dashboard and profile pages only)		This block displays a grid of your friends. It only shows a certain number of friends.
			It is on your profile page by default, but you can also add it to and remove it from your dashboard page as you like.

Category	Name	Image	Description
	My Groups (Dashboard and profile pages only)		This shows a list of the groups of which you are a member. It is on the profile and dashboard pages by default, and can be removed or added as you like.
	My Pages (Dashboard and profile pages only)		This shows a list of pages that you have created. If placed on your profile page, this shows other users which pages you have been creating recently that they can access.
	Profile Information		Use this to display information from your profile. You can use this to display your profile icon if you wish. You also have the option to enter an introduction to your profile information.
	Wall (Profile page only)		Other users can add short messages to your profile page by using this block. It is on the profile page by default and can be removed or added as you like.
Résumé	Your Entire Résumé		With this, you can display the whole of your résumé. All sections, including personal information, employment history, cover letter and so on, will be displayed.
	One Résumé Field		Use this to display just one field from your résumé. Only the fields that you have already completed in your résumé will be available to include in your page.
External Content	External Feed		This block allows you to display valid RSS or ATOM feeds from other websites. You get the choice of whether to show a summary of the feed items or to show their descriptions as well, or not. Your page may be an analysis of current trends, for example, in global climate conditions. By including RSS feeds to weather stations/meteorological sources, you are keeping your page up-to-date without having to alter the content by yourself.

Category	Name	Image	Description
	External Media		Use this to link to multimedia from an external website. In the configuration settings, enter the URL link to the video that you want to include in your page. You can embed from: <ul><li>YouTube (`youtube.com`)</li><li>TeacherTube (`teachertube.com`)</li><li>Scivee (`scivee.tv`)</li><li>Glogster</li><li>Slideshare</li><li>VoiceThread</li><li>WikiEducator</li><li>Prezi</li><li>Vimeo</li><li>Voki</li></ul> You are able to set a width and height for the multimedia that you embed. Media makes your pages more interesting. You could include a short educational clip or presentation from any of the sites listed above to exemplify and support any other content in your page.
	Google Apps		You can use Google Apps's API to embed books, calendars, docs (spreadsheets, docs, and presentations), and maps right into your Mahara page. All you have to do is copy and paste the URL or embed code of the widget, and it will be rendered on the page. You also get an additional height parameter to help you control the size of the content.

Copying pages

You learned how to make your own pages copyable earlier in this chapter, but what about if you want to copy somebody else's page into your own portfolio? The ability to copy someone's page is a really useful thing. This feature is all about saving time and sharing ideas.

Neil from Training for Work thinks:

I think the ability to copy other people's pages will be really helpful for my assessors and learners. For my assessors, I want to create a template page that will contain all blocks that the learners need to submit their evidence with. It'll make life much easier if each assessor can copy the template for each of their students rather than starting from scratch. As the learners gain confidence, they can learn how to change things around later.

Time for action – copying a page

You can follow these next steps to copy a page:

1. Return to the **Pages** section of your portfolio. Click on the button called **Copy a page**:

2. You will now see a screen showing all the pages that you are able to copy in the Mahara site. You can use this screen to search for pages by both name and owner. Search for and find the page that you would like to copy.

3. Find a page you would like to copy in your own Mahara site. To copy the page, click on **Copy a page**. Punam has found the page that she would like to copy. It is called "The Vikings" and was created by Stewart from Schools Online:

Copy a page

Here you can search through the pages that you are allowed to copy as a starting point for making a new page. You can see a preview of each page by clicking on its name. Once you have found the page you wish to copy, click the corresponding "Copy page" button to make a copy and begin customising it. You may also choose to copy the entire collection that the page belongs to by clicking the corresponding "Copy collection" button.

Search pages:

Search owners:

Page name	Collection Title	Owner	
The tudors		Punam	Copy page
The Vikings		Stewart	Copy page

4. Then, you will be taken to the screen that allows you to re-edit the page—should you wish to-and see a message indicating how many blocks and artefacts (files, journals, and so on) were copied. On the details page, you will see that your page now has a prefix **Copy of** in its name—decide whether you would like to keep this or change the name to something of your own choice.

5. None of the access rights have been copied (unless the author has decided to retain access to the copied page), so decide to whom you would like to give access to the copied page.

6. When you have finished, click on **Save** at the bottom.

What just happened?

You have just copied a page. This is a really useful feature if you wish to create consistency between pages, either for you personally, or between different staff members. Also, if you have someone new to Mahara, it may be really helpful to provide a template page for them to copy, to get them started. As an assessor, you may wish to create a template page for your learners to copy with a variety of sections, and then just ask them to populate the various sections with their evidence. You will be seeing more about this in *Chapter 6, Course Groups and Other Roles in Mahara*.

You may have noticed that when you were searching for pages to copy, some of your own pages appeared. This is because you have the ability to copy all of your own pages, whether they have been made copyable or not.

Also, when you copied the page, there may have been some files or journals that were also copied. These will now have appeared in your own file and journal areas. Copied files are all put into a new folder called **viewfiles**:

| viewfiles | Files from copied pages | 06/01/2012 | |

Journals are renamed with the **Copy of** prefix. As you saw earlier, journals and other artefacts may not always be copied depending on how the copyable page has been set up.

Pop quiz – copying pages

1. Once you have copied a page, can you tell the difference between that and a standard page?

2. When you copy a page, which parts aren't copied?

Page feedback

This is a useful feature of Mahara. You have the ability to give feedback on any page that you have access to. This might be useful in the following situations:

◆ You might have asked a peer on a course for feedback on some work that you are doing—in exchange for feedback that you can give on their work.

◆ A tutor may have added your page to their watchlist. You may then be getting some informal feedback from your tutor on your work before you submit it for formal assessment (see more on formal assessment in Chapter 6, *Course Groups and Other Roles in Mahara*).

Watchlists

In Mahara you can add pages to your watchlist. By adding a page to a watchlist, you will receive updates (usually an e-mail notification depending on how you have things set up) about when it has been changed. This is useful for keeping track of any pages that you are interested in.

◆ You could be using the feedback functionality as a communication vehicle. You may raise a topic for the discussion for your workmates, for example, and get them to answer the core question posed in your page by using the feedback option.

◆ You may have used a page in Mahara to share highlights of a recent holiday experience with your friends. They could then use the feedback option to tell you how jealous they are of your rich experiences or at least of your sun tan!

The feedback that you give can be both private or public (although anonymous comments may have been turned off by the site administrator). When you send private feedback, the feedback is sent to the person who has created the page and nobody else can see it. With public feedback, all users who have and will have access to this page can see the feedback, and it will appear at the bottom of the page. Any public feedback that is submitted is public unless and until the person who owns the page decides to make it private. If you own the page on which feedback is being placed, you have the right to remove that feedback.

So, let's now look at the process for giving feedback on a page.

Time for action – feeding back on a page's content

Let's leave some feedback on a page:

1. Start by finding the page on which you would like to give feedback and open it.

2. At the bottom of the page, you will see a section with four options listed. Click on **Place feedback**:

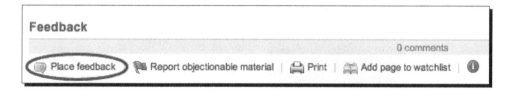

3. You will see a box open as shown in the following screenshot. Enter the message that you would like to send to the person who owns the page.

4. By default, the **Make public** option is checked, leave it like that to make your first feedback public.

5. You also have an option to attach a file, if you want to, to give more meaning to your message. Why not give multimedia feedback by attaching an audio or video response?

6. When you are happy, click on **Place feedback**. Stewart from Schools Online has found Punam's page and decided he would like to give it some public feedback:

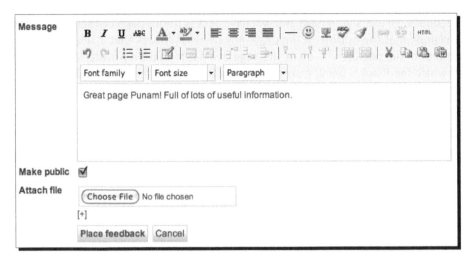

7. You will now see the feedback displayed at the bottom of the page:

What just happened?

You just gave feedback on somebody else's page content. It is important to think carefully about what you are going to write to the person, especially if your feedback is for a learner and has a critical tone. You don't want people to be offended by your comments—be constructive—you want them to feel reassured. You should certainly think carefully before making the feedback public. It is advised that you only make positive and enthusiastic feedback public; if the user may take offense, you should make it private.

If your administrator has decided to enable comment ratings, you may have also seen the **Rating** option. This allows you to leave a rating on a five-star scale in addition to the comments and files that you may have already added. This allows you to give a really simple visual indication of how highly you rate the page. Here is what the rating feature looks like:

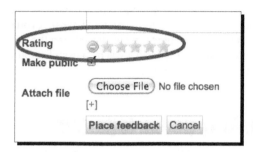

You just saw how to give feedback, but what about the other three options that were listed? Following are the things that you can do with a page:

♦ **Report objectionable material**: If you see anything on the page that is objectionable or offensive to you, you can report it to the site administrator. Do this only if you are sure the content is offensive. Remember users don't always manage the content of external links, so if the content of an external link is objectionable, it may not always be the user's fault—in this case, message the user to check first.

♦ **Print**: This gives you a printout of the page.

♦ **Add page to watchlist**: By adding a page to a watchlist, you can get regular updates as to when it has been changed. This is useful for following pages that you found interesting. Whenever the user adds more information, you can then find out and revisit the page. This is great for checking on learner's progress. You may receive a notification e-mail when a page changes by default, but that depends on how you have configured your notifications.

You have seen how to place feedback, let's now look at responding to feedback placed on your own page. Punam has now found the feedback that Stewart placed at the bottom of her page by checking her e-mail account. She decides that because the students will see the page, she doesn't want any public feedback to be there, however glowing it was! You will see that for any feedback placed on your page, there will be a delete button on the right. Simply click there to remove the feedback.

Feedback on your own page

Don't forget that you can give feedback on your own pages. This could be a good way of telling a group of people about why you created the page without writing it into the content itself. Although it's tempting to delete feedback that you have read, why not let it stay there? People have taken the time to give you some good advice and it will be a useful resource when you revisit your page in future.

Collections—linking pages together

Collections are simply a way of combining several pages together into one entity. They are really useful for creating a coherent story when you feel that one page alone doesn't give you enough space to do so.

Here are a few things that you can do with collections:

♦ Link pages together and give them a navigational block, so that they can be easily navigated between

♦ Order the pages to your liking, not necessarily alphabetically

♦ Give access to a whole collection rather than each page at a time

♦ Copy a whole collection

With pages in Mahara, you can create a mini-website with individual pages, a navigation system, and the ability to share it with whoever you like. Let's have a look at a few ideas for how you can use collections:

♦ **In a topical approach to a school project**: The students might prepare a "The Tudors" collection of different pages including, for example: "Science and the Tudors", "Language and the Tudors", "Theatre and the Tudors", "Politics and the Tudors", "Religion and Tudors", and so on.

♦ **A rich and immersive résumé/CV**: Create an impressive and in-depth résumé/CV collection. Allow the audience to see projects that you've worked on or some of the work that you've produced. Provide downloads of a corporate scannable CV, but really show off what you're capable of!

- **A modern style scientific paper format**: You could use a collection to structure a science report. This could have images, videos, hyperlinks, reflective journal entries, and perhaps embedded presentations that you've used! Use a page for each section such as "Introduction", "Research", "Results", "Conclusion", and so on.

- **In a business context**: A Project Manager may wish to submit a collection of pages, for example, "Finance", "HR", "Vision", "Partnerships", and so on, for a review in a meeting.

- **Supporting notes for a presentation**: Put together notes on different subjects, for example, "Free Software for Education", "What is Open Source?", "Lists of popular Open Source tools", "Open Source legal and licensing issues", and so on.

Christophe from Silverworks University thinks:

Collections are an absolutely wonderful feature! I will ask my students to put together a collection of their final project showing off all the work that they have been doing. I will recommend to them that they structure their collection to show the development of their work, with four pages—overview, inspirations, development, and final work. Having said that—I'm going to keep the brief quite open to give them flexibility and see what they come up with. When they've made their collections, we'll be able to allow access to the public and share the links on the Silverworks Final Show website as a promotional tool for our students.

Christophe is due to give a demonstration of the collections feature to his tutor group before they get going on creating their own and is going to use one of his own recent projects as an example. So, let's show you and Christophe how to make your first collection.

Time for action – create a collection

Let's see how you can link some pages together to make a collection:

1. Before you can get going on creating your collection, you will need to have all the pages ready to put into it. Start by creating some pages. Don't worry, they don't need to be complete and have all the content in, just to exist in your portfolio. Christophe has begun creating his pages. Here is the overview page for his collection:

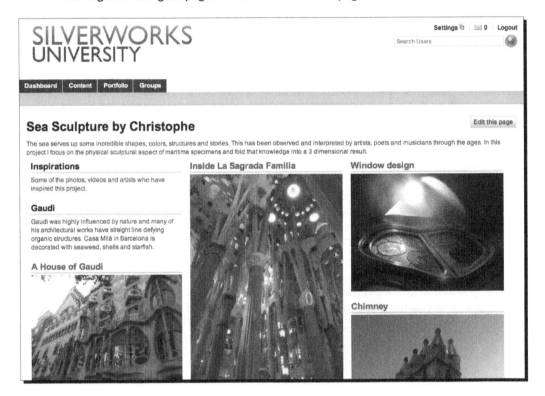

2. Now that you have your pages ready to add, click on **Portfolio** from the main menu and then **Collections** from the submenu.

3. On the resulting page, you will see that you don't have any collections at the moment, click on **Add one!** or the **New collection** button in the top-right to start creating one.

4. The next page is where you can give your collection some details. Think of a relevant collection name and give it a collection description.

5. Next, decide if you would like to give your collection a page navigation bar. It is recommended that you do to start with, just to see the feature in action. When you are ready, click on **Next: Edit collection pages**. Here is what Christophe selected for his collection:

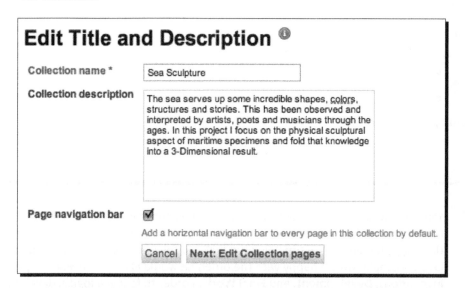

6. On the page that you now have on your screen, you will see that you are invited to choose all the pages that you wish to add to your collection. Use the check boxes to the right of the pages to add them one at a time. You can add as many pages as you like to your collection. Christophe has selected his four pages. Then, click on **Add pages**:

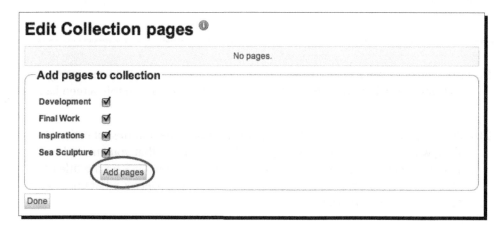

7. You will then see that all the pages you added have jumped to the top section below the **Edit Collection pages** title:

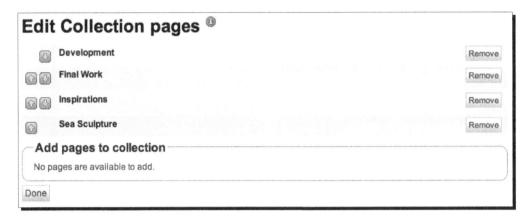

8. You will also see that you now have some options for rearranging and removing the pages. Reorder your pages as you would like. Use the arrows on the left to rearrange the pages, the one at the top being the first and the one at the bottom being the last. Christophe wasn't happy with the order, he would like it to be **Sea Sculpture**, **Inspirations**, **Development**, and **Final Work** in order to follow a logical development progression and so reordered his pages:

9. Now that you're happy with the pages in your collection, and their ordering, click on **Done** at the bottom to finish. You can always come back to this screen later to reorder your collection.

10. When you've finished, you will see your collection appear in the collections listing along with some metadata showing you the description that you entered earlier as well as those pages that are included in the collection. Click on the title of your collection to open it up and get your first glimpse. Here is what Christophe's collection listing looks like:

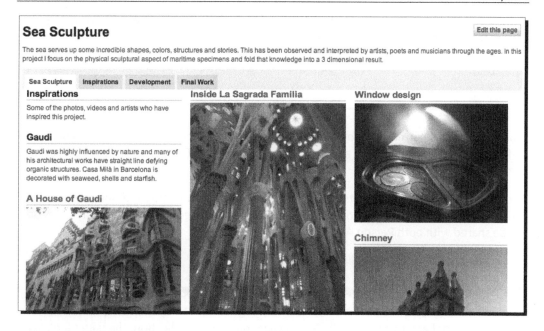

Sea Sculpture

Edit this page

The sea serves up some incredible shapes, colors, structures and stories. This has been observed and interpreted by artists, poets and musicians through the ages. In this project I focus on the physical sculptural aspect of maritime specimens and fold that knowledge into a 3 dimensional result.

Sea Sculpture Inspirations Development Final Work

Inspirations

Some of the photos, videos and artists who have inspired this project.

Gaudi

Gaudi was highly influenced by nature and many of his architectural works have straight line defying organic structures. Casa Milà in Barcelona is decorated with seaweed, shells and starfish.

A House of Gaudi

Inside La Sagrada Familia

Window design

Chimney

What just happened?

You just created your very first collection of pages in Mahara. You learned how to add some information for your collection. You also saw how easy it is to add and edit the pages for your collection by pulling from those pages that already exist in your portfolio.

You chose to add a navigational bar to your collection, which for Christophe looks like this:

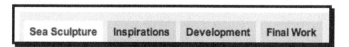

You may be wondering what the collection would look like if you hadn't decided to include this navigational bar. The simple answer is, the individual pages would simply act as if they didn't belong to a collection and appear exactly the same as a normal page to a viewer.

So the question is, why would you put a page into a collection and not include a navigational menu? The answer basically relates to access. As well as being a way of linking pages together using physical links, a collection also links the access permissions of all the pages it contains.

If you had decided not to include the horizontal navigation bar, you could (and probably should) choose to add a vertical navigation block instead. You will learn about the vertical navigation block later in this chapter.

If you revisit the **Share** section of your portfolio that you looked at earlier, you will notice that your collection has appeared there:

Collections	Access list	Edit Access	Secret URLs
Sea Sculpture			

You can set access permissions for the whole collection in exactly the same way as you would do for an individual page as well as when adding secret URLs. Of course, you can go back and edit this access at any time.

A collection automatically inherits the access of all the pages it contains. If one of your pages in the collection is being shared only with Person A and another with Person B, the collection will be shared with both Person A and Person B.

Pages can only belong to one collection at a time.

Have a go hero – add a navigation block to your collection

We've just seen that when you don't allow navigation on your collection, the pages look just as they would do as normal pages. There is a way to add a different navigational menu to your collection without using the default one that runs across the top of the pages—using the **Navigation** block.

Try removing the top navigational menu from your collection and copying in the navigation block. You will need to put the block on every page in the collection.

Here is what Christophe's collection looks like when using the navigation block rather than the default top menu:

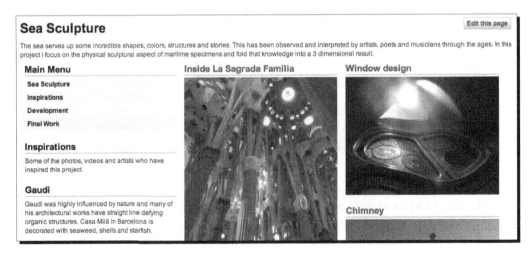

Assessing the quality of your page/collection

So by now, you should have had plenty of practice at setting up pages and collections. We would like to encourage you to think about the quality of your page. The quality of your page is very important. If your page is to be available for others to see, you want them to be enthused to read, watch, or listen to what you have to say. If the page is just for personal reflection, you still want to be able to return to the page at a later date and understand it, especially if you are going to use it in some kind of revision program.

We have devised a list of guidelines for you to assess your pages against. This list is grouped into two key sections that we believe are important in page quality—Content (what you are adding, how relevant it is, and so on) and Aesthetics (layout, graphics, and so on).

You may not agree with all of the guidelines, but hopefully it provides a good basis from which you can assess the quality of your page. This checklist will be available to download from the logged-in links and resources menu from this book's demonstration Mahara site at `http://maharaforbeginners.tdm.info/`. To the right of the criteria points, we have provided simple tick boxes for you to fill in if you wish to.

Page quality checklist

The page quality checklist is divided into two sections—**Content** and **Aesthetics**.

Content

This section contains the following list:

♦   **C1**: The content isn't simply a repetition of fact. The page contains personal responses to the content. Arguments/opinions are included.

♦   **C2**: The thoughts are well structured and original.

♦   **C3**: The page has a clear purpose/objective.

♦   **C4**: Linked to point C3, an introductory sentence or paragraph could be included to communicate the key objective of the page.

♦   **C5**: Paragraphs are used appropriately.

♦   **C6**: The content is free of grammatical/punctuation errors.

♦   **C7**: Colloquialism/slang is used only when appropriate to the subject of the page or to your style of reflection.

♦   **C8**: Video included should be short, succinct, and add value to the page content. As a guide, videos longer than two minutes should be considered before inclusion (this is a rough guide, teaching videos or music tracks may be longer, for example).

◆ **C9**: Audio should also add value to the content and be of a high quality. Audio hasn't just been included for the sake of it.

◆ **C10**: Content is interesting. Even if what you are writing about isn't to the readers' normal interest, they should be hooked by a well presented, convincing, and structured page.

◆ **C11**: Any arguments you make are polite and respectful. You show sensitivity to different audiences and do not offend them by your content.

◆ **C12**: None of your content is repetitive in a single page. You haven't duplicated images or ideas.

◆ **C13**: Where relevant, you have summarized your content with an indication of what has been learned.

◆ **C14**: Your content shows research into the subject being discussed. A certain amount of work required prior to page creation is evident.

◆ **C15**: In the case of collections, there is a logical order to the pages. Each tells a separate section of the whole story.

◆ **C16**: All links in your content are live. None of them link to dead pages or pages that have altered from the originally intended content.

◆ **C17**: Linked-to content is of a high quality. Content in external web sites is relevant to the original subject.

◆ **C18**: Links are well-labeled. They give a clear indication of what content you should expect to see when you click on them.

Aesthetics

This section contains the following list:

◆ **A1**: Main body font is consistent throughout the page, apart from where changes are absolutely necessary (for example, to highlight a different point or to make a comment).

◆ **A2**: Main body font is relevant to the content. Use of Serif/Sans-serif fonts are appropriate.

◆ **A3**: Main body font isn't garish, it should be simple. Commonly used web fonts are Serif—Georgia, Times New Roman, Book Antiqua and Sans-serif—Helvetica, Verdana, Arial.

◆ **A4**: Images in your page are of a sensible size. They don't dominate other content by being too big.

- **A5**: Images are cut/cropped to the correct size before you upload them to your page. You don't have unnecessary detail in your images.

- **A6**: Images are of a good coloring. Your images don't look washed out or too bright.

- **A7**: Images are of good quality resolution. Your images don't look pixelated or low quality. Remember though—you have a limited file quota, so don't upload huge images to your portfolio otherwise you will soon run out.

- **A8**: The page is visually attractive. It includes a graphic of some kind. People looking at your page should want to read it.

- **A9**: There is an element of user initiative/creativity in the aesthetics of the page. This may include the creation of your own image for example.

- **A10**: Bullet pointed/numbered lists are used to break up long sections of text.

- **A11**: If you have developed a collection, the layout/design of each page should be consistent. Each page doesn't use vastly different font/image styles.

- **A12** :The page doesn't appear too cluttered. There shouldn't be lots of text/images packed into one section of the page.

- **A13**: Don't adjust the link color unless you really need to. The CSS styling of the web page will help to keep these consistent.

Page inspiration

Remember, you can visit `http://groups.diigo.com/group/everything-mahara` and filter by the `mahara_portfolio_example` tag to see plenty of good quality pages.

Have a go hero – make a top quality page

You have learned a lot about creating your own page in Mahara and seen two case studies—a page on the Tudors by Punam and a collection by Christophe. Use this information, and the page quality guide that you have just seen, to create a page in the demonstration site or your own Mahara site. Your page could be on anything you want—sport, politics, hobbies, art, music, film, and so on.

It doesn't matter what topic you choose as we just want to see you coming up with ideas for making your pages interesting, innovative, and of a good quality.

Let's finish the chapter by looking at how you can export your portfolio.

Exporting your portfolio

Mahara allows you to export your whole portfolio. This is a great feature because it means that your portfolio isn't trapped inside the Mahara website in which it resides. You can set it free whenever you want to! This helps your life long learning—work that you have done in one school, college, university, company, or other training provider—to be transferred and developed upon as you move from institution to institution.

In Mahara, you currently have the ability to export your portfolio into the following two formats:

- **Standalone HTML website**: This option creates a self-contained website with your portfolio data. This means that you can view your portfolio in a standard web browser such as Firefox, Chrome, Safari, or Internet Explorer. This is great, because it also means that you can easily show off your portfolio to others via your own website on the Internet rather than the Mahara page owned by your education institution.

- **Leap2A**: This is a format that allows editable portfolios to be transferred from one portfolio system to another. This means that you can move your portfolio not only between different Mahara sites, but also to and from any other ePortfolio system that supports this open format (for example, PebblePad at `http://www.pebblepad.co.uk/`). Unlike the HTML format, Leap2A is difficult for people to read and should only be used for moving your portfolio around.

Let's see how you can export your portfolio into the two formats by using an example from Derrin Kent's portfolio:

Time for action – exporting your portfolio

Let's see how you can export your portfolio in Mahara:

1. Under the **Portfolio** tab on the main menu, click on **Export**.

2. On this page, you will see the two options for exporting your portfolio. Let's start by making a standalone HTML website. Make sure the **Standalone HTML Website** option is selected (it should be by default).

3. Next, you have the choice of exporting all of your portfolio, or just one or more pages. Let's export just one of Derrin's pages to be displayed as an HTML webpage. To do this, first click on the **Just some of my Pages** link under **What do you want to export?**.

4. You will see a section drop down that invites you to choose which pages you would like to export. Derrin has chosen his **Free Software for Education** page and ticked the box next to it to select it:

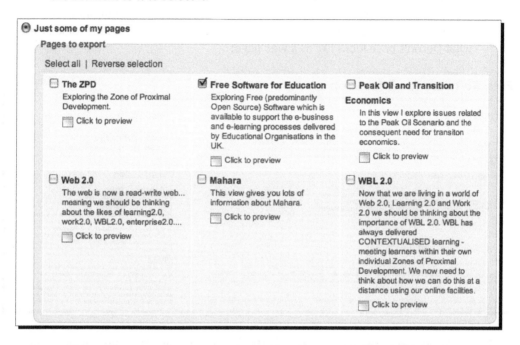

5. Remember, you can choose as many pages or collections as you would like to export.

6. Decide if you would like to include user feedback in your export.

7. To export, click on the **Generate export** link at the bottom of the page. You will see a progress bar telling you the details of the export as it progresses. When finished, the resulting ZIP file will be automatically downloaded to your computer.

8. Now, let's have a look at the file that you just created. It will be a ZIP file, so before you do anything else, you will need to de-compress it. When you have done that, you should see a folder named something like **portfolio-for-derrin**, but with your username on the end. Open the folder and you will see all the content of your export. To view your new website, click on the `index.html` file in the folder. Here is what Derrin's page looks like as a web page:

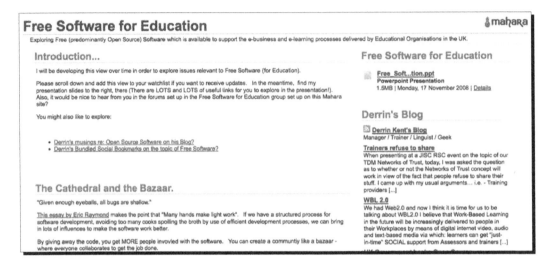

9. You've exported and viewed your portfolio as a web page. Now, let's export your portfolio to Leap2A format. Return to the export page in your portfolio. This time, select the **Leap2A** option and generate the export. You will be asked to save the result in the same way that you did with the HTML website export. Again, you can choose individual pages for export.

10. This time, once unzipped, your export will be named something like **mahara-export-leap-user1-1259342849 Folder**.

11. That's it! You've just exported your portfolio to two different formats using Mahara's export facility.

What just happened?

You just exported your portfolio to both a standalone HTML website and Leap2A format.

HTML export

The **hypertext markup language (HTML)** is the most common language used on the Internet. The option to download to this format allows you to keep a copy of your own work on your own computer and view it whenever you want to with your favorite Internet browser. Nowadays, it has become incredibly cheap to rent some web space on a web server—just Google search for cheap webhosting! So, if you want to show off your own work after you have left your educational institution, you can just upload the exported HTML to your web browser and point a website address to it (`http://www.yourname.com`).

Leap2A export

Leap2A is an open format that doesn't belong to any company or individual. In an age where data is commonly being used by large organizations and governments, it is good to think that you can maintain control over your own learning data in a Leap2A format, which will always be available for you to use.

Another good thing about this format is that more than one ePortfolio system has adopted it. This means that you can move your own stuff not only from Mahara site to Mahara site but from various ePortfolio sites to other ePortfolio sites.

You are probably wondering how you can import your Leap2A data from another Mahara system into this one. You can't do this by yourself—the site administrator or institutional administrator (refer to *Chapter 6, Course Groups and Other Roles in Mahara* for an example) has to do this for you. So, either e-mail them if you know their e-mail address, speak to them in person, or send them a message via Mahara.

While the import between different systems is a great idea in theory, it doesn't always work out perfectly in practice. This is because different ePortfolio sites may have implemented the Leap2A format slight differently.

It is also a good idea to regularly take a backup of your portfolio, say every semester or year, so that you have your own personal copy of your data.

Pop quiz – export

A student is moving from one school to another. Both schools have a Mahara ePortfolio system. The student would like to take their portfolio with them when they move and have it imported to the new Mahara system. To which format should they export their portfolio?

Have a go hero – show off your portfolio by exporting to an HTML website

Try using the HTML export function to create yourself a standalone version of your portfolio. Now, you have a simple but effective way of creating your own website and showing it off to others. If you're feeling adventurous, you could learn some basic HTML and CSS to tweak the resultant website to be more presentable. The best place to start learning HTML and CSS is at `http://www.w3schools.com/`.

Summary

In this chapter, you learned a lot about pages. You saw how you can make a new page from scratch and edit it to contain the kind of content that you want to add. You also saw how to control who can see your page as well as when they can see it. You saw how to go back and edit your page once you have created it. Also, you copied someone else's page into your portfolio area.

You had an introduction to the page feedback system in Mahara and placed your first feedback on a page, deciding whether you wanted to make it public or not. You saw how to link pages together by using collections.

Finally, you thought about the quality of your pages by looking at some page quality guidelines and found out how to export your portfolio.

Now that you've learned about your profile, files, journals, and pages, you're ready to learn all about the social networking facilities in Mahara. We started to discuss social networking in this chapter when we mentioned groups and friends. That is the topic of the next chapter.

5
Share and Network in Groups

By now, you must have added your stuff to Mahara and discovered how to organize it into pages and collections. In this chapter, you will find out how you can connect with other Mahara users, using groups and friends. This is where Mahara really comes to life, with people being able to discuss topics of common interest in forums and share pages with each other. So what are you waiting for, let's get social!

In this chapter you will:

- ◆ Learn how to make your own groups
- ◆ See what you can do in a group
- ◆ Create and participate in forums
- ◆ Learn how to find and join other groups
- ◆ Start building your network of friends

Groups

Groups in Mahara are a way of bringing users together into places where they can collaborate and share ideas. Groups may be created for a number of different uses. You might, for example, create a group based around a common interest area or hobby. For example, if you are interested in playing guitar, you might create a group called Guitar playing techniques. In an educational context, you could create a group for a study topic to share ideas and questions. Groups may also be based around a course in which all learners on the course are members of the group.

You can give your group a name and description, and decide who can enter the group. Here is what you can do in a Mahara group:

◆ **Set up and participate in discussion forums**: This is where all the group members can discuss issues related to key topics in the group.

◆ **Create group pages**: Here, users can view group pages. They can also collaborate to create new group pages.

◆ **Share group files**: You can allow members of the group to upload their own files to share with other group members.

Janet Norman from PI Inc. thinks:

This is really where Mahara gets very interesting for me. I want my users to be communicating in common interest groups that relate to the type of research and development they are involved in. We want to use Mahara for improving communication between staff members in other roles as well. Communities of practice can form where marketing experts share their ideas and techniques by sharing pages they have created. Managers can use forums to discuss practical applications of procedures and compare experiences, giving advice wherever they feel they can. Strategists can work collaboratively on tenders. In many different ways, Mahara groups can offer PI Inc. staff a real digital place where we can share innovative ideas and chat to each other about questions and problems that we are facing.

Let's get started by showing you how to set up your first group. Note, you will only be able to create a group if your site administrator has allowed this ability to standard users.

Time for action – creating a group

Let's first learn how to create a Mahara group:

1. Click on the **Groups** option on the main menu bar. This is the area that contains all the options you need to access the social aspects of Mahara.

2. By default, now you will be on the **My groups** page. Currently, you don't belong to any groups, but that's about to change. Click on the **Create group** button as shown in the following screenshot:

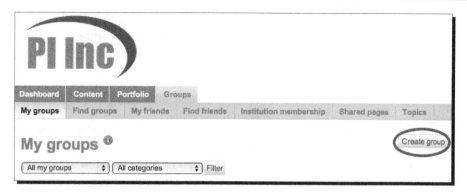

3. Now, you will see the **Create group** page. This contains all the options you need to configure your new group. Start by giving your group a relevant name in the **Group name** box.

4. Next, take some time to fill in the **Group description** section. The information you enter here will show up in the group's **About** page.

5. Click on the **Settings** link to open a drop-down list. First look at the **Membership** section. This lets you decide how other users can join your group.

6. The first decision to make is whether you would like to make your group open or not. Open means that anyone from the Mahara site can join. Janet has made a Clinical Trials group and decided that she doesn't mind it being open, so left the **Open** option checked:

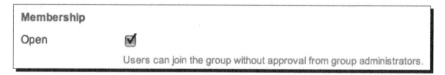

7. Notice that if you have unchecked the **Open** option, the **Request** option becomes available. This allows users to request membership of the group.

8. Look at the two other options in the **Membership** section—**Friend invitations** and **Recommendations**. Decide whether group members can invite their friends or if they can send recommendations to join the group. It is only possible to have one of these options selected. So, choose which you would prefer. Janet has decided it would be nice to have a button on her **Group homepage** for recommendations, so ticked that option:

9. Next, choose who can create and edit group pages. There is the choice between the options **All group members**, **Everyone except ordinary members**, and **Group administrators**. You will find out more detail about group roles in the next chapter.

10. Now look at the **Visibility** section. Here you can decide if your group will be shown up publicly for users who aren't logged-in to the site; this will enable logged-out users to see the group's **About** page and forum posts. Janet has decided that her Clinical Trials group could have sensitive information in it and so left this option unchecked. You can also decide to hide a group so that it can't be found, to hide membership so that non-members don't see who's in the group, and to even hide membership from members so that only the group admin knows who's in the group.

11. Finally, you can decide if you would like to allow notifications on the **Shared** page. This option sends notifications if and when a member shares a page with the group. Janet doesn't want her group members to receive these messages and so left it unchecked.

12. When you're happy with your settings, click on **Save group** to finish.

What just happened?

You just saw how to make a new Mahara group.

Revisit the **My groups** screen. Here, you will see the group that you have just created along with the title and description that you entered earlier. It is important that you choose a sensible summary for your group, so that when you are looking through all your groups on this page later, you will know exactly what the different groups are for. You will notice that the **My groups** page also shows the number of members that currently belong to the group (if the group admin hasn't decided to hide the group members). Here is what Janet Norman's **Clinical Trials** group looks like:

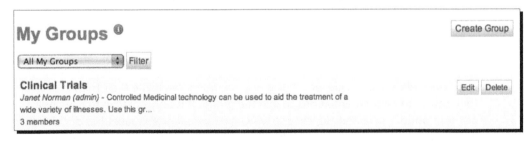

Finally, this is the place you should come to if you want to edit or delete the group. The **Edit** option allows you to change any of the group settings that you chose originally. Clicking on the **Delete** option brings up a warning page asking if you would like to delete the group, as shown in the following screenshot:

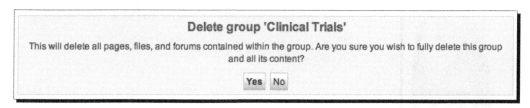

Always be certain that you know you are doing the right thing before you decide to delete your group. There may be important forums or pages in there that other users want to keep. Once the group has been deleted, it can't be retrieved!

Now, before you go on to explore what else you can do in your group, let's go back and have a look at some of the settings that were available when you created the group.

Membership

In the preceding *Time for action – creating a group section*, you discovered that when you create a new group, you can decide how to allocate membership for it. You saw that there are two main types of group in Mahara for a standard user:

- ◆ **Open**: Any user of the site can join your group, they don't need approval from a group admin.
- ◆ **Request**: Users can send requests to group admins to ask to join a group.

To get a better idea about how these different group types affect how people join your group, let's discuss each type in more detail and think up a few scenarios where they might be used.

Open membership groups

When you choose to make an open membership group, you are opening your community up for participation by all registered site users. In making this decision, you are saying that you don't mind who joins your group and, in fact, that you want to encourage participation by as many users as possible. You are also giving your users the freedom to leave the group at any time. This group type is great for a community space where you want to encourage large numbers of people to join in and to participate in open discussion. Many of the groups on the mahara.org website for example are open membership. Why restrict community interaction unless you really need to?

Neil from Training for Work thinks:

I would like to set up a social area for my learners called "Sports". I want anyone to be able to participate without any restrictions on joining. I want joining up to be as simple as clicking a Join button for the group. Open membership seems to be the option I should go for.

Request membership groups

This is where you start to get more protective of your group. You aren't opening the group up to all users, but getting users to send a request—asking for your permission before they can join in. This is a good way of restricting group access to users who have an active interest in joining you. When users request to join your group, they can give a short description explaining why. You should think carefully before creating this group type because it means, potentially, that you will have to monitor and respond to lots of requests to join.

Janet Norman from PI Inc. thinks:

I'm really excited thinking about all the different groups I could make. I have already practiced by making a Clinical Trials group, but I have another idea—to have a company wide PI Inc. policy discussion group. I want to encourage those who are interested to join, but still maintain some control over the membership.

Friend invitations and recommendations

These settings are a really useful way for users to organically spread the word about your group. Rather than the administrator of a group having to send out requests to all the people they would like to join, group members themselves can get in touch with their friends and let them know that they should join and get involved.

Often you're much more likely to join a group that a colleague or friend has told you about than a group administrator who you may not know in person. This can help your group and its community to grow more quickly.

So, which option should you choose since you can only tick one? Let's have a look at the difference between the two:

- **Friend invitations**: This gives your group members the freedom to invite their Mahara friends to join your group themselves. The invited friend can then decide to accept or decline the request. If they accept, they are auto-added to the group and the group admin doesn't have to do anything. This option also adds a button to **Group homepage** to allow members to invite friends.

- **Recommendations**: This puts a button on **Group homepage**, which allows group members to recommend the group to their Mahara friends. When the friend receives the recommendation, they then still need to join the group according to the group settings. So, they would need to request membership if it is a request group, for example. In this sense, a recommendation is less active then a friend invitation.

Both of the above options put a button on **Group homepage**. Using this button, you can invite group members to actively spread the word about your group to their friends.

The main difference between the two types is that friend invitations give group members the power to allow their friends directly into the group by accepting the invitation. With recommendations, the invited friends still have to go through the normal process before they're allowed in—if the group is open, this of course would mean that they can just join up as usual.

Christophe from Silverworks University thinks:

I'm going to create a Mahara group for my tutor group. I'm not that interested in the group being completely closed to just my tutor group members, though, I'm going to allow them to send friend invitations. This is so others can get in on the action and see what we've been doing.

Regardless of which type of group you choose and how you allow your users to recommend your group, you are always able to invite anyone you like to join your group.

In Mahara, there are other group types and role allocations that are available only to administrators and staff members. These are known as **controlled membership groups** and **course roles**. Controlled groups allow you to oblige people to become members of your group without them responding to a request or deciding to join—they are instantly put into your group. Course roles allow you to set up different group roles, including tutors. Neil is an admin in his Mahara site and has indicated that he is interested in using controlled groups. See Chapter 6, *Course Groups and Other Roles in Mahara*, if you think this is what you want to do.

Group categories

You may have found in the last activity that you had an additional option in the general group settings to add a group category. For you to see this, it would have to be set up by a group administrator. This option allows you to choose a general category for your group from the options that your admin has added. This can be really useful for people who want to search for your group from the find groups page as they can filter by category.

Now let's see what you can do in your new group.

Navigating your new group

Before you start looking at group members, forums, pages, sharing, and files, you should get used to navigating around your group and take a look at the **About** page.

Time for action – opening up and navigating around your group

Let's have a look around your group:

1. In the **My Groups** section, open up the group that you would like to navigate around by clicking on its name. Janet decides to open up the **Clinical Trials** group that she created:

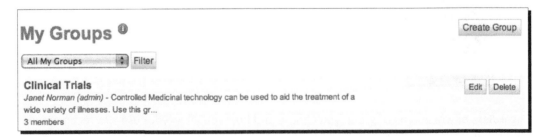

2. Now, you will see all the options available for your group in a menu bar. The tabs are **About**, **Members**, **Forums**, **Pages**, **Share**, and **Files**. Try clicking on each of these to get used to navigating around your group:

3. Return to the default group page by clicking on the **About** tab.

4. The **About** page gives you an overview of the group. It includes a description of what the group is about, who administers it and moderates the forums, the group type, when it was created, how many members, pages, files, and folders there are, and latest forum posts. You can also edit or delete the group from the **About** page.

5. The **About** page is actually another type of page that belongs to your group. You could think of it like the profile page for the group. You can edit this page by clicking on the **Pages** tab. You will see that you have the **Group homepage** page there:

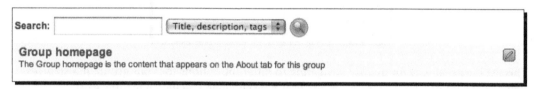

6. And that's all there is to navigating your group!

What just happened?

You just had a brief introduction to what a group looks like and how to navigate it by using the group tabs. You also had a look at the group's **About** page and how it is just another type of special page in Mahara. You can use the **About** page to give group members an overview of what's going on in your group. Make this page as attractive as possible, it's a really useful way of communicating with your group members.

There is another quick way to navigate your group. You will quickly look at it now.

The groups shortcut side block

Whenever you are doing anything with group, a handy little feature of Mahara is the group's shortcut side block. It will usually be on the right-hand side of your screen and look a little like the one shown in the following screenshot for the **Clinical Trials** group:

This list is a great way for quickly navigating to different options for your group. It also gives you a snapshot of what's going on in the group by showing you which forums exist.

Have a go hero – set up some new groups and create their About pages

It is time to set up some of your own groups. If you do not have your own Mahara site yet, feel free to register yourself at `http://maharaforbeginners.tdm.info`. This site offers a safe haven where you can experiment with group creation.

If you already have a Mahara site, you might be wisest to put in a bit of advance thinking before you start clicking on the Mahara buttons. Why not brainstorm a list of groups that you would like to set up on a sheet of paper first? You could then start deciding what group type you think you should choose for each of your new groups. When you are ready, go ahead and start setting up your different groups in the Mahara space. There may well already be some groups in your Mahara site, so check that you aren't creating a group that isn't the same as one that already exists. As you set up each and every group, put a little bit of thought and love into your **About** page. It is, after all, the first introduction to your group that your new group members will have.

As we said, you could put anything on this **About** page. You have the same scope as a normal Mahara page, so you can include text boxes, image galleries, and media to make it as attractive and dynamic as possible.

Joining an open membership group

By now, you should have an empty group set up with the relevant settings. But a group is nothing without its member community!

Let's see how you can join an open membership group.

Time for action – joining a group in Mahara for Beginners

Let's join an open membership group:

1. Log in to http://maharaforbeginners.tdm.info with your username and password.

2. Click on **Groups** on the main menu bar.

3. Click on the **Find groups** submenu tab.

4. You will see all the groups that are available to you in `http://maharaforbeginners.tdm.info`. Browse through the groups until you find a group called **ePortfolios: Best Practice**. Remember, you can always use the **Search** box to search for any group you want, if you already know its name.

5. When you have found this group, you will see that you have the option **Join this group**. This button is present on all open membership groups. Click on **Join this group**.

6. That's all there is to it. You have just joined your first Mahara group.

What just happened?

You just joined a group at `http://maharaforbeginners.tdm.info`. We think it would be great if readers of this book could use the groups and discussion area in this site to give feedback on things that they have read in the book or generally to discuss Mahara and ePortfolios.

Have a look around the other groups in the site and see if there are any that grab your interest. Why not join up to some more groups or even set up some new groups of your own? When you've had some practice, move over to your own Mahara site or one of the mentioned free alternatives.

Managing your group members

If, when you made your group earlier, you made an open group, it may be that people have already started joining you. If you chose a request membership group, you won't have any members so far. Later in this chapter, you will see how to invite members and respond to other users' **Join** requests.

Janet Norman can now see that new users have started to join her **Clinical Trials** group. She would like to know how she can see more detail about who is in her group as well as how to manage them. So, let's get going and find out how to manage your group members!

When we talk about **managing members**, we mean the ability to decide who stays in your group and to determine what roles users in the group have assigned to them.

Time for action – managing group members and changing roles

Let's see how to manage you group members:

1. Start by clicking on the **Members** tab of the group menu bar.

2. You will now see a screen with all your group members listed. In Janet's **Clinical Trials** group, currently there are three members indicated by the box similar to that shown in the following screenshot:

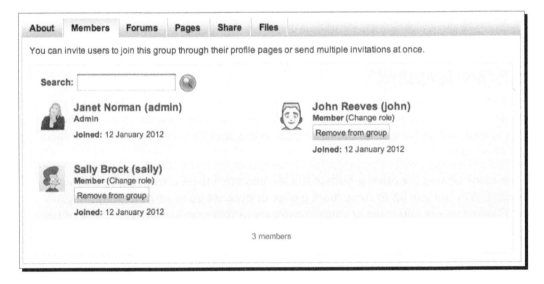

3. When your group starts growing, it will be more difficult to find your users. You can use the **Search** box to find the user you are looking for. Type the name of the person that you would like to search for in your group, and hit the **Enter** key or click on the search icon. Janet Norman has decided that she would like John Reeves to become a group administrator as he is head of the **Clinical Trials** group. She has typed **John** in the **Search** box:

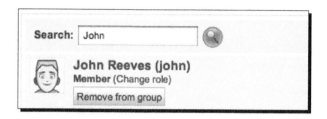

4. Now, change the role of your new group member by clicking on the **Change role** button:

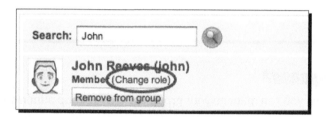

5. Next you will see a screen inviting you to switch the role of the user. Switch your group member to have an administrator role by selecting **Admin** from the drop-down box. To complete the action, click on **Submit**:

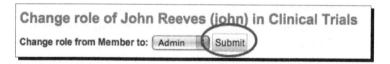

6. Finally, you may want to remove a user from your group completely. To do this, click on the **Remove from group** button next to the users' name. You must be sure before you do this, because you don't get a second chance, the user will be instantly removed (although you could of course reinstate the user later):

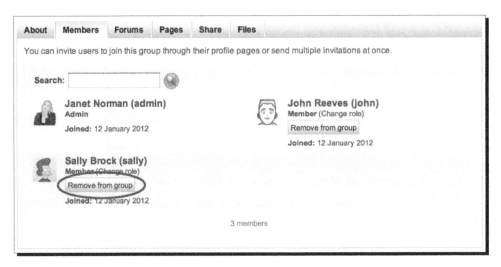

What just happened?

You just learned how you can manage your group users as a group administrator.

In the preceding *Time for action – managing group members and changing roles section*, you saw that you are able to assign roles to your users (choose whether to make them a group administrator or not). Let's have a look at the difference between a group administrator and a group member:

- **Group administrator**: A group admin can do anything in a group, including managing users, editing the group settings, creating forums, editing forum posts (it will be obvious that an administrator has done this, so they can't pretend to be a user), creating pages, sharing pages, and uploading files. The person who creates a group is automatically a group administrator.

- **Group member**: A member can create forum topics, group pages (provided the group is set up that way), and upload group files. Members are simply users in your group who aren't administrators.

You should carefully think about who you want to administer your group. Adding new administrators helps to ease the pressure on you for updating and monitoring your group, because you can share the load with another member of staff. On the other hand, you must be sure that your group administrators know what they are doing, otherwise they could do some damage such as deleting a forum or accidentally removing users. In that case, they should probably be handed this chapter to read!

Your group now has some members, so it's time to start getting them talking and interacting in your group forums.

Pop Quiz – creating Mahara groups

1. Who is allowed to join an open membership group?
2. What does it mean to make your group publicly viewable?
3. What can a group administrator do that a group member can't?

Group forums

The Cambridge Online Dictionary (`http://dictionary.cambridge.org`) defines a forum as a situation or meeting in which people can talk about a problem or matter. Traditionally, a forum was a physical place where people could join together and share ideas (think of the Romans). Nowadays, thanks to the Internet, people don't even need to be on the same continent to discuss things in this way!

Forums are one of the most important features you will use for socializing. Group members are able to talk about a topic and can comment on each other's ideas or suggestions.

Mahara groups give you the ability to add forums, allowing your group members to discuss any issues if they would like to. Each forum can have lots of users in it—all of them can make posts. Posts are simply a text comment, and they can be used to ask questions or to respond to elements of a discussion. Each group can have more than one forum, each with a different topic.

Let's go back to Janet and see what ideas she has for how she can use forums in her Clinical Trials group.

Janet Norman from PI Inc. thinks:

We know how important it is for our clinical trials to be conducted in a legal and moral way. To help with this, it would be great to get a legal and ethical discussion forum going where our experts can talk about latest legislation and ethical issues that are relevant to the way we conduct our clinical trials.

The forum that Janet has suggested is great for gathering information from different users in one place.

Here is what Neil from Training for Work thinks about forums.

Neil from Training for Work thinks:

We are coming to the end of a program for some of our learners. It would be great if we could get a discussion going on the users' experience of using Mahara for reflective learning. A course experience forum in the course group would be perfect for this, so that the users can let us know what they think of the online and offline elements of our training program—and suggest what improvements we can make next time we run it.

Hopefully, now you may have got some ideas about the different kinds of forum that you may want to have in your own group. You could also look at the `mahara.org` forums for some inspiration as there is lots of activity there.

Now, let's go ahead and see how you can set up a group forum.

Time for action – creating a forum

Let's create a forum for your group:

> *1.* From the **Group homepage** page, click on the **Forums** tab.

2. To start with, you will see that you already have the **General Discussion** forum in your group, but start by making your own new forum by clicking on the **New forum** button:

3. The **Add forum** page will now open. Give your forum a relevant title.

4. Then fill in the **Description** section by giving a simple explanation of what the forum will be used for.

5. Next, choose how you would like topics in your forum to be expanded. You can select **Fully expand**, **Expand to max**, or **No indents**. Janet has decided to leave it set to the default—**Fully expand**. These options will be discussed later in this chapter.

6. You will also see a link that says **Settings**, click on it. This shows a group of options for your forum. The first option is an option to automatically subscribe users. If this is set to **Yes**, all group members will start receiving e-mail updates about this forum. Janet wants her users to decide for themselves if they would like to subscribe, so left it set to **No**.

7. Choose how you would like to order your forum compared to the other forums in the group by using the radio buttons. Janet thinks that the discussion forum should always remain at the top and so selected the button below that:

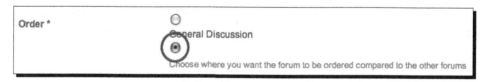

8. There is also an option to add moderators for the forum. Moderators are non-admin members who you have confidence in to edit and delete other peoples' topics or posts. Janet has decided that she would like to have one moderator called Sally Brock who is the head of the Clinical Trials steering group. To make someone a moderator, simply click on his/her name under the **Potential Moderators** section and click on the right arrow. You will now see him/her listed under **Current Moderators**:

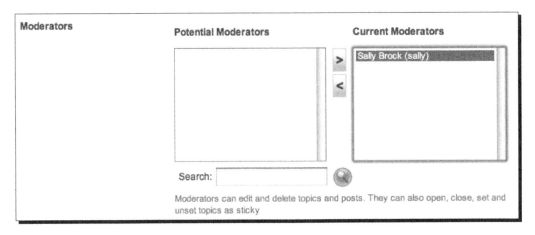

9. Finally, there are a couple of other options available. You can decide who can create topics. With this, you can limit creating topics to just moderators and admins. Under this scheme, members are still able to respond and reply to the created topics. You can also choose to close new topics for standard members, so that only admins and moderators can reply.

10. Click on the **Save** button to finish. You will see a screen similar to this showing your newly created forum:

What just happened?

You just saw how easy it is to create your first group forum.

The Mahara forums are as good as any you will find on the Internet—so take advantage of the feature. Think about discussions you have at the moment that require meeting up in a physical location and consider making an online Mahara forum for them, so that you can chat at distance. Why spend hours talking in face-to-face meetings? You could get all the serious discussion done before you turn up to a meeting, cutting down meeting time to focus on making the decisions, and socializing with each other a bit more. Why not use the online forums to debate issues and meet face-to-face to make decisions.

The other great thing about Mahara forums is that they can serve as a permanent online record of thought. Often, people tend to craft their thinking more carefully when they put their thoughts into writing than they do when they are speaking aloud. Users can go back again and again to revisit carefully-crafted comments that were made a long time ago but which may still be useful today.

With group forums, you are able to keep the discussions in relevant and controlled areas. You can decide who does and doesn't see the forum, and who you would like to administer or moderate it.

You were also introduced to the concept of a forum moderator. Let's have a look at this in more detail.

Forum moderation

It may be important to you that your group forums are moderated. In a Mahara group, a forum can be edited by group administrators and forum moderators.

Moderators have the ability to edit and delete forum posts to remove any posts that may break the house rules or that are irrelevant to a discussion and require moving elsewhere. Mahara moderators also have the ability to respond to closed topics to which standard members cannot reply.

By forum moderation, we mean the allocation of a few special people to actively make the discussions happen. A moderator will generally conduct the following phases of a forum:

- Clearly presenting the topic up for discussion
- Engaging participants
- Managing the discussion process by linking the thought threads, widening out the topic, engaging responses from the more passive, and so on
- Ending the discussion when appropriate—perhaps with personalized feedback to some of the participants and a generic discussion summary or conclusion for the benefit of all

Not all forums have to follow the framework suggested in the preceding list, of course. Many forums are more open-ended in nature and many can be much more passively moderated.

Another responsibility of a forum moderator is to ensure that people are behaving themselves. What is exactly meant by behaving yourself is entirely up to you. Typically, a forum moderator should establish a set of ground rules for what is and isn't the acceptable behavior. Common rules might include the exclusion of abusive language, or a negative attitude to other people's postings.

Once the ground rules are established, it is a good idea for a moderator to make them clear and available to forum members. Perhaps they could include a link to the code of conduct in the forum description. This way the users will know the ground rules before they even start posting.

It is a good idea to replicate forum moderation standards across the entire Mahara site. Your Mahara site administrator may even have set up a code of practice for forum contribution as an element on your site's **Terms and Conditions** page. The important point is that you should be seeking to develop community standards from the onset, which become the culture for how people behave.

These extracts from a classic article called netiquette by Gary Alexander get you thinking about how people should expect to behave in forum settings:

`http://sustainability.open.ac.uk/gary/netique.htm`

Moderators should also try to be active in discussions. Here are a few things you could do as a moderator:

- Encourage users to send requests to you for how the forum should operate.
- Reply to threads, giving useful information.
- Take time to listen to people, praising good postings or topics with useful information.
- Be diplomatic with users who aren't following guidelines. Message them privately, not publicly. Usually a polite request to tone down their behavior will do the job.
- Be the most obsessive user of the forum. Be interested in the discussion. Spark discussion yourself.

Forum topic expansion

In the preceding *Time for action – creating a forum* section, you also saw that you are able to select how you would like the topics in your forum to be expanded. Let's have a look at the difference between the three types of expansion on offer.

◆ **Fully expand**: Under this scheme, the topics in your forum will keep indenting to the right as more replies are added. Here is what the full expansion looks like:

- **Expand to max**: This is similar to the previous option in which the topics' responses automatically expand to the right, but this time you are able to choose a maximum level of expansion. This is really useful because when the **Fully expand** option is set and there are lots of replies in the forum, things can begin to look a bit messy. The following screenshot shows the expansion to the first level only:

- **No indents**: After the first topic, there are no indentations or expansion levels.

Now, going back to the forum page you will see there are a few options for managing your new forum. You will briefly look at these now.

Managing your forum

You may want to edit your forum after some time. To do this, simply use the pencil **Edit** button next to the forum. You will see all the same options that you were presented with when you created the forum.

You may also want to delete the forum. Perhaps you realize that nobody is engaging in discussion with that particular forum and it doesn't matter if you delete it because there aren't many topics or it is no longer in use. To do this, click on the small cross button to delete the forum. You will get a message prompting you to confirm the action.

Be careful when deleting forums

When you delete a forum, all of the content will be removed, including topics, posts, and moderators. You really need to be sure before you delete any forums in Mahara, because they could contain valuable information.

Finally, you are able to subscribe to forums (if you have decided to subscribe to all forums, you won't have this option as you are already subscribed). Subscription is just like subscribing to a weekly magazine. Instead of receiving mail through your front door, you will get live Mahara notifications giving you details of new forum posts that are added. Click on **Subscribe** to do this:

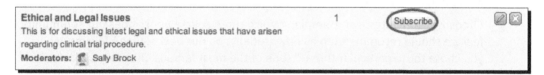

If you want to stop receiving notifications of forum posts, click on **Unsubscribe**:

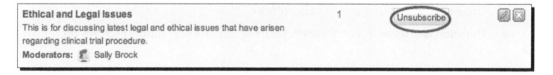

If you are subscribed to a lot of forums in groups, your e-mail inbox can soon pile up with lots of messages from forum posts. We recommend that you switch to using a daily digest for your e-mail notifications to prevent this from happening. This way you get a short daily summary of forum activity rather than a separate e-mail for each update. See Chapter 2, *Getting Started with Mahara* for more information on how to set this up.

Forum topics

Now that you have your forum in place, it's time to start adding the questions and comments that will make it into a lively social discussion area. To do this, you need to start using topics.

Topics are exactly that... topics. They are issues that people want to discuss. A forum that works, remember, will usually be one where the group members have an extrinsic necessity (for example, part of their job role) or an intrinsic desire to engage with it (useful information to gain, important decisions to be made, fun, and laughter to be had).

Forum discussion frameworks

A forum can be made up of many different topics with a wide range issues. The best discussion frameworks are those which lead to some sort of outcome or conclusion. Some generically useful discussion frameworks include:

- **Comparing**: For example, "What are the similarities and differences between food we eat today and food they ate in Tudor England?".

- **Detecting differences**: For example, "What different reactions are there to our company's marketing campaigns in different countries?".

- **Putting in order**: For example, "Put this list of our ten course topics in order from one to ten. Number one was the most interesting and number ten was the least interesting. Then tell us why you felt like this.".

- **Choosing candidates**: For example, "Which three course books does our community feel we should recommend to all new students on our next course? Tell us why you chose those particular three?" (one of the most famous Choosing Candidates discussion is the "Hot Air Balloon debate" in which participants have to decide who gets thrown overboard from an air balloon, which is falling fast towards the ground).

- **Layout problems**: For example, "Let's discuss how we layout our group page" or "How shall we set up our open plan office?".

- **Question and answer**: For example, Many of the practical support forums on `http://mahara.org`.

- **Ideas from a central theme**: For example, "Let's discuss new research approaches". This then gets broken down into sub-discussions as to the relevant merits of the individual approaches.

- **Implications and interpretations**: For example, "What would life have been like when people didn't have the advanced medical facilities we have today? " or "How do you think Henry VIII would have practically coped or suffered with the gangrene in his leg?".

- **Surveys of opinion**: For example, "Tell us three things you think we should do differently in our course next year".

- ◆ **Planning projects**: For example, "1. Brainstorm ideas, 2. Prioritize actions, 3. Allocate responsibilities, 4. Report back on progress, 5. Celebrate successes".

- ◆ **Combining versions**: For example, "Let's read all the pages that individual users have submitted to our group and then identify which are the most important elements we think we should include in a common group page on this topic".

This is not an exhaustive list, of course. The most important thing is to try to set up discussions with a clear sense of purpose or outcome to the debate. You do this because you need to give your forum participants a reason to post.

Don't get us wrong, depending upon the engagement and motivation of the group a generic forum title such as "Talk about Dogs" could, in fact, generate just as much discussion as a "Choosing Candidates" discussion like, "The Queen of England likes corgis and Winston Churchill should have had a bulldog. Say which breed of dog you think is best suited to (for example, Queen Elizabeth I or for example the CEO of PI Inc.) and tell us why you chose this breed."

There is nothing to say that you have to use Mahara forums to set up outcome-oriented discussion frameworks, we are simply putting this idea forward for you as food for thought.

Let's go back to Janet and see what kind of topics she thinks could be included in her legal and ethical forum for the Clinical Trials group.

Janet Norman from PI Inc. thinks:

One of my colleagues has said that they would like a place where they can discuss if withholding medicine for a control group is still scientifically justifiable and ethical. There are implications and interpretations to be discussed here, so I instantly suggested that we set this up as a topic in the Clinical Trials group's Legal and Ethical forum.

Time for action – adding a discussion topic

Time to create your first forum discussion topic:

1. Start by reopening the forum that you created earlier. To do this, click on the **Forum** tab of the **Clinical Trials** group. You will see all the forums that exist in this group. Click on the name of the forum to which you would like to add a topic.

2. Then, you will see a screen listing all the options for managing your forum that we discussed earlier. Click on **New topic** to start creating the topic.

3. Use the following screen to add a subject and a body. The subject should be descriptive of exactly what you will be talking about in this topic. The body information should give some more information about what it is that you want to discuss, perhaps giving examples or posing questions to other users. You may want to set up an outcomes-oriented discussion framework in your description to stimulate conversation. The screen will look as shown in the following screenshot:

4. There are two other options on this page to make the topic sticky or closed. These options are available only to a group administrator or forum moderator. Leave these set to the default option of unchecked for now; you will find out what they mean later in this chapter.

5. When you are happy with your topic, click on **Post** to add it to the forum, otherwise, click on **Cancel**. And there you go, you have added your first forum post!

What just happened?

You just saw how easy it is to create your first forum topic. You gave it a relevant name and description and posted it to the forum. Now all you have to do is wait for people to start responding to you so that you can develop the discussion.

Let's take a brief look at how adding this post has affected the options available to you in the forum. Navigate back to your forum. You can now see the topic that you just created, its description, as well as who posted it. As an administrator you have the option to delete or edit the topic. Normal members do not have this option.

There is also the ability to quickly apply actions to any topic. To do this, check the tick box to the left of the topic box. Then use the **Choose an action** option box at the top or bottom of the page to select your action. When you have chosen an action, click on **Update selected topics**. This is a good way of applying changes, such as making topics sticky to more than one topic in your forum. See the following screenshot:

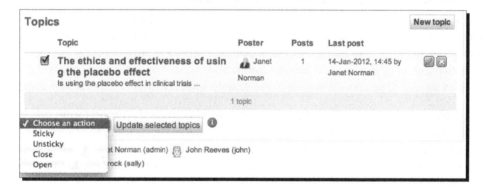

In the preceding *Time for action – adding a discussion topic*, you also saw that group administrators and forum moderators have two extra options when they are making a new topic. These are to make a topic sticky or closed:

- **Sticky**: Choose this option if you have lots of forum topics and you would like this particular one to stand out from the rest by staying glued to the top of the forum.

- **Closed**: This option can only be replied to by forum moderators and administrators for the group. Use these topics if you don't want other users to comment.

Sticky topics are really useful. Imagine that your forum is now really popular with lots of good advice going into the various posts and topics. This is when it becomes likely that topics start getting replicated and people begin discussing issues that have already been discussed. A good idea would be to create a sticky topic that stays at the top of the forum and brings together all of the topics that are commonly discussed in the forum, linking the user to the correct area of discussion. This means that users won't have to spend a long time searching through all the forums to find the answer they are looking for.

Such a topic could also be made closed. You wouldn't want this topic to be added to by general group users. It could be organized and managed by the group moderator.

Closed topics can be a useful way to get news out to your group members. Since e-mail notifications are sent to group members that are subscribed to a forum in your group, they will receive the updates as you add them. How about posting a weekly news update?

Earlier, we briefly mentioned subscribing users to your forums automatically. This is a useful way of ensuring your group members receive e-mails on important posts. Remember though, group members will also receive notification e-mails when any other replies are made in the forum, so you might want to create a completely separate forum just for news.

To turn on automatic subscription, revisit your forum options and check the **Automatically subscribe users**? option in the settings of the forum.

Naming forums and their topic subjects

Now that you've just created your first forum, let's think a little bit about how you want to name your forums and topics. Each forum in your group should be given a sufficiently general name with the idea being that it will be made up of a number of different topic threads that are all related to it. While the forum titles should be sufficiently general, the topic titles should all be specific and describe exactly what it is that will be spoken about.

For example, one Mahara site may have a group called "Olympics". A good forum title would be "Track and Field", because it is general and covers a wide topic. Then, the "Track and Field" forum could have topics, such as "Not enough funding for UK athletics" or "Which country is the best at track and field?" The topic subjects are more specific and targeted.

Posting to a topic

So you know how to make a new forum topic and how to administer it, but what if you have found something in the forum that interests you and you want to respond to it? This is where posts come into the picture. You can have any number of posts for a topic in your forum.

Janet Norman has seen that a member of the site has added a response to the topic that she created. She would really like to reply.

So let's find out how to reply to the posts.

Time for action – replying to a topic post

Let's find a topic and post a reply:

1. Find and open the topic to which you want to reply. You can do this by clicking on **Latest Forum Posts** link in your group's **About** page. More commonly though, you would click the **Forums** tab in the group.

2. Then click on the link to the forum, which contains the topic you want to reply to. Janet has clicked into her **Ethical and Legal Issues** forum:

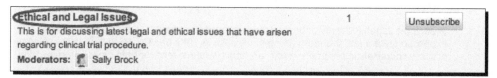

3. You will now see the topics listed in the forum. Click into the topic that you want to add a response to. Janet has clicked into her ethics and placebo effect topic:

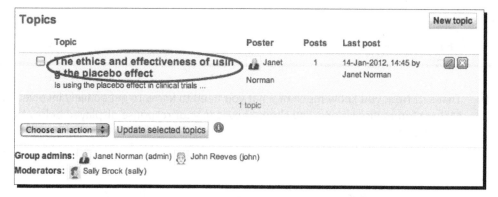

4. For each topic post, you will see that there are options to the bottom right—**Reply**, **Edit**, and **Delete**. You will only see all three options if you are a forum administrator or moderator. A standard group user will just have the ability to reply. Click on **Reply** to make your response to the post:

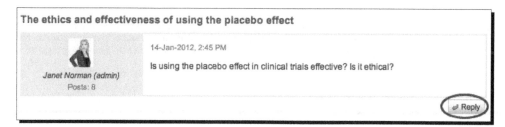

5. Then, you will see an editor that you can use to enter your response. Optionally, you can also click on **Click to set a subject**, but often you will want the subject to stay the same as the original topic for consistency. When you are happy with your response, click on **Post**:

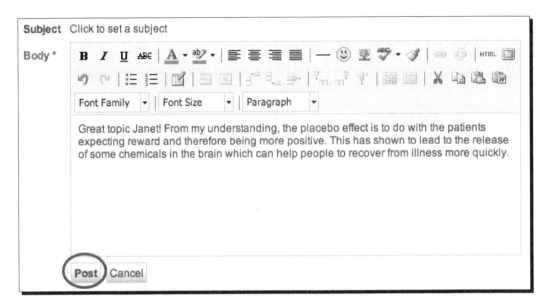

6. That's it! Now, you know much of what you need to know to get actively involved in Mahara forum discussions. You should now see your response displayed below the original post:

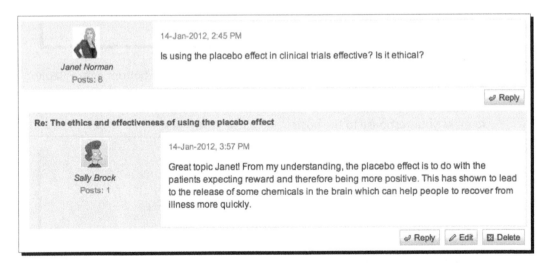

What just happened?

You have created some forums in your site, and seen how to start discussion topics as well as how to respond to other user posts.

One thing to note about posting to forums is that you can edit any posts that you create, so you don't have to worry about making sure they are perfect first time.

When you post in the forum, there is usually a lag time until a notification is sent out about the post. This is to give you some time to review your post and make changes.

You will now move on to look at the other shared features of a group—files and pages.

Pop Quiz – group forums

1. What is the job of a forum moderator? What can they do?
2. What is a sticky forum topic? When might you use one?
3. What is a good system for naming your forums and topics?

Group pages

The next feature of a group that will be useful for you is the group pages option. Click on the **Pages** tab to navigate here. As you saw earlier, the **Pages** section for your group will currently only have one page available—**Group homepage**.

You would have learned a lot about Mahara pages in Chapter 2, *Getting Started with Mahara* and Chapter 4, *Organize and Showcase your Portfolio*. So you won't repeat that here. Instead you will find out what is different about a group page and start thinking about how you can use them to improve your communication and to share information.

Group page is simply a normal page that can be seen (and edited if allowed by the group admin) by all members of the group. When you are creating a group page, you will notice that you don't have access to all the same blocks that you did when making your own pages. You can't add any of your own profile information, résumé, plans, or journals to a group page. The only blocks that you are able to add to a group page (unless any extensions have been enabled) are:

- **Files, images, and videos**: File to download, folder, image gallery, image, some HTML, and embedded media.
- **General**: Creative Commons License, recent forum posts (of the group), and text box.
- **External content**: External feed, external media, and Google Apps.

So why would you want to create a group page? Group pages are great for sharing ideas collaboratively. Different users can work together to edit a web page. It is a great way of keeping common information sheets, which could contain instructions or ideas. The ability of pages to pull in image and video media from external sources will enable you to quickly show your group a host of rich interactive content without sending them a list of links. Let's hear what ideas Punam, Neil, Janet, and Christophe have for how the group pages can be used:

Punam from Pennytown Primary thinks:

Group pages will be excellent for me, because I can effectively create interactive online worksheets that are organized into specific areas of my site. I can share a worksheet page that I have just created about rivers in a geography group. I can use a text box in the page to get learners entering factual information they discover about named rivers (length in kilometers, geographic location, and so on). I can also encourage the children to collaborate further by adding more blocks to this group page, getting them to add their own artwork and web links in order to make an online collage that they can go home and show their parents.

Janet Norman from PI Inc. thinks:

Group pages will be useful for us to work together in our Clinical Trials group to produce a document showing and summarizing key action points that have arisen in our group discussions. This will be helpful to steer company thinking with respect to the current situation with our clinical trial procedures. The page we create could be used as a reference document in any strategic meeting that we have in the future.

Neil from Training for Work thinks:

I am going to set up a group page for Electrical Engineering topics of the day, related to information that I read in monthly magazines. This will go into our Electrical Engineering group. Users of the group can then all access the page for up-to-date information about Electrical Engineering. This will be completely separate from our formal accreditation process, as it will be more of an informal interest group.

Christophe from Silverworks University thinks:

My tutor group and I are having weekly creative sessions where we come up with ideas for projects and pieces. We're using the group pages collaboratively to add our ideas together. Some of my tutor group add sketches, images, or even concept videos to the group pages. It's working really well and we've got a record of the creative sessions that we've had in the past.

The only thing to watch out for, while working on collaborative group pages, is that you have no history of who did what and when. If all of the information suddenly goes missing, there's no easy way to tell who was responsible. You need to be very trusting when working with group pages.

Just like your own pages, if you are the owner/admin of your group, you can pick how your group pages are shared. If you allow your group members to edit pages, they will also be able to change the **Share** options. You can use the **Share** tab of your group to access group page sharing options.

Group files

In your group, you can also add files to share with everyone. The files you add to the group can then be used in group pages or downloaded by other group members. The group's file area works in exactly the same way as uploading your own file. Click on the **Files** tab in the group menu bar and have a go at uploading a file into the group.

Those who have an eagle eye will notice that there is a slight difference in the options for uploading a file to a group. You are given options for deciding what the permissions are for the file:

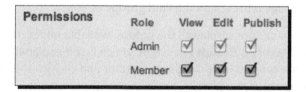

By default both admins and members are able to view, edit, and publish the file. If you want, you could decide to reduce the permissions to just allow group admins to see a file you upload; the choice is yours. This facility could come in very handy if you want to include progress reporting spreadsheets that only the tutors (but not the learners) get to see, for example.

If you set this possibility of fine-tuning access and permissions to one side, though, the great thing to notice about group files is that everyone in the group can access, edit, and publish any of them, if you allow them to. This facility becomes even more useful when you think that you are able to link to these files from within Mahara group pages.

Finding groups

Now that you have covered many of the features of a Mahara group, let's start thinking about joining other groups. Now, it's all well and good having groups in your Mahara, but what happens when it starts to get overloaded with not just tens, but potentially hundreds of them? How will you find not only your own groups, but also groups that you don't own? The answer is Mahara's **Find Groups** option.

Back to Janet to find out how she would like to use the Find Groups feature:

Janet Norman from PI Inc. thinks:

I've heard that my colleague Fernando has created an interest group about allergy research. I'm really interested to see what's going on in this area, because I hear there have been some recent breakthroughs. I'm going to use the Find Groups feature to find his group and see what's going on.

Time for action – finding and joining a group

Let's see how you can find a group and join it:

1. Under the **Groups** tab, click on the **Find groups** option.

2. The drop-down options display all the groups available under different categories. The default category is **Groups I'm not in**, which is self-explanatory. To change categories, you can use the drop-down selector and click on the search icon (in this case a magnifying glass):

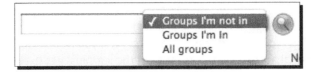

3. Have a go at changing the search category and see what effect it has on the groups that are displayed below. If there aren't many groups in your site at this point, it is likely that some of the categories won't contain any groups. The other categories to choose from are **Groups I'm In** and **All groups**. When you have chosen your filter, click on the search button. For Janet, the **Groups I'm not in** drop-down revealed the group she is looking for:

Allergy Research

Fernando Canizares (fernando) - This group is for all PI Inc members who are interested in the allergy research department discus...

1 member

Request to join this group

4. When your site starts getting really crowded with groups, it won't be enough to simply choose one of the categories and be able to find a specific group. You can improve your search by typing the group name in the search box provided before you click on the magnifying glass icon (or equivalent – depending upon your Mahara site theme). Nevertheless, just for the experience of it, try searching now for one of the groups you have already created, or a group you are a member of, to see how the Mahara search functionality narrows it down to the one you actually want to see.

5. And that's it! That's all you need to know about searching through your groups.

What just happened?

You have just seen how easy it is to find groups in Mahara that you want to join.

As you are searching for a group, it will probably come to your attention just how important it is for people to set up a clearly named group title with a clear and useful description. For example, compare:

Group 1.

Problems at work: Let's talk.

with...

Group 2.

Drilling, Milling, and Turning: In this group, you discuss practical techniques for working metal—sharing pages, celebrating your work, and collecting and evaluating our best practice tips and ideas.

Hopefully, you can see that the purpose of Group 2 is much more clear than Group 1.

Earlier you saw how to join an open membership group. Now, let's look at how you can join a request membership group that you have been invited to. To join groups that are setup this way, requires a few extra steps. Let's look at the request membership process.

Joining a request membership group

As you know, some groups require you to request membership. You will need to give a reason why you want to join the group and wait for the group administrator to accept your request, if they think you are a suitable group member. The process for joining a group is:

1. You find a group to which you would like to request membership.

2. You then request to join the group, indicating why you would like to join.

3. The group admin decides whether they would like you to join or not.

Now let's have a look at the process in more detail.

Time for action – requesting to join a group

Let's request to join a group:

1. Start by finding the group that you would like to join.

2. You will see that instead of the **Join this group** button, you have the **Request to join this group** button; click on it:

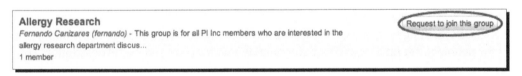

3. Next, you have a page that invites you to enter a reason for why you want to join the group. Think carefully about what you will write in here. It is usually a good idea to give well thought out reasons for why you want to join as well as expressing enthusiasm for wanting to get involved. When you have given your reason, click on **Request**:

4. That's all there is to it! You have requested to join the group. When you return to the group listing, you will see that it now says **You have requested to join this group**.

What just happened?

You have just requested to join a group. Now, you must wait for the group administrator to decide whether you should be accepted or not.

Accepting/denying requests to join a group

When someone has requested to join your group, you will see a message appear at the top of the group's **About** page:

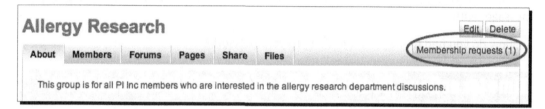

Click on that link. You will then see a page showing you who wants to join your group and the reason why. You will also receive a notification that somebody would like to join the group. If you are happy to add this new user, click on the button to add the user:

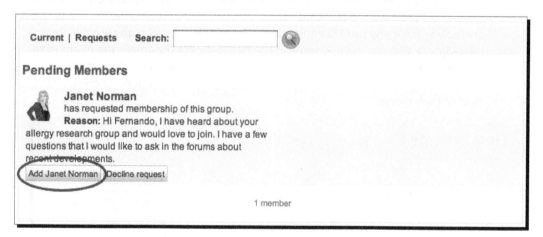

This group will now be available in Janet's **My Groups** listing.

To finish this chapter, you will have a look at how you can make friends in Mahara.

Making friends!

At the moment, you will be feeling quite lonely in your site, because you don't have any friends! The Mahara friends feature allows you to find other people in the site that you would like to connect with. Being someone's friend allows you to do a couple of important things. Firstly, all your friends show up in your profile. This is a great way of being able to quickly and easily find all the people in the Mahara site that you regularly contact. Secondly, you can assign page access only to your friends. This is useful, if you only want people you know to be able to see one of the pages you have created (as an alternative to making it publicly available or available to all logged-in users, for example).

Some people like to think of friends in Mahara as contacts. They are all the people you want to connect with in the learning environment and the people who you are likely to exchange messages with.

So, how do you find friends and add them to your network?

Time for action – finding friends and adding them to your list

Let's start making some friends in Mahara:

1. Return to the **Groups** section of your site and click on the **Find Friends** tab.

2. You will see a screen that lists all the people that are in your Mahara site. Notice in the top left you have the standard search box. Use this to search for the friend you are looking for, if you can't see them in the list. If there aren't many users in your own Mahara site, try and find some in the demo site for this book. You might even be able to make friends with Janet Norman, if you can find her. When you have found the friend you would like to add, simply click on **Send Friend Request** to the right of their name:

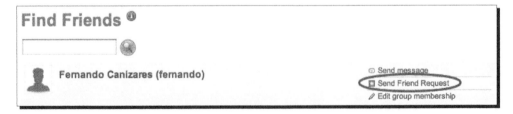

3. On the following page, you can fill in a form to tell them why you want to be their friend and send it off.

4. You have now requested to be someone's friend. You have to wait for their response before you are accepted as their friend (or not, as the case may be).

What just happened?

You have just requested to be someone's friend.

Sometimes you may find that the person you want to add doesn't have the **Send Friend Request** option, instead it might say **Add to Friends**. This is because that person is very sociable and has decided that they are happy for anyone to be their friend! When you click on one of those buttons, you automatically become that person's friend. You can toggle your own friend options on your settings page that you saw in Chapter 2, *Getting Started with Mahara*.

Similarly, you might find that there is no button there at all. That is because the person has decided that they don't want any friends. Instead, it will say **This user doesn't want any new friends**.

Responding to a friend request

So, how do you know when someone wants to be your friend?

And what do you do if they do?

Responding to a friend request is easy. You will spot that somebody has requested to be your friend from the main side block on your **Home** page (as well as receiving a notification in your inbox):

The message should read something like **1 pending friend** (or more). Click on that link to see who it is requesting to be your friend. If someone has sent you a message along with the request, you will see that too. All you need to do now is to decide whether you want him/her to be your friend and, if so, to confirm him/her as a friend, click on **Approve Request** to the right of the screen:

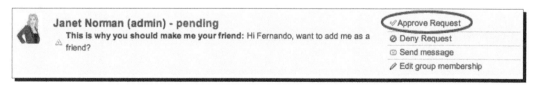

If you deny the friend request, that person will receive a notification.

Managing your friends

When you start getting lots of friends, it will be useful for you to be able to filter through them and find someone you are looking for. To do this, you will be using the **My Friends** page. You may also want to remove a friend.

Let's find out how to do both.

Time for action – filtering and removing friends

Let's see how to manage your friends:

1. Return to the **Groups** section of your site and click on the **My Friends** tab.

2. You will see a page, which lists all of your friends. Start by clicking on the drop-down box in the top left corner as shown in the following screenshot:

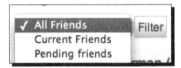

3. As you can see, there are three options for filtering your friends. You can choose to show all of your friends, those who are confirmed and those to whom you have sent a request with the **All Friends** option. Alternatively, with the **Current Friends** option, you might want to show just the friends that have definitely accepted your request and are now your friends. Finally, by clicking on **Pending Friends**, you can show all the friends who you are waiting for to confirm your request. When you have decided which group you would like to see, click on the **Filter** button.

4. You will now see all the friends that belong to that group. You will also see that for each friend, there are two options. Click on **Send message** to get in contact with your friend. If you no longer want to be someone's friend, click on the **Remove from friends** button.

5. When you choose to remove a friend, you get an option for explaining the reason for removing him/her, type in a reason and click on **Remove friend**. The person will receive this reason as a notification:

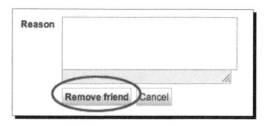

What just happened?

You have just learned how to view and filter through your friends, as well as how to remove friends from your list.

Whenever you send a message to a friend in Mahara, that message can be found in your notifications.

Summary

In this chapter, you learned a lot about how you can be more collaborative and social in Mahara by using the groups and friends features. Specifically, you looked at creating groups, group types, forums and discussions, group pages, group files, and making friends.

We also discussed how you might use Mahara to encourage collaboration and social interaction in your organization through sharing. We saw discussion represented by the four fictional case study characters. Hopefully, now you have a good idea of how you can use the social facilities of Mahara to get people connecting and sharing ideas.

In the next chapter, you will be looking at some more advanced roles in Mahara including institutional administrators, staff members and group tutors, as well as the controlled membership group type.

6
Course Groups and Other Roles in Mahara

So far, you have been looking at how you can use all the standard features of Mahara to put together your own eye-catching portfolio and work together with other Mahara users in groups. In this chapter, you are going to look at roles beyond that of a standard user.

In the first part of the chapter, you will look at institutions in Mahara and some of the things that an institution administrator can do.

In the second part, you will be exploring special course group roles, controlled groups, and the ability to submit pages to controlled and request groups for assessment.

In this chapter you will:

- ◆ Explore the options available to an institution administrator for managing members, including how to set up staff members in your institution
- ◆ Choose some settings for your institution
- ◆ As a staff member, find out how to set up a controlled group to which users can submit work for assessment
- ◆ Discover how to turn your group into a course group, using course roles
- ◆ Find out what a group tutor can do in these course groups and how to create one
- ◆ Learn how to submit work to and release work from a controlled or request membership group
- ◆ See an example of using groups for assessment of work

Less learner-driven aspects of Mahara

Mahara is, quite rightly, set up as a learner-driven community site. It is important for us to see a Mahara site as a space where learners with their own personalized learning materials can choose whether to allow access to them, or not. The learner can also choose whether or not to interact with other site users with reference to the materials they create.

However, this does not mean that there is no useful role for an administrator or tutor in such an environment. Here are some of the things that a tutor might want to do in an ePortfolio system:

- Monitor their learners' work and get ready to feedback on it
- Decide who's in and who's out of particular areas of the site (such as institutions or groups)
- Scaffold learners' work by creating templates, which they can work from and go on to extend creatively
- Have work submitted to them for formal assessment
- Allow others, such as teaching assistants, inspectors, or verifiers, to access pages that have been submitted for assessment

Mahara has provided the features needed to achieve all of the things mentioned in the preceding list.

In Neil's case, there are clear reasons for him to want to exert some control over the learning process. He needs to give some of his colleagues a way to supervise and structure the work that their learners are doing. In this chapter, you will look at how Neil can use Mahara to meet his particular needs. You will get thinking about how you might want to use Mahara in different institutions, for the delivery of formally assessed programs, and for monitoring project-based or evidence-based learning.

Neil from Training for Work thinks:

I have a colleague called Graham, also an Engineer, who is interested in using Mahara for his students. I would like to allow Graham to manage his own users in his own section of Mahara.

Neither Graham nor I want to inhibit our learners' creative learning process. However, we do feel a need to manage some aspects of our users' work in a more formal way. We would like our learners to submit their work to us for assessment. We will then be able to give feedback on their pages that have been submitted. Most of the content will be locked until we release the pages back to the users. We can then ask them to submit their work again, when they have improved it, and we can invite external verifiers from an accrediting body to have a look.

Institutions

We will discuss institutions in Mahara with the help of the following sections.

What is an institution?

An **institution** is a sub-division of a Mahara site that can have its own administrators. The four main advantages of using institutions are:

◆ A consortia of different institutions can share a common user base on a single Mahara site. This allows users to network with others across institution boundaries.

◆ A Mahara site administrator can devolve much of the responsibility for user management to institution administrators.

◆ Each institution can be given its own theme.

◆ Each institution can have its own preferences, such as authentication methods and whether or not to show public pages and the online users side block.

A group of schools in a local area, for example, may wish to share a single Mahara installation. This may be because students naturally migrate from one school to another, but will want to retain access to their lifelong learning. It may be because a teacher of a subject teaches learners from a variety of schools. Finally, it could be that the schools have seen the advantage of encouraging common interest groups across the region.

While the local area wants to promote collaboration between the schools, each school will want to retain control over their users. They will also want users from their own school to be clearly identified as they operate within the Mahara site. Even on a shared Mahara platform, each institution can achieve this localization by having their own look-and-feel with an institution theme.

Users can even belong to more than one institution in Mahara. This is useful if a user requires a different role in each institution. Perhaps they are a staff member at one college (institution) and at another they are taking a vocational language course in their spare time.

Punam from Pennytown Primary thinks:

Pennytown Primary has been set up as one of the many institutions in the Schools Online Mahara site. We have our own school theme, which the site administrators have created for us (our institution administrator is able to change this if she wanted to). Other schools in our local area also have their own themes. I have not been set up as the institution administrator for Pennytown Primary; this is the responsibility of one of the school office staff called Susan. I advise Susan when I want a new institution member to be added.

Janet Norman from PI Inc. thinks:

At PI Inc., it makes sense for us to have an institution administrator for every branch. That way, somebody with their fingers on the pulse can maintain the institution user membership, and keep it all live and current. I thought about giving each branch its own theme, but decided against it. At the end of the day, PI Inc. has an international brand and it is unnecessary to distinguish between the different branches.

Administering an institution

An institution administrator can manage most aspects of their institution as if it were a separate Mahara site. This includes users and institution settings. They are also able to create groups, but only via CSV files and they cannot get into these groups without joining the groups. Specifically, an institution administrator can:

- Configure institution settings
- Manage new user subscriptions and deal with requests to join the institution (this includes the ability to add users via Leap2A)
- Suspend, reactivate, and fully remove users
- Monitor abusive behavior in the institution
- Allocate institution themes
- Decide what information users of their institution will provide as a minimum when joining up
- Allocate roles to staff members and to other administrators of the institution
- Add groups by CSV files
- Create institution pages and allocate sharing for them
- Upload institution files

Let's find out how you can manage your institution. To follow the tasks in this section, you need to be set up as an institution administrator.

Time for action – adding users to your institution

Let's start by seeing how you can add new users to your institution:

1. Log in to your Mahara as an institution administrator (if you do not have these permissions, ask your site administrator to give them to you—they may need to set up a new site institution for you to work with). Once you have these permissions, you will see that you have a new tab called **Institution administration**:

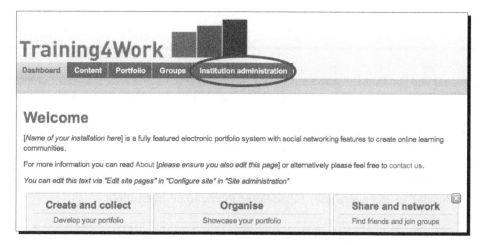

2. You will see that you have entered a new area of the site where you can manage your institution and that you have a different main menu bar. You can return to the main Mahara site whenever you want to, by clicking on the tab called **Return to site**. To start, you will be in the **Manage users** area:

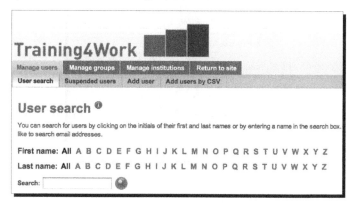

3. You are going to start by adding some users to your new institution. Click on the **Add user** submenu item. You will see the following screen:

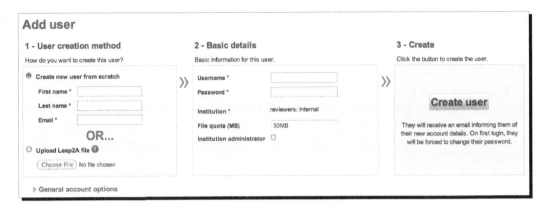

4. You will see that the **Add user** page has three sections. In section **1 - User creation method**, you can decide how your users are created. You can create a new user from scratch or upload a Leap2A file. Use the check box to decide which option to use. In Chapter 4, *Organize and Showcase your Portfolio*, you saw how you can export to Leap2A—this can now be used to create a new user and to add their existing portfolio (profile, pages, and so on) at the same time. For now, you will probably want to create a brand new user. Enter the name and e-mail address. Graham has decided to add a new user called Peter Tooley to his institution:

5. In section **2 - Basic details**, add a username and password for your user. The user will be invited to change the password, when he/she logs in for the first time. You are also allowed to change the **File quota** for your user. This setting controls how much space the user will have to upload files. You also have the option to make the user an Institution administrator. Graham has made Peter Tooley a standard user and given him a username and password:

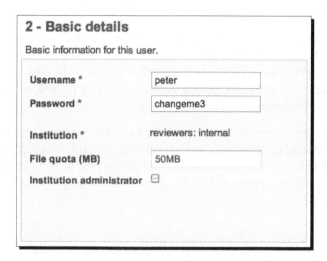

6. Finally, in section **3 - Create**, simply click on the **Create user** button.

What just happened?

You have just learned how to add users to your institution.

When you added your user, you had to allocate him/her a username and password. It is a good idea to keep the user naming scheme consistent across the whole institution. A common scheme, for example, is to use both first name and surname in the username, such as `peter.tooley`. This method would reduce the likelihood of duplication.

Bulk uploading users to your institution

When administering your institution, you also have the option to bulk upload users by CSV. The letters **CSV** stand for **comma-separated values**. This simply means that you can set up lots of users in one single action by uploading a simple text file that you have created. This text file will list lots of your users and identify their particular attributes. This CSV file trick will save you time, if you have lots of users to upload.

Time for action – adding institution users by CSV

Let's find out how to add some users to your institution by using a CSV file:

1. Click on the **Add users by CSV** tab in the **Manage users** submenu. On this page, you will read some very useful instructions explaining how you should set up your CSV file.

2. There will be at least five mandatory fields for a CSV file. As an Institution administrator, you may have set up more mandatory fields for your institution (you will see how to lock fields in the *Configuring the institution settings* section of this chapter). If you have already done so, your CSV file will also need to include a reference for these fields for each learner.

3. It is a good idea to create your CSV files in a plain text-editing software application, such as Notepad on Windows, TextEdit on Mac, or Gedit for Linux. Imagining that you had locked the additional field for **city** in your institution (again, see the institution settings section to find out how to lock fields), an example CSV file might look like this:

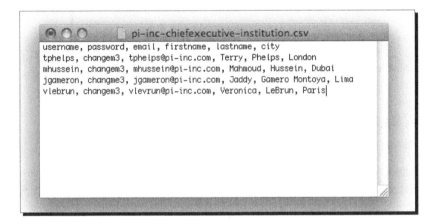

4. Now make a CSV file of your own for some users, which you would like to upload, and save it to your computer.

5. Use the **Browse** button to find the CSV file, which you have created on your computer.

6. Decide whether or not to force a password change (which is recommended for new accounts, especially if the passwords are the same) and whether you would like to e-mail users about their account, telling them they have been added to the system. You can also use a CSV file to update users that currently exist in the system. Also, notice that you have some general account options available, so that you can set the default settings for a user. When you are ready, click on the **Add Users by CSV** button:

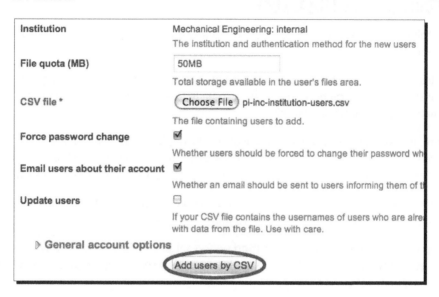

What just happened?

You have just used a CSV file to set up new users in bulk for your Mahara institution.

You saw that you can build your CSV file, using a plain text editor as well as some examples of programs that people use. Some people find it easier to use a spreadsheet software such as Open Office Calc or Microsoft Excel to build the list of users. If you are using this method, remember that the first line needs to be the fields that you are adding and the resulting lines contain the data for your users. When you have finished, you can save your spreadsheet and export the data to the CSV format. Some spreadsheet software gives you various options for CSV files, such as separating values with semi-colons, commas, or tabs. For Mahara, check that you have comma-separated values.

With all that in mind, it's always a good idea to check the resulting file just to make sure everything looks to be in the right format before uploading.

You have just looked at some internal methods for adding users to your institution. Mahara also provides a number of other options for authenticating users including IMAP, LDAP, SAML, and XMLRPC. If you're interested in using these options, you can find out more on the Mahara wiki at `http://manual.mahara.org/en/1.5_STABLE/site_admin/institutions.html`.

Approving pending users

If your Mahara site allows self registration, users are able to join up without you adding them manually.

Whilst this is a great time saver, it can also mean that you will find users adding themselves to your institution that you don't really want to be in there. This can be particularly problematic if spammers join your site.

Therefore, it makes sense for most administrators to deploy more control over the registration process by enabling the **Confirm registration** option in the institution settings. You can see how to allow this when you edit your institution settings later in this chapter.

As an institution administrator, this setting allows you to respond to these pending requests. You can decide if you would like that user to join.

Assuming you have the **Confirm registration** option set in your settings, start by clicking on **Manage institutions**. Then, click on **Members**. You will see a page showing you all the members who have requested to join.

For each member, you can decide whether to approve or deny them. Graham saw that somebody called Juliet has applied to join his **Mechanical Engineering** group. He knows Juliet and decided to allow her to join, so clicked on the **Approve** button:

On the following page, you are asked to confirm the action. Again, click on **Approve** to finish adding the user to the institution.

Editing user account settings

By now you have begun to add some users to your institution, but you may want to go back and change some of the details that you entered when you first created them. You can do this, using the **User account settings** section. Each user in your institution has his/her own site account settings. You can reach this page by clicking on a username on the **User search** page.

These account settings subdivide into three sections—each with configurable options for your user:

- ◆ **Site account settings**
- ◆ **Suspend user**
- ◆ **Institution settings**

Site account settings allow you to create a new password for your institution users (provided they are internal and not authentication via a different method). This comes in handy later if your users ever forget their old one. It is also useful to notice that you can set an account expiry date and that you can reconfigure the user's file quota limit (given that the site administrator has allowed you to do this).

You can also suspend a user under the option to suspend/delete user. Suspending the user has the effect of stopping them from logging-in and using the Mahara system. There are many reasons why you might do this, ranging from response to inappropriate behavior through non-payment of user fees (some organizations charge their clients to use Mahara) to termination of a paid course. Whatever your reason, it is a good idea to use the text entry box provided to explain to the user why their access has been suspended. It is shown to the users the next time they try to log in. Once you have suspended a user, you can delete them completely by entering into the **Suspended users** tab. You can tick the check boxes for all the users you wish to erase, and then click on the **Delete users** button. You will, naturally, receive a warning asking you if you are sure you want to take this (irreversible) action before you do. If you are sure, go ahead and delete these users permanently—remember they cannot be retrieved easily (if at all), if you do this.

Janet Norman from PI Inc. thinks:

I like that the institution administrators can delete a user if they choose to, but I actually encourage them to do no more than suspend these users from their institution. This is partly because when an employee leaves one PI Inc. branch, they might move to another one of our branches, elsewhere.

Finally, you can set **Institution settings** for your user. Here, you will notice that you can choose to automatically expire a user's membership of your institution at a certain point. You may also choose to give the learner an ID number within your institution. The final thing to note is that you can use this page to turn a user into an institution administrator or alternatively set them up as an institution staff member. You will look at the type of things a staff member can do later on in this chapter:

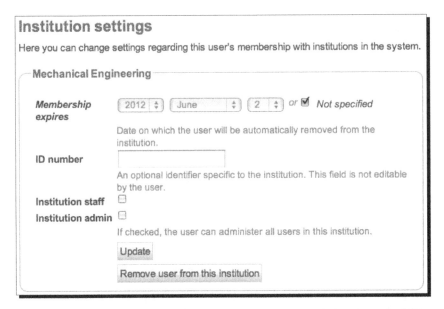

Time for action – finding and suspending a user

Let's look in more detail at how to suspend users in your institution. Remember, this is quite a serious action to take on a user. So, only work with a test user when you are working through this example:

1. Start by searching for the user that you would like to suspend (remember to find a test user rather than a real member of your institution). Click on the **Manage users** main menu tab, then click on **User search**.

2. On this page, you will see all the users in your institution listed. You can search alphabetically, or by typing a query in the search box. Find the test user you are looking for and click on his/her username.

3. This will take you to the user's account settings page. As discussed earlier, this page is split into three sections. To suspend a user, look in the right hand section entitled **Suspend/delete user**. To suspend your user, type a reason in the box, and click on **Suspend user**:

4. That's all there is to it. You have just suspended the user. Now, visit the **Suspended users** page of the admin area by clicking on **Manage users** on the main menu, then clicking on **Suspended users**. This page displays all the users that have been suspended. You have the option on this page to unsuspend users from the Mahara system. To do this, just click in the select box to the right of the user's name and click on **Unsuspend users**. Graham has decided to unsuspend the user, because they have now promised to improve their behavior in the forums:

What just happened?

You have just learned how to find users in your institution, and how to suspend and unsuspend them.

You should have a good reason before you suspend somebody, because it could be potentially disturbing to their work. Someone will almost certainly be offended if you suspend them without a good cause. Users are usually suspended if they are displaying poor behavior to other users throughout the system, through messages or forums. Other bad behavior may include allowing someone else to log in as them and to unfairly alter their ePortfolio.

In the preceding *Time for action – finding and suspending a user* section, you may have also noticed that you can use the **Suspended users** page to view those users whose accounts have expired. This is useful for reinstating users whose time limit has run out, but who have perhaps decided to continue onto another course after theirs is over. Expired users aren't deleted from the site, but simply redefined as expired so that you then have the choice over their removal.

Switching user roles in your institution

In early chapters, you looked at Mahara through the eyes of a standard site member. In this chapter so far you have been working as an institution member. There is a third site role that you haven't looked at yet called **staff**.

Staff have the ability above a standard member to:

◆ Create controlled groups
◆ Allow course roles in their group—turning them into course groups that can have tutors

Moving people in and out of the member, institution staff, and institution administrator statuses of your institution couldn't be easier.

Time for action – creating institution staff and institution administrators

Let's look at how you can turn standard members into institution staff and institution administrators:

1. To begin, click on the **Institution staff** submenu option in the **Manage institutions** section.

2. On this screen, you will see all the members who can potentially become staff in your institution as well as those who are already staff members. To create a new staff member, first click on the user that you would like to make staff. Then, click on the right facing arrow. Alternatively, you could just double-click on the user's name:

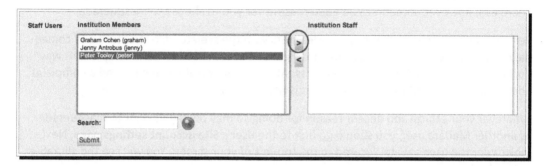

3. Then, you will see that user's name appears on the right hand side under the label **Institution staff**:

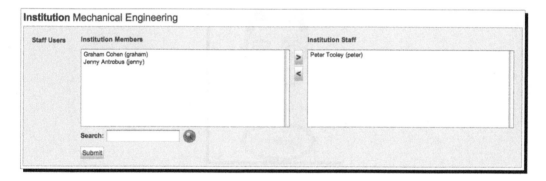

4. You can also manage your administrators in the same way, using the **Institution administrators** submenu tab.

What just happened?

You have just seen how you can assign roles in your institution.

You looked at how to turn a user into a staff member in the institution. Remember, an institution staff member is simply a person in your institution who has the ability to create controlled groups and to allow course roles such as a tutor in your group. You will be finding out more about both of these later in this chapter.

Masquerading as another user

It is worth drawing your attention to the fact that, as an institution administrator, you can also choose to masquerade as one of the Mahara users in your institution. In principle, it feels wrong and unfair to use such a privilege to edit another person's ePortfolio work. There can, however, sometimes be good reasons for you to choose to masquerade.

Perhaps you would want to set up new learners with the skeleton file structure and copied pages that they would need. You could masquerade in order to set learners up in this way during an organization's user setup process. Alternatively, maybe you have had a complaint about a user and need to investigate what is happening in their learning space.

Whatever your ethical and decent reason for doing so may be, if you want to masquerade as another Mahara user, you should go first to the user's **Site account settings** page. Next, look under the user's avatar located to the top-left of your screen. You will see the clickable option **Login as**:

Peter Tooley (peter)

Login as

If the user is new and you have forced the user's password change, you will see a screen inviting you to change the user's password. If this is the case, just click on the link **to log in anyway**:

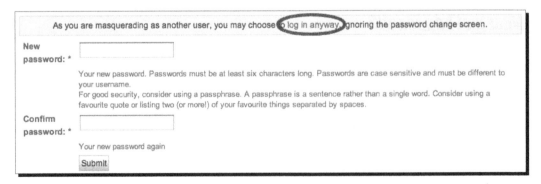

As you are masquerading as another user, you may choose to log in anyway, ignoring the password change screen.

New password: *	
	Your new password. Passwords must be at least six characters long. Passwords are case sensitive and must be different to your username. For good security, consider using a passphrase. A passphrase is a sentence rather than a single word. Consider using a favourite quote or listing two (or more!) of your favourite things separated by spaces.
Confirm password: *	
	Your new password again
	Submit

You will now find yourself masquerading as that particular user.

When you are ready to finish your masquerade, click on the banner at the top of the screen, which gives you the option to become the institution administrator again:

Configuring your institution's settings

Now that you've looked at your institution's members and their settings, let's move on to configure the settings for the institution. To find your institution settings, click on **Manage institutions** on the main menu. You will find yourself, by default, on the **Settings** page, which looks something like this:

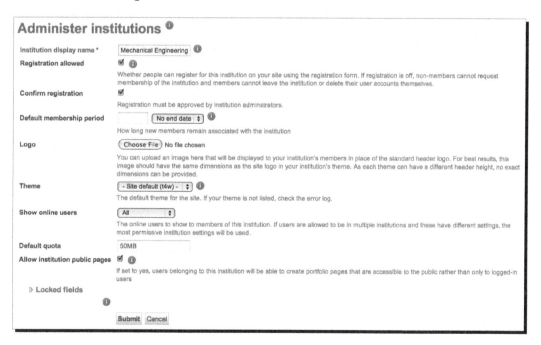

Firstly, you can edit your **Institution display name** here to another name if you prefer to.

Next, there is the **Registration allowed** checkbox option asking if you wish to set registration allowed. As you have already seen, if you set this to yes, you are allowing users to register themselves as a member of your institution, using a registration form. Some people will prefer to decide for themselves who becomes a member of their institution rather than letting people register for themselves, so turn this off if that's you.

Earlier in the chapter, when showing you how to confirm pending users, you saw that you can also choose to set the **Confirm registration** option. The need to confirm users places a bit more administrative duty on you, but it will mean that user accounts aren't automatically created when a user registers. You have to confirm a user before allowing them in. This is very useful in a controlled school or university setting.

You can set the **Default membership period** option. This option is useful if you have a regular term of membership for your institution. You can set the number of days, weeks, months, or even years for which you might wish to allow members to access your site. A university offering a three year undergraduate degree program, for example, might set a membership of a Mahara degree course institution to four years. They would then advise their new cohort of students that they will be able to access the content of their Mahara ePortfolios for one year (only) beyond the termination of their degree program.

This is also the page where you can determine the logo and theme for your institution, which is displayed when users access the Mahara site. Use the drop-down box here to choose your favored theme and logo. By default, Mahara provides a range of themes to choose from including, **Aqua**, **Default**, **Fresh**, **Raw**, **Sunset**, and **Ultima**.

If you don't think any of the default themes are suitable and you haven't been able to create your own theme, you can select the **Configurable Theme** option from the drop-down. This is great! You are able to select your own set of colors that correspond to different features of the site, such as the links or the main menu bar. You can use the color drop-down to select your preferred shade. If you would like a specific color, you can also enter a six digit hexadecimal value. There is no visual indicator of what features these colors affect, so you will have to try some out and come back to this page if you want to make further changes:

Configurable Theme	ⓘ

The default theme for the site - if your theme is not listed, check the error log.

Custom theme configuration

Background	#685A33
Text on Background	#FFFFFF
Link	#D66800
Headings	#182768
Side block background	#182768
Side block content background	#F1F2F8
Side block link	#182768
Navigation background	#F6871F
Navigation text	#FFFFFF
Sub navigation background	#FFF4EA
Sub navigation text	#14336F
Row background	#FFF4EA
Reset colours	

Restore default colours

Next, you will see that you also have the **Show online users** options to show online users and to set a base quota (again, only if the site administrator has allowed this) for the file space of users in your institution. Choose the options that you would like.

You can decide whether or not to **Allow institution public pages**. If selected, users in the institution are able to create pages that are viewable publicly. Otherwise, any pages they create will only be seen by other site users who have permission to view them.

Finally, you may wish to lock some user data fields for your institution by using the arrow icon to the left of the words **Locked fields**. This prevents users from editing the fields that you lock. You may for example decide to lock a student ID for security purposes.

Dealing with admin notifications

As an institution administrator, you will have the responsibility to respond to learner activity. Under the **Admin notifications** tab, you will see that you will be advised about, and have the chance to respond to, the following circumstances:

- **Objectionable content**: At the bottom of learner pages (excluding profiles pages), users will find the option to report objectionable content to the Mahara administrators. You will receive notifications when this happens. Then, you will need to go and investigate the reported incident. While inappropriate behavior can't be completely thwarted—in the same way that you cannot stop this sort of thing from happening in a real-world environment—you can at least use this facility to responsively investigate any reported incidents.

- **Repeat virus upload and virus flag release** (this requires your site to have additional virus software installed): Unfortunately, some users are not as careful at protecting their computers from viruses as they should be. Mahara has a facility, which can spot many of the files that have been affected by many of the viruses. If an infected file is identified, Mahara will disallow the user from submitting the file, requesting that they run the file through an anti-virus application before resubmitting. Repeat attempts to upload files containing viruses will be brought to your attention as an institution administrator on this page.

Institution pages

Click into the **Pages** tab and click on the **Create page** button. You will notice that when you edit the content, you have the tabs to drag and add blocks for external content, files, images, and video, and the general options. But you do not see the options to add blocks from your profile, your résumé, or for your journals.

This is because these latter tabs represent more personalized content. The institution pages are intended to carry person-neutral content—representing more generic content, which can be made available to institution members. If one of these pages has been made copyable, any user can then go on to add more personalized content to the pages they create from this institution page, which has been provided as a starting point.

Otherwise, the setting up of an institution page follows much the same process as that of setting up a page for yourself as a user.

There is also a feature whereby you can select **Copy for new institution members**. This automatically adds the page to new institution members' portfolios. To set this up, visit the **Advanced** options of the share options for your institution page. You will see this option appear once you select **Allow copying**. This is really useful if you are adding, for example, some help pages to get your user started with using Mahara, or some templates for them to start creating their own pages.

Institution files

The files you upload into your institution will be available for use by all of your institution members. These could be general information documents, such as a code of practice or user guide, that you would like the whole institution to read.

Now, let's move on to look at controlled membership groups and what you can do with them as well as how to set up course roles in your groups (providing you are a staff member or an administrator).

Pop Quiz – managing your institution

1. Sometimes uploading one user at a time can take too long, especially when you have a list of over a hundred. If you were an institution administrator, what type of file could you use to make life easier for yourself?

2. Name three things that an institution administrator can do to manage their users.

Controlled membership groups

In Chapter 5, *Share and Network in Groups*, do you remember when setting up groups that you were able to select how users were added to your group? You chose between open and request membership groups as ways for users to join your group.

Administrators and staff have an additional option for adding users to their group—controlled membership. This option gives you ultimate power over who belongs in your group. You can pick any user in the site and force him/her to be a member. There is also the added factor that once a user has been added, he/she cannot leave without you removing them.

You will notice this additional option pop up in your group settings:

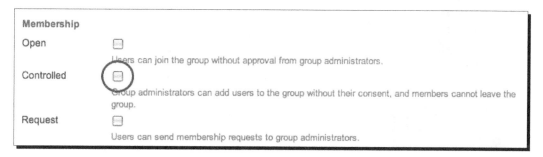

Note that your group can be controlled as well as request. That is, users can be forced to join and if they aren't members, can still request to join your group.

Controlled membership is a very useful feature for an admin. You can get all the members you want in your group without having to wait for users to join themselves. This is great for a course where your need a discrete set of users to join up and you don't want them to leave until you have said so.

This setting can be used in combination with group roles to create a group that is used for the purpose of managing a set of learners.

Course group roles

There are two types of staff members within Mahara—site staff members and institution staff members. So far in this chapter, you have seen how you can set up an institution staff member, but there is no difference as to what they can do.

You learned that a staff member is allowed to assign course roles to their groups. Let's have a look at the two different sets of roles that you can assign to your group as a staff member or administrator:

- **Standard—Member and Admin**: This is the default setup for a group and these are the only roles available to a standard user when setting up a group. Only group member and group administrator roles are allowed under this scheme.

- **Course—Member, Tutor, and Admin**: This can be chosen by site staff or administrators when setting up their groups. Notice how there is one extra role under this scheme—group tutor. Later on you will see what a group tutor is able to do in a group with course roles enabled.

Punam from Pennytown Primary thinks:

Although Susan, the Pennytown Primary institution administrator, has had to set up the new learners for our school, I still have control over my own English Tudor Monarchy group's membership and permissions. This is because I have been set up as a staff member in my school's institution. As I set up this particular controlled membership group myself, I am in complete control of my class' English Tudor Monarchy group and have decided to allow course roles too, so that I can set up some tutors.

Create a controlled membership group and allow course roles

Now that you've learned what a controlled membership group is and what course group roles are, it's time to have a go at putting things together to create a controlled membership group with course roles allowed.

Returning to the example from Training for Work, Graham has now made the user he created earlier—Peter Tooley—into a staff member. Peter is the course leader for an evidence-based qualification (for example, NVQ Level 2 in the UK) in Mechanical Engineering, which is why he belongs in this institution. He and his tutors would like to be able to assess evidence submitted by the learners through Mahara. He is going to need either a request or controlled group and to allow course roles, so that he can create some tutors.

Time for action – setting up a controlled membership group with course roles

You must be set up as a staff member or an administrator in your Mahara site—or a Mahara institution, in order to complete the procedure mentioned in this section. If you do not have these permissions, ask your site administrator, or your own institution administrator, to set you up. You are going to set up your first controlled membership group and to allow course roles, so that you can set up some tutors:

1. Log in to your Mahara as either a general staff member or a staff member of an institution.

2. Click on the **Groups** tab in the main menu bar.

3. On the **My groups** page, click on the **Create group** button.

4. As you did in Chapter 5, *Share and Network in Groups*, create your group in exactly the same way by giving it a relevant name and description.

5. In the **Settings** drop-down list, make sure you tick the **Controlled** check box to set up a group that you can oblige members to join.

6. Under **Roles**, choose **Course: Member, Tutor, Admin**. Here are the settings for the group created by Peter Tooley, the staff member that Graham Cohen added to his institution:

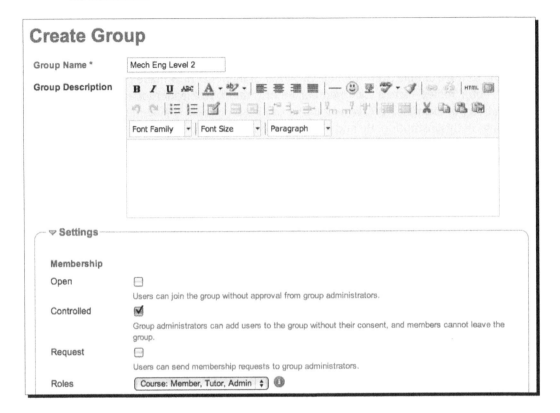

7. Click on **Save group** to finish!

8. And that's all there is to it, you now have a controlled group with course roles.

What just happened?

You just learned how to make your own controlled group with course roles as a staff member.

In the last *Time for action – setting up a controlled membership group with course roles*, you may have noticed that as a staff member you have a new option to make your group **Publicly viewable** (depending on whether this is allowed by administrators). This option was not available as a standard user. Let's have a look at what this means.

Publicly viewable groups

When creating a new group, a staff member also gets the option to make a group publicly viewable. This allows anyone, both within and outside the Mahara to access the group, including any forums that may exist. People outside the site can only view the group, not take part in discussions.

As you saw, the option to make your group publicly viewable appears on the **Create group** page, when you are setting up your group:

A good example of a time when you might want to use this is when you want users to join your site. A potential user may find your group via a search engine and discover a forum topic. On realizing that they want to post a response, the user will then need to sign up to join your Mahara. This is great for Mahara sites and groups that reach out into the public domain, but is not recommended for those who want their site to be more of a walled garden. You should consult with your site administrator before making a group open to be publicly viewed to find out if there are any site policies on this.

Now, Peter Tooley, although he is responsible for the Level 2 NVQ for Mechanical Engineering course, isn't the only assessor of the work that gets submitted. Learner assessment is also undertaken by one of his colleagues, Sally O'Leary.

Peter would like to allow Sally to use the controlled group that he has just created, in order to assess the work of the learners without having to let her use his own login details. But, Peter doesn't want Susan to have any administrative rights over the group. He just needs her to have the ability to see the pages, which have been submitted in order for her to assess and feedback on the work submitted.

Luckily, Mahara makes this possible with the group course role known as a tutor.

Tutors

The tutor role can be enabled in any group by allowing course roles as you saw earlier in this chapter. A tutor within a group has the ability to view all the work that has been submitted there. They are also able to release the work back to the learner once it has been assessed. They don't, however, have the ability to manage the group users or forums.

Time for action – adding a tutor to your controlled group with course roles

Let's set up your very first tutor in your course, controlled group:

1. Log in to your Mahara as the same staff member seen in the previous *Time for action – setting up a controlled membership group with course roles*. The controlled group you created should still be there.

2. Search for a user in your site that you would like to make a tutor in your course group. Click on the user to access his/her profile.

3. Then, from the user's profile page, add that user to your group by selecting the appropriate course from the **Add to** drop-down box. Then click on **Add**:

4. Navigate to your controlled group by using either the **Groups** and then **My groups** menu options, or more quickly by clicking on the group in the groups list to the right of your dashboard screen.

5. Click on the **Members** tab of your group. In there you should see the user that you have added in step 3. Peter Tooley of Training for Work has identified Sally O'Leary as a tutor of his NVQ Level 2 group:

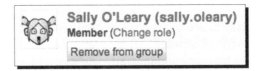

6. Currently, you should see that your user is set as a member of the group. You want them to be a tutor. Click on the **Change role** link next to the text saying **Member**:

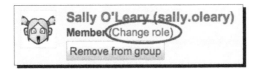

7. You will now see a screen that invites you to change the role of the user. Currently their role is set as **Member**. Use the drop-down box to the right of the text saying **Change role from Member to** and select **Tutor** from the available options:

8. To finish, click on **Submit**. And that's it! You have a tutor in your controlled group. You should see that your users' details have now changed from **Member** to **Tutor** in the description next to their name:

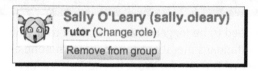

What just happened?

You have just learned how to create a tutor within a controlled group that has course roles enabled.

Sally O'Leary has become a tutor because she needs to assess work submitted by learners as evidence of their competencies for an engineering qualification. There are other reasons why you might set up tutors, though. Punam from Pennytown Primary might set up some of her teaching assistants as tutors in order that they too can view and feedback on work that gets submitted during their course. Staff members in PI Inc. might use tutors in controlled or request groups to approve information submitted about pharmaceutical processes.

Human Resources Managers might use Mahara for monthly **Continuous Professional Development (CPD)** reports and a departmental director might use the tutor role to delegate supervisory responsibilities to departmental subordinates.

Have a go hero – set up some tutors in controlled or request groups

Think about some of the courses that you currently run offline in your institution. Could your learners create some pages that can be submitted to you for assessment? Create some controlled or request membership groups for those courses and set up some tutors who will be helping you to manage and assess the work that is submitted to you.

Submitting work for assessment

Mahara is a learner-centred environment and any assessment process you conduct within it should not sacrifice its learner-driven principles. Controlled or request groups that allow page submission make this possible. It is the learners themselves who get to choose exactly what work they submit and when. This, we believe, is the way things should be.

Let's see what a learner has to do to submit a page for assessment by a tutor or administrator in a controlled group that has page submission enabled in its group settings.

Time for action – submitting a page to a course group for assessment

For this section, you will need to be logged in as a standard user who has been added to your course group. Add a standard member to your group, if none already exist. As group administrator, Peter Tooley of Training for Work has added one learner who he knows will be taking his NVQ Level 2 course, called Ravinda Pavel:

1. Log in to your Mahara as a standard course member belonging to the course group that you created earlier. For testing purposes, remember you can masquerade as a standard user, so do that if you think it is easier.

2. Using everything you learned in Chapter 2, *Getting Started with Mahara*, and Chapter 4, *Organize and Showcase your Portfolio*, create a page that you think would be of a good quality to submit to your group for assessment. Save your page when you are happy with it. Ravinda has created this page to submit for assessment:

3. Find the page that you created in step 2 in the **Pages** section of your portfolio and open it up.

4. Where it says **Submit this page to**, which enables you to select the appropriate course group from the drop-down list, it is likely that you only have one course group to submit to at the moment. However, in the future you might belong to more than one course and want to select a specific group to submit to. Ravinda wanted to submit his page to the **Mech Eng Level 2** group, so he selected **Mech Eng Level 2** from the drop-down list:

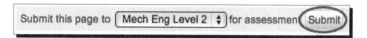

5. Click on **Submit**. Remember, you don't have to share your page with the group in order to do this. You can just submit it and it will be accessible only by tutors and administrators—not other group members.

6. When you submit your page, you will see a box explaining that you won't be able to delete or edit your page until your tutor has marked it, click on **Yes** to finish:

> If you submit 'PEO: Performing Engineering Operations' to 'Mech Eng Level 2' for assessment, you will not be able to edit this page until your tutor has finished marking it. Are you sure you want to submit this page now?
>
> Yes No

What just happened?

You have just seen how easy it is for a learner to submit work to their tutor in controlled or request groups with course roles and page submission enabled.

You saw that the page, once it has been sent and is in the hands of the tutor, cannot be edited by the learner. This is true in the sense that the learner cannot access his/her page to edit and move their blocks around.

At this point we need to make clear that the page a tutor sees may still not be displaying exactly the same content that the user saw when they submitted it.

The reason for this potential variation is because the page may contain content that is being linked to, or updated. For example, if a learner has added a journal post or an RSS feed to their page, it is likely that they have added to their journal since submitting. In this situation, the journal posts in the page will also update and be different to those that were originally there at the time of submission. Similarly, any externally linked websites may be displaying different text/video at the time of assessment.

With that qualifier acknowledged, page submission is clearly a great assessment technique for a tutor. The tutor knows that the user cannot edit the page in any way other than those you just saw. This gives them time to look at the page, and to grade or assess it. When the tutor has come up with a mark for it, they are then able to (should they choose to) release the page back to the learner—leaving them free again to extend and re-use it in the future.

Copy your page before submitting

Once you have submitted your page to a course group for assessment, you cannot access it for further editing. It is, therefore, a good idea to copy your page before you submit it. This way you can access your work and edit it, if you want to whilst your other copy is still locked for assessment. It is also possible to copy a page after submitting your work, so don't worry that your work is uneditable forever. Remember, though, that when you copy a page that feedback for the page is not copied.

So, you've seen how to submit a page, now let's find out how a page is returned to a learner once it has been assessed.

Time for action – releasing a page submitted for assessment

It's time to see how you can release a learner page back to them, once it has been submitted to your group:

1. Log in to Mahara as either a tutor or administrator of the course controlled group (that has page submission enabled) you have created.

2. Navigate to your course controlled group.

3. The first thing you should notice when you enter your group is that you have a new section at the bottom of the group's **About** page called **Pages submitted to this group**. Here, Sally O'Leary, the tutor on the NVQ Level 2 for Mechanical Engineering can now see the work that Ravinda has completed and when it was submitted:

Pages submitted to this group	Time of submission
PEO: Performing Engineering Operations Ravinda Pavel	22 January 2012, 9:16 PM

4. Click on the page that has been submitted for assessment.

5. At this point, imagine yourself in the role of a tutor. You have the time to carefully consider the submissions without the user being able to edit the page (apart from updating their journals or feeds).

6. When you have decided what mark the work deserves, you can release it back to the learner. Click on the **Release page** button at the bottom left of the page. Sally O'Leary releases Ravinda's page back to him:

This page was submitted to Mech Eng Level 2 on 22 January 2012, 9:16 PM (Release page)

What just happened?

You just found out how a tutor can release a page back to a learner once it has been marked, completing the assessment process.

In Chapter 4, *Organize and Showcase your Portfolio*, you saw how you can give feedback on pages. Use this feature to give your learners constructive advice on what they did/didn't do well. It is probably best if you make this feedback private, so that only the user can see what you have written. Remember, you can also add files as feedback—so why not add an attractive certificate of successful achievement, if relevant?

Putting it all together into an assessment process

So far in this chapter, you have seen how powerful institutions, controlled groups, course roles, and page submission can be in providing a bit more control for administrators and staff. You have also seen the basis of a simple assessment process based around learners submitting pages to a controlled or request membership group that has this page submission enabled. Now, let's combine all that you've seen to create an assessment process in Mahara.

First, we'll hear again from Neil from Training for Work.

Neil from Training for Work thinks:

It is looking great now that Graham has his own institution; he was telling me how he's set up Peter Tooley as a staff member, so that he can create a course, controlled group for his Mech Eng Level 2 course.

As part of the assessment process, I've decided to explore the idea of using the templating feature that I read about earlier in the book to set up some pages, which will be a base for our learners to work from.

Neil is right, the page templating system in Mahara is a great way of creating standard layouts for work to be submitted by all learners.

Of course, a learner could take the template, change it completely, and then submit that completely new set of information. But, depending on the course, they may then be failed for this level of creativity. The decision here is up to the assessor concerned. The important thing is that Mahara believes that a modern learner need not sacrifice his/her right to personalize the presentation of his/her own content, even if it may still remain wise for him/her to follow the conventions suggested by a tutor.

Let's show Mahara in action by devising a full assessment process, including the use of templates and showing how you can involve people external to the Mahara site (such as somebody verifying the standard of the submitted work for an examining body) in the process. The process described works for the UK-centric NVQ delivery example, but is general enough to apply to any qualification that requires work to be submitted for assessment. You can use Mahara to submit work digitally in a similar way to how learners have submitted a paper-based portfolio and worksheet for assessment in the past.

Time for action – an example assessment process with Mahara

Let's see an example of an assessment process in action in Mahara:

1. As a staff member, create a controlled group that has course roles and page submission enabled.

2. Add all your learners to the group that you just created. You saw how to add members to a controlled membership group in the *Tutors* section of this chapter.

3. In the **Pages** section of your course group, create a page and make it copyable by ticking the **Allow copying** box in the page share settings.

4. To the template, add a basic description of what the learner should be loading into which sections. Here is a very simple example of the kind of template you may create:

> ## Evidence Template by Mech Eng Level 2
>
> ### Evidence Part 1
> Enter your evidence in this area for Part 1 of the NVQ
>
> ### Evidence Part 2
> Enter your evidence in this area for Part 2 of the NVQ
>
> ### Evidence Part 3
> Enter your evidence in this area for Part 3 of the NVQ

5. Save your page when you are happy with it. It should now be seen by all your learners in the group.

6. Encourage your learners to copy the template page to their own portfolio area. Here, they can make adjustments to it, adding their own information.

7. When they are happy with their work, the learners should submit their page back to the group for assessment. Remember, the learner doesn't need to allow any additional sharing options for his/her page—it will be viewable by tutors and administrators on submission.

8. You can assess a learner's work, choosing to add feedback to their work if you want them to review it and resubmit it to you.

9. Now, in the files area of the group, you can upload documents and make them only viewable by tutors/administrators. One idea is to share a spreadsheet showing the marks for all of the students at this point—showing their progress on the course. This spreadsheet can then be displayed to people verifying the quality of the work (either internal or external to the Mahara site). This spreadsheet would need to be uploaded every time it is updated. See the next *What just happened* section for an alternative based on Google documents.

10. At this point, tutors are ready to look at all the work that has been submitted.

11. When marks have been decided, pages can be released back to the learners.

What just happened?

You have just looked at a simple process for how you could use Mahara templates along with controlled groups to assess learner evidence.

Monitoring and assessing learners' work

Many tutors giving feedback on a learner's work like to use the facility that Mahara provides to add a file to the feedback they provide. This could be a spreadsheet or word processed document giving feedback according to a formalized assessment criteria. Tutors can also attach audio/video feedback, if they require. The files that a tutor uploads automatically get placed in the learners file area in a folder called `commentfiles`, so the learner can add those files to their pages.

Other tutors like to make use of the **Add to watchlist** option, where a learner allows a tutor (or any site user for that matter) to watch and feedback on the way they are developing their page before it gets submitted for assessment. For this to happen, the learner has to share access to his/her page by allowing access by the tutor on his/her page's share settings. While a learner may want to engage a tutor's support in the development of his/her work in this way, he/she also may retain his/her right to choose for themselves which of their pages the tutor gets to see and which ones the tutor doesn't.

Earlier in this chapter, you saw how you can work collaboratively with your tutors to share the results of your assessment. We mentioned that you could share a file in the files area with permissions set, so that file isn't editable or readable by standard users (you probably don't want learners seeing the progress of and marks awarded to their colleagues). Another idea is to set up a Google document (spreadsheet or word processed file—visit `http://docs.google.com`), which contains all the results. Again, permissions settings would be important here and this could be linked to from a private page in the course group or even embedded in the group's **About** page, using the Google Apps block. This would perhaps be easier than having to upload assessment documents each time they are edited.

Link to a Moodle course

Do you also run a Moodle installation for your institution/business? Why not put a link to a related Moodle course page within the description on the **About** page of your Mahara group? This way, learners can access Moodle course materials whilst working within the Mahara group. Your Mahara site will need to be linked to a Moodle installation for this to work and for single sign-on to be enabled.

You also saw that as part of the process for assessment in Mahara, you may want to include people external to the group or Mahara site to verify the quality of work.

Here are a couple of ideas for how you could do this:

- **Secret URLs**: Encourage learners to create and send you a secret URL linking to their pages. These links could be collated and sent to an external verifier.

- **Create an assessment page**: The staff member for the group could create a special assessment page. This page could contain secret URLs of all the pages that require external review. This page could also contain links to a mark book in course management system such as Moodle to show results of quizzes.

In this chapter, it is important to note that, while Mahara has facilitated assessment of learning in this way, Mahara has no intention of ever becoming a Learning Management System or an eAssessment/eTracking platform. Moodle is a formalised course and Learning Management System, Mahara isn't. Instead, Mahara is, and will always remain, an informal and personalized learning environment.

One of the reasons Mahara is so keen on maintaining its symbiotic relationship with Moodle (`http://moodle.org`) is that Mahara sees the benefits of the integration of its own informal learning model with Moodle's Gradebook.

Useful notes on Moodle and Mahara integration (creating what the community have affectionately named a "Mahoodle" environment) can be accessed via the Mahara wiki at `https://wiki.mahara.org/images/d/d5/Mahoodle.pdf`. It is possible to submit pages created in Mahara to a Moodle course for assessment. Visit `https://wiki.mahara.org/index.php/System_administrator%27s_Guide/Moodle//Mahara_Integration/View_Submission`.

It is also worth pointing out the extremely useful work that has been done by a Mahara partner in the UK, the **University of London Computer Centre (ULCC)**. In a highly pedagogically-sound quest to promote the delivery of personalized learning, they have developed a personalization of Learning Framework at `http://moodle.ulcc.ac.uk/course/view.php?id=139`.

This framework elegantly integrates Mahara and Moodle with two Open Source Moodle Modules, which they have written:

- **Assessment Manager**: For progress tracking and verification of evidence towards formally accredited qualification (a significant improvement on the spreadsheet in the course group files area or the Google Doc mentioned earlier). Visit `http://moodle.ulcc.ac.uk/course/view.php?id=140`.

- **ULCC ILP**: For facilitating tutor support, including target setting and progress reviews. Visit `http://moodle.ulcc.ac.uk/course/view.php?id=107`. This ILP Module can be configured to "listen to" data sent to it from many of the popular Management Information Systems used by schools, colleges, universities, and other training providers.

Pop quiz – course groups, staff members, and tutors

1. What is a staff member able to do that standard users can't?

2. What is possible with a course group that isn't with a standard group?

3. What can a tutor do?

Summary

In the first part of this chapter, you looked at institutions in Mahara. You found out some of the things that an institution administrator can do when managing an institution. This included adding new members, managing members, and choosing some institution settings. You also learned how to change the role of your members, including turning a standard member into a staff member.

In the second part of the chapter, you learned what a staff member is able to do. You also saw how you can create controlled groups and what these are. You also saw how a staff member can allow course roles in their group and what these are. You learned about the tutor role, which allowed you to see how Mahara can be used to develop an assessment process, with pages being submitted to group tutors and group administrators for marking before they are released back to learners.

While you saw that Mahara can be used to assess and feedback on learners work with your tutors' hats on, we pointed out that Mahara is, in itself, making no attempt to become a formalized Learning Management System. Mahara is happier, instead, to work in symbiosis with Moodle or other systems/plugins for this more formal type of gradebook-centred progress tracking.

The next chapter is all about extensions in Mahara—the bells and whistles that can be added to give a Mahara site that little bit extra.

7
Mahara Extensions

Mahara is modular, and has been written so that its functionality isn't confined to the core code. Developers are able to contribute plugins that extend the main functionality of Mahara.

In this chapter, you will have a look at the parts of Mahara that can be extended and be introduced to some of the extensions that are currently available.

Since they are extensions and don't come packaged with the default Mahara download, you may not have them installed in your own Mahara site. In this chapter, you will be using `http://foliofor.me` *to work through demonstrations of the extensions as it is already configured to use them.*

In this chapter you will:

- ◆ Look at which features can be extended in Mahara and which extensions are currently available
- ◆ Continuing professional development
- ◆ Look at the My Learning artefact
- ◆ Look in detail at the Embedly block type
- ◆ Look at the social sharing block types (Twitter, Facebook, and LinkedIn)
- ◆ See how to embed a LinkedIn profile in a page

Extending Mahara

Mahara has been written to be pluggable, and this means that anyone with the knowhow and inclination can put together his/her own additions to the code, because the source code is open.

Think of it like LEGO when you were younger. You've got that super-cool pirate ship that has everything you need to start playing—cannons, masts, monkeys, and treasure. But, one day you find out you can get a separate harbor to dock your boat to and new special characters to go on your ship. You don't need these extras, but they would make it more fun to play with.

The extensions don't meddle with the core code. When you have a plugin installed, on occasion it can cause problems for you when you come to upgrade as it is now part of your system. If its functionality breaks when you upgrade your Mahara site, users won't have access to some of their content anymore.

This extension/plugin system means that administrators can pick and choose which extensions to add to their site. In Mahara you are able to plug in content as:

- ◆ **Artefacts**: Completely new sections of content for your portfolio
- ◆ **Blocktypes**: Available when editing a page, artefacts often include a blocktype
- ◆ **Authentication**: Facilitates the integration of user login between different systems
- ◆ **Search**: Plugs in to/extends the Mahara default search

In this chapter, you will look at a few of the artefact and blocktype plugins in detail. Authentication and search plugins are really useful too, and we advise you to look into what's available if you're a more technical reader. If you would like to install any of the plugins in this chapter, it's best to talk to your Mahara site administrator.

All of the plugins that have been made available to the community are listed on the Mahara Wiki at `https://wiki.mahara.org/index.php/plugins`. This list will be the most up-to-date, so we suggest you hop over and have a look.

Mahara extensions list

Here is a summary of some currently available Mahara plugins:

Name	Description	Author(s)	Link
Artefacts			
CPD (showcased in this chapter)	A way of recording **Continuing Professional Development** (CPD) activities—tracking their time and location.	James Kerrigan, Geoff Rowland	`https://wiki.Mahara.org/index.php/Plugins/Artefact/My_CPD`
My Learning (showcased in this chapter)	Allows you to determine your multiple intelligences and learning styles by answering a series of questions. Graphical results can be displayed.	Gregor Anželj	`https://wiki.Mahara.org/index.php/Plugins/Artefact/My_Learning`
Problems and Conditions	Gives a student the ability to create case notes that are related to particular medical conditions.	Catalyst for the University of Cambridge	`https://wiki.Mahara.org/index.php/Plugins/Artefact/Problems_%26_Conditions`
Blocktypes			
Embedly (showcased in this chapter)	Provides the ability to embed all sorts of web 2.0 content in pages.	Gregor Anželj	`http://Mahara.org/view/view.php?id=35826`
Facebook Like/ Recommend (showcased In this chapter)	Adds a Facebook **Like** button to Mahara pages. When clicked, this sends updates to the Facebook feed of the user.	Gregor Anželj	`http://Mahara.org/view/view.php?id=35645`
LinkedIn Share button (showcased in this chapter)	Adds a button to a page, which will update LinkedIn profile feeds.	Gregor Anželj	`http://Mahara.org/view/view.php?id=35645`

Name	Description	Author(s)	Link
Twitter Tweet button (showcased in this chapter)	Gives the **Tweet** option to a Mahara page so that Twitter feeds can share content.	Gregor Anželj	`http://Mahara.org/view/view.php?id=35645`
LinkedIn Profile (showcased in this chapter)	Gives the facility for adding LinkedIn profile content within a Mahara page.	Gregor Anželj	`http://Mahara.org/view/view.php?id=35645`
FreeMind Flash	Renders a FreeMind application in a Mahara page.	James Kerrigan, Geoff Rowland	`https://wiki.Mahara.org/index.php/Plugins/Artefact/FreeMindFlash`
Chem 2D NIH	Displays an image of a chemical structure in a Mahara page. The image is produced by using the NIH NCI/CADD Chemical Identifier Resolver service.	Geoff Rowland	`https://wiki.Mahara.org/index.php/Plugins/Blocktype/ChemNIH`
Jmol	Renders a 3D chemical structure in a page. The structure is interactive.	James Kerrigan, Geoff Rowland	`https://wiki.Mahara.org/index.php/Plugins/Blocktype/Jmol`
Jmol NIH	Renders an interactive 3D chemical structure in a page. The structure is produced by using the NIH NCI/CADD Chemical Identifier Resolver service.	Geoff Rowland	`https://wiki.Mahara.org/index.php/Plugins/Blocktype/JmolNIH`

Name	Description	Author(s)	Link
Authentication			
Web Services	Web Services in Mahara provide REST, XML-RPC, and SOAP alternatives for any Mahara function that is registered.	-	`https://wiki.mahara.org/index.php/Plugins/Auth/WebServices`
Jahrain Engage	Single sign on to Mahara from Google, Facebook, Twitter, Yahoo!, and more—Based on the Jahrain Engage service.	LUNS Ltd. for Learning Arabia	`https://wiki.mahara.org/index.php/Plugins/Auth/Janrain_Engage`
LDAP sync	A plugin that syncs LDAP user accounts and LDAP groups with Mahara.	Patrick Pollet	`https://mahara.org//interaction/forum/topic.php?id=4303#post19025`

Janet Norman from PI Inc. thinks:

I didn't realize there were so many extensions for Mahara!

One of the reasons we chose the platform originally was because it was Open Source. We saw the benefits of it being free both money-wise and code-wise. Now, I'm starting to see how it also benefits from a developer community.

The chemical structures plugin is interesting for us as there is a chemistry element to our learning units. I'm going to contact the administrators to see if we can get a demo running.

Continuing Professional Development (CPD)

CPD is an essential element of many learning programs. It is the practice of keeping tabs on your skills and how they have improved over the course of time.

As you've seen, Mahara is already great for CPD—you can write journals logging your progress and display them in pages. You can also plan your actions using plans.

Sometimes, however, when monitoring CPD, it's necessary to have the ability to log more specific information related to the activity undertaken, for example the location of a CPD activity and the time spent on it. Some courses, for example, require you to demonstrate a specific number of hours of CPD before you can complete them.

Fortunately, the CPD Mahara artefact allows you to do just that. Built in a similar way to plans, it allows users to log their own CPD activities, and group these into lists for easy management. You may, for example, have a group of CPD activities for each course undertaken or for each personal area of interest (for example, JavaScript programming, cooking, and climbing).

An example of a CPD activity list based around JavaScript development is shown in the following screenshot:

CPD Javascript activities					New activity
Start Date	End Date	Title	Description		Hours
20 January 2012	12 February 2012	Created color box JQuery plugin at Hom	Dedicated a few weekends to creating my first JQuery plugin - a colorbox input. Users are able to select colors in RGB and HEX and have these inputted into a web form field.		40.0
10 January 2012	10 January 2012	Online JS forum at Online	A four hour webinar looking at the future of javascript and its role in dynamic web applications of tomorrow. Chaired by leaders in javascript development.		4.0
19 December 2011	21 December 2011	JQuery Course at South East University	A three day JQuery beginners course. Learned the basics of JQuery and developed a very simple front-end application based on fake music ticket sales website.		24.0
				Total hours	68.0

CPD isn't only useful for students, it should also be conducted by staff and employees. According to the developers, "One rationale for this plugin was that if lecturers/teachers found Mahara useful to record and reflect upon their own CPD, they would be more likely to use Mahara with their students".

So let's have a look at the CPD Mahara extension and see what you can do with it:

Time for action – create a list of CPD activities

Let's create a list of CPD activities:

1. Log in to http://foliofor.me if you have set up an account, or your own Mahara if you have the CPD artefact installed.

2. Click on the **Content** tab on the main menu, followed by **CPD** on the submenu:

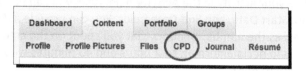

3. You will see that under the title **Continuing Professional Development**, you currently have no CPDs. So let's make a new one! Click on the **Add one!** button, or **New CPD** to the top right:

4. On the next page, you will see that you can give your CPD a title and description. Here, by CPD, we simply mean a group of activities that you are likely to conduct related to your development, so think of a good title for grouping your activities. Subject area, course, or time frame are the most common. For example, you might create a CPD for a Spring term:

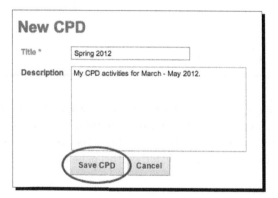

5. Now, you will see that your CPD is ready for you to begin adding activities. Click on the **New activity** button to start creating your first activity.

6. The following screen is where you can really get into adding the detail of your CPD. You can name your activity in the **Activity** field. Also, you can fill in the details in the **Location**, **Start Date**, and **End Date** fields. You can provide a description of your activity as well as the number of hours that you spent on the activity. You should put your hours in decimal format, so 2 hours and 45 minutes would be 2.75. Click on **Save activity** to finish.

7. On the following screen you will see your activity appear with all the details that you added, displayed neatly in columns. One thing you will notice is that you are provided the **Total hours** indicator field. This is the sum of the number of hours that you took for all activities as listed on this page of the CPD:

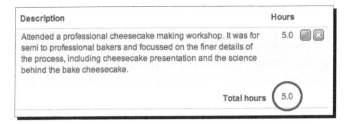

What just happened?

You just had a look at the CPD extension.

Functionally, you can think of the CPD plan as doing the opposite job to the plans feature. With plans you are deciding what you are going to do, whereas with CPD you are logging what you have done. Together they are really useful for managing your reflective learning portfolio. When you look back, you will be able to see exactly where you have come from and how much you have learned.

You can ask yourself questions such as, "Why did I improve so much in that skill but not in another?" Perhaps you can trace it to a particular course or experience you had.

It would be easy to fall into the trap of thinking that CPD is all about fulfilling the CPD element of a course, but you should think of it in terms of capturing useful experiences and assessing what you have gained from them.

The CPD artefact also comes with its own blocktype. The block shows up under the **General** tab in the page editor. When you drag the block into the page, you have the option to select a CPD that you would like to embed in the page:

Once embedded, the CPD block shows all the details relating to its activities and also provides the total number of hours.

My Learning

This artefact, called My Learning, actually includes two different tools. One measures your multiple intelligences and the other, your learning styles.

Multiple intelligences

The theory of multiple intelligences was developed in 1983 by Dr. Howard Gardner. It is the simple idea that intelligence isn't simply based on logic (as with IQ tests), but rather it comes up with a number of different intelligences a person may have. These range from visual-spatial to musical-rhythmic.

Knowing where your intelligence lies will help you to understand your strengths and weaknesses. This is useful in thinking about the way you approach a task.

Deciding your multiple intelligences is a simple matter of answering a few questions. Let's take the plunge and see where we're intelligent (and not so intelligent).

Time for action – determine multiple intelligences and display them

Let's see how you can determine your multiple intelligences by using the My Learning artefact:

1. Log in to the `http://foliofor.me` website, if you have set up an account, or log in to your own Mahara, if My Learning is installed.

2. Click on **Content**, then on **My Learning**.

3. At the top of the page, you will see a description of multiple intelligences, their history, and what the intelligences are in detail. When you have completed reading it, click on the **Multiple Intelligences** link:

The theory of multiple intelligences was developed in 1983 by Dr. Howard Gardner. It suggests that the traditional notion of intelligence, based on I.Q. testing, is far too limited. Instead, Dr. Gardner proposes seven different intelligences to account for a broader range of human potential in children and adults. An eighth intelligence was defined and put forth in the mid '90s also by Gardner. These intelligences are:

- **Linguistic.** The ability to use spoken or written words.
- **Logical-Mathematical.** Inductive and deductive thinking and reasoning abilities, logic, as well as the use of numbers and abstract pattern recognition.
- **Visual-Spatial.** The ability to mentally visualize objects and spatial dimensions.
- **Body-Kinesthetic.** The wisdom of the body and the ability to control physical motion.
- **Musical-Rhythmic.** The ability to master music as well as rhythms, tones and beats.
- **Interpersonal.** The ability to communicate effectively with other people and to be able to develop relationships.
- **Intrapersonal.** The ability to understand one's own emotions, motivations, inner states of being, and self-reflection.
- **Naturalist-Environmental.** The ability to make distinctions in the natural world and the environment.

 Multiple Intelligences

---

4. You will see a series of questions drop down. Tick all the boxes that are true for you. Answer them as honestly as you can. When you are done, click on **Save**.

5. You will see the Learning survey saved notice pop up at the top of the screen. If you click on the multiple intelligences link once again, you will see that all your options have been saved there and can be edited if you wish to do so. Now, you need to display the results, so start creating a new Mahara page.

6. Click on the **Profile** tab. Open a page in editing view. You will see that there is a block for multiple intelligences:

7. Drag the block into your page. In the options, choose a title for the block and select if you want to set a graph color and select the legend type.

8. You should see your intelligences appear in the page. The following screenshot shows my results. Looks like I've got strong visual-spatial and musical intelligence, but my verbal-linguistic tendencies are non-existent:

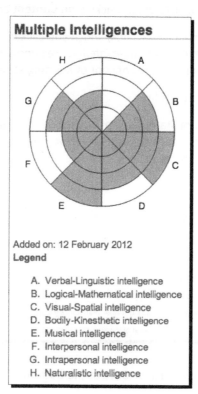

What just happened?

You just answered some questions to determine your multiple intelligences and displayed the results in a Mahara page. Now, let's move on to have a look at your learning styles.

Learning styles

There has been a lot of work around the idea of using learning styles to decide how you should plan your learning activities. These can be roughly classified as visual, auditory, reading/writing, and kinesthetic/tactile. While many have turned to this as a method for matching style to activity, it must be said that its effect on learning is somewhat disputed. Whether you believe in the success of learning styles for guiding learning or not, it's certainly fun to find out what they are.

Time for action – determine your learning styles and display them

So let's find out your preferred learning styles:

1.   Revisit the My Learning artefact by clicking on **Content** and then **My Learning**.

2.   Below the **Multiple Intelligences** link, which you clicked during the preceding *Time for action – determine multiple intelligences and display them*, you will see a paragraph introducing the concept of learning styles.

3.   Click on the **Learning Styles** link.

4.   You will see a long list of statements about specific learning situations. You have a number of options for each statement—**Never, Rarely, Sometimes, Often**, and **Always**. Answer all of the questions:

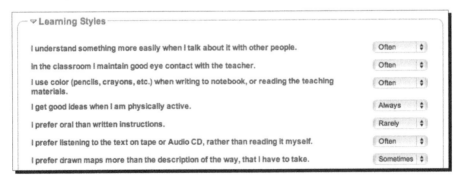

5.   When you have finished, click on Save at the bottom of the page.

6. Now, as with the multiple intelligences, you need to add the learning styles block to a page in order to see the results. Open up a new or existing page in editing view.

7. Under the **Profile** block tab, you will see an icon for learning styles.

8. Drag the block onto your page. You will see some options for editing the colors of the pie chart and its legend. Click on **Save**.

9. In your page, you will see a pie chart displaying your preferred learning styles.

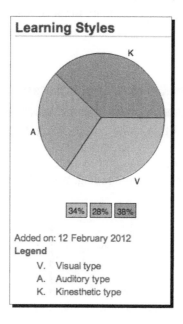

10. Looks like I'm more of a kinesthetic/visual learner.

What just happened?

You just learned how to work out your learning styles and display them in a Mahara page.

Were you surprised by the results? Next time you take a course why not tailor your studies to your preferred learning styles? On the VARK website, there are some useful help sheets that give you some ideas for learning strategies once you know your results (http://www.vark-learn.com/english/page.asp?p=helpsheets).

Embedly

The Embedly blocktype allows you to embed content from certain Web 2.0 services right into a Mahara page. For those who aren't familiar with Embedly (`http://embedly/`), it is a service that converts URLs into rich content. In their own words:

> *Embedly provides a powerful API to convert standard URLs into embedded videos, images, and rich article previews.*

Embedly has 218 leading Web 2.0 services in its supported list (`http://embedly/providers`).

So let's see how it works:

Time for action – embed some content using Embedly

Let's add some Web 2.0 content to a Mahara page, using the Embedly block:

1. Create a new page in your `http://foliofor.me` portfolio. Switch to edit view and look under the **External content** heading. You will see that you have the Embedly block available:

2. Drag the block onto your page as you would do with any other block in Mahara.

3. You will see the options box pop up. You need to do a couple of things before you can fill these out. Sign up for a free Embedly API account, and find the URL of what you want to embed. Let's sign up.

4. Visit `https://app.embedly/pricing/free` and fill out the form with your own details. With the free plan, you can embed 10,000 links per month—that should be plenty! Once you have signed up, you will see a page that shows you **Your API Key**. Leave this page open for now and you will come back to it later.

5. Now, let's find some content to embed. Visit `http://embedly/providers`. This shows you all of the services that you are able to embed into a Mahara page. There are lots of them! They range from commonly used services such as Facebook and Flickr to the more obscure Ultra Kawaii and SmugMug.

6. By hovering over each service, you can see which URL patterns are accepted. Let's try embedding a video from the SoundCloud—a music/audio sharing service. At the time of writing, these are the URL patterns that are accepted:

- `http://soundcloud.com/*`
- `http://soundcloud.com/*/*`
- `http://soundcloud.com/*/sets/*`
- `http://soundcloud.com/groups/*`
- `http://snd.sc/*`

7. So, you can embed from most locations on the SoundCloud website.

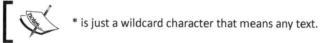 * is just a wildcard character that means any text.

8. Let's visit the SoundCloud website and choose an audio clip. Go to `http://http://soundcloud.com/`. I searched for music by one of my favorite bands—**Fleet Foxes**—and chose their track **Helplessness Blues**. I listened to the track and decided I would like to add it to my page about 21st Century American Folk Music.

9. Copy the link of the audio URL, which in this case is `http://soundcloud.com/subpop/fleet-foxes-helplessness-blues`. A quick check against the URL patterns shows that this video is fine to embed because of `http://soundcloud.com/*/*`.

10. Back to Mahara. Let's fill in the settings for Embedly. First paste the **Embedly API Key** that you found in step 4.

11. Then paste the URL in the **Content URL** field for the content to embed.

12. Next, decide if you would like to show content description—this is a little bit of auto generated text that gets displayed below the embed. Fill in the usual block title, description, and so on. Here are the options for the SoundCloud embed:

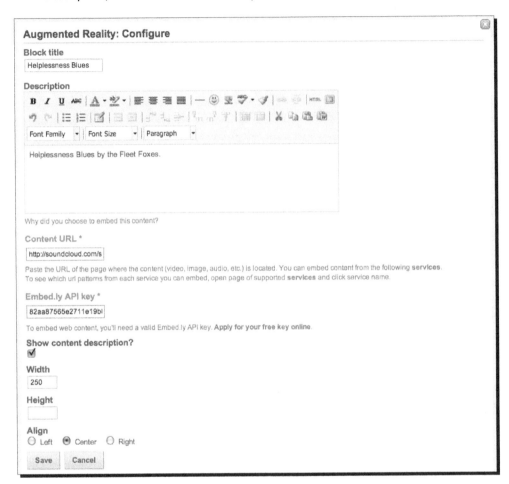

13. That's all there is to it. You will see your content embedded in your Mahara page:

What just happened?

You just saw how to embed some content from the SoundCloud website into a Mahara page, using the Embedly blocktype.

Isn't that great? This opens up a whole world of possibilities for your Mahara pages. With so many different services to choose from, there's no longer any excuse for a text-only, bland Mahara page. Make it dynamic and interesting.

Let's have a look at a few ideas for the other services that you can embed and what they look like in a Mahara page.

Mixcloud

This is an online radio service that serves up podcast and live streaming broadcasts. You can access content from a variety of talk categories, including comedy, technology, sport, politics, and business. Why not include a talk in your Mahara page to show you understand a topic or give weight to an argument?

Here is what the embed looks like, taken from a radio show by the comedian Dave Gorman:

SchoolTube

SchoolTube (http://www.schooltube.com/), along with TeacherTube (http://www.teachertube.com/) is one of the most popular video resources out there dedicated solely for education. It hosts many videos from students and academics alike. You're sure to find something useful there.

There is a fun stop motion video, about lab safety, made using LEGO characters—`http://www.schooltube.com/video/8abf3e870635c885a3d3/Lab-Safety`. You can imagine this being useful in a chemistry induction class. This is what it looks like once embedded:

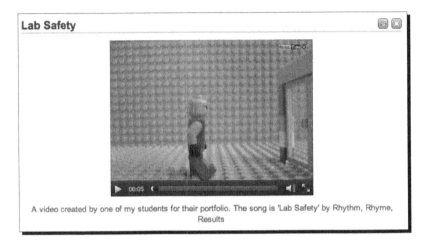

A video created by one of my students for their portfolio. The song is 'Lab Safety' by Rhythm, Rhyme, Results

Social sharing—Twitter, Facebook, and LinkedIn

There are a number of extensions that allow you to connect your Mahara page with some of the most popular social networking spaces out there. Here, you will have a look at a few of them—Twitter, Facebook, and LinkedIn.

Each plugin is similar, in that they put a button on your page, which allows readers to send updates to their social networking pages linking your work.

Time for action – add a Twitter Tweet button to a Mahara page

Let's start by looking at how to add a Twitter Tweet button:

1. Visit *http://foliofor.me* once more or log in to your own Mahara instance and start creating a new page.

2. In **Edit Content** view, click on the **General** tab. You will see an icon called **Twitter Tweet**:

3. Drag the block onto your page. There are a few options that you can choose. For layout style, decide where to display the tweet count. This refers to the box, next to the Tweet button, that shows how many people have shared it. Choose either vertical, horizontal, or no count.

4. Next, choose the Tweet text that is displayed along with the link when the content is shared on Twitter. This should be something relevant to the content on the page. For example, Amazon Biodiversity, if the page is about bio-diversity in the Amazon rainforest.

5. Click on **Save**. Here is what the **Twitter** button looks like on the page:

6. That's all there is to it. Viewers of the page can now send updates to Twitter informing others of the content.

What just happened?

You just saw how to add a Twitter Tweet button to your page.

The Facebook Like/Recommend and LinkedIn blocks work in much the same way. You simply drag the block onto the page, set the options, and that's all there is to it.

Should you go social?

These are great blocks to have in any Mahara installation. They enhance the sharing features that already exist, encouraging feedback and comments on your portfolio beyond that permitted within the walled garden. The question is, when is it a good idea to add these buttons to a page?

When you add these social links to a page, you are basically saying to the world, "Go ahead and let other people know about the content I have created".

Self-promotion isn't a bad thing! Maybe you have an interesting idea or take on an idea that you think is worth the world knowing about. If the content is good enough, people will naturally let others know about it. In fact, there's no reason why you can't use a Mahara page with the specific purpose of selling a product or to show off your work. This would be useful for, say, photographers, artists, authors, or freelancers in general.

As with setting up your page share settings, you should think carefully about whether the content in your page should be available to be shared with the outside world via social sharing buttons. Here are some situations when it's probably not very clever to allow social sharing:

◆ Your page contains information sensitive to other people in your class or organization, and you haven't asked their permission to share it with others.

◆ Your page contains private information from your organization. Perhaps a trade secret/intellectual property or simply meeting notes.

◆ Your content contains incorrect facts or uninformed conclusions. What you put out there, should be well thought out and true at the very least—unless, of course, you are writing in a satirical/ironic tone.

◆ The content you're sharing might be offensive to a particular person or group.

If you decide to add a share button to your Mahara page, it's probably a good idea to make sure that your page itself is public or at least has a wide audience in the Mahara site, so that enough people would actually be able to look at it. You're likely to get more shares that way.

Ok, so you've decided that you would like to share your page with the world. The question now is, which social networking site(s) to choose? Let's look at each of them a bit closer.

Twitter

Twitter is a micro-blogging site and lets you share mini text updates with a limited character count. When viewers of your page share it on Twitter, it is their followers who will be notified as well as those who subsequently find the tweet through search engines and retweets.

Facebook

Facebook is used for individuals to share content with their friends, although it is gaining more traction with professionals and universities too. Facebook shares are in the forms of "Likes", so by clicking the button, the sharer is saying they like your content.

LinkedIn

This is a professional profile and networking site. When users share content here, it is usually in a strictly professional context. Add the LinkedIn button, if you would like to promote your content with other professional working groups.

Christophe from Silverworks University thinks:

I'm putting together a Mahara collection that promotes our degree show. It includes lots of images of student work as well as details about the event. I'm going to link to this from our social networking pages.

These buttons will be really useful—I'm going to add them to the collection home page, so that students can reshare the collection with their friends and followers.

LinkedIn profile

In this book, you've already seen how Mahara can be used to manage your professional profile. LinkedIn (`http://www.LinkedIn.com/`) is a professional social networking website that allows you to do very much the same, you can fill out your résumé as well as your skills, introduction, picture, and so on. The advantage of LinkedIn over Mahara is that you have access to a world of other professionals. Colleagues, peers, head hunters, and so on are all able to communicate with you via LinkedIn through messages, groups, and connections.

The LinkedIn profile block provides a closer integration between your personal portfolio profile and your socially networked professional profile out there.

It allows you to embed your LinkedIn profile into a Mahara page.

Time for action – embed your LinkedIn profile in a page

Let's see how you can embed your LinkedIn profile in a Mahara page:

1. You will need to have your own LinkedIn profile to complete this procedure. If you don't have one already, visit LinkedIn (`http://www.LinkedIn.com`) and get yourself set up. Take some time to fill out your professional profile there. Add a photo, introduction, some work experiences, and skills. LinkedIn will give you instructions for completing your profile. If you have a LinkedIn profile just move onto the next step.

2. Log in to LinkedIn. You need to find the URL of your public profile page. Open up your profile page. In the box to the top left that shows your profile image and profile summary, you should see a field labeled as **Public Profile**, copy the URL listed there. If you don't see a link, you will need to enable your LinkedIn profile for public sharing.

3. Open up Mahara (either `http://foliofor.me` or your own installation if you have this block installed). Start creating a new page, or edit an existing page.

4. In editing view, click on the **Profile** tab. Drag the LinkedIn Profile block icon onto your page. You will see the options box pop up:

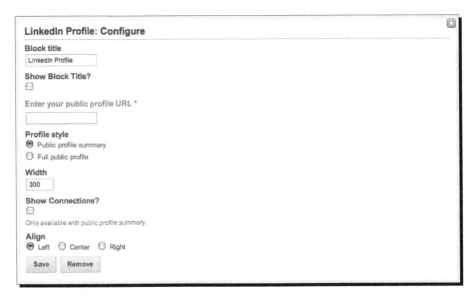

5. In the **Enter your public profile URL** field, paste the URL that you copied in step 2. You can also choose whether to show a full public profile or just the summary. Let's tick the box to show the full profile. Also, you can decide whether to show connections or not. Click on **Save**.

6. You should see your full LinkedIn profile embedded in your page. Here's a snapshot of Richard Hand's profile in a Mahara page:

Linked in®

Richard Hand

Front-end Web Development Consultant

Berlin Area, Germany | Internet

Join LinkedIn and access Richard Hand's full profile.

As a LinkedIn member, you'll join 150 million other professionals who are sharing connections, ideas, and opportunities. And it's free! You'll also be able to:

See who you and **Richard Hand** know in common

Get introduced to **Richard Hand**

Contact **Richard Hand** directly

View Full Profile

Richard Hand's Overview

Current	**Front-end Web Development Consultant at** TDM Ltd
	Web Development Internship at pidoco° GmbH
Past	Learning Technologist at TDM Ltd
Education	University of Bristol
Recommendations	**2** people have recommended Richard
Connections	**50** connections

Richard Hand's Summary

- User interface designer and front-end web specialist.
- Worked on the design and implementation of international-scale e-Learning products.
- Developed wireframes and skins for Drupal, Wordpress, Joomla and Moodle websites.
- Worked in small, focused, development teams.
- Delivered public product launches.
- Published author of the Mahara e-Portfolios Beginner's Guide.
- Specialist in Open Source Software.

What just happened?

You just saw how to show your full LinkedIn profile in a Mahara page.

This is what the embed would look like, if only the summary is included:

Richard Hand

Front-end Web Development Consultant at TDM Ltd

Web Development Internship at pidoco° GmbH

Berlin Area, Germany

View Profile

Neil from Training for Work thinks:

So far I've seen Mahara as a personal, reflective walled garden where our learners can put together their files, plan, journals, and pages to document their learning progress.

We have promoted LinkedIn as a tool that our learners should consider using in order to show off their skills and to connect with potential employers.

The fact that the two can now be used in tandem by embedding LinkedIn profiles into Mahara pages, is great news.

Summary

In this chapter, you had a look at some of the extensions that are available for the Mahara platform.

You saw examples of how to use these extensions on the `foliofor.me` platform. Perhaps now you've had a look through some of them, you can see their value and would like to persuade your system administrator to install a few for your Mahara site.

You specifically looked at CPD for logging continuous professional development activity, Embedly block for allowing the inclusion of Web 2.0 embeds in a page, the My Learning artefact (Multiple Intelligence and Learning Style assessments), social networking share buttons (Twitter, LinkedIn, and Facebook), and embedding your LinkedIn profile.

That's all for the book proper—we hope you have enjoyed finding out about the Mahara platform and felt inspired to make use of its many features. Read on to find a pre-implementation guide and a guide for installing Mahara, in the appendices.

Mahara Implementation–Pre-Planner

In this appendix, we have laid out and sequenced some of the important questions that your organization will need to address should you want to get your ePortfolio system set up efficiently and for it to be a success. This appendix serves as a pre-planner, not as a planner. It is intended to get you thinking through some of the important issues behind organizational ePortfolio platform implementation. After you have worked through this Appendix, you should then go on to draw up an Implementation Action Plan.

One action plan format, for example, could be based on the following. The items styled in Italics are example objectives:

Mahara Implementation Planner

Overall Aim:

PHASE ONE: Analysis and Specification

Objective 1: *Decide which ePortfolio tool is* best *for us*

Action	Who?	By when?	Resources required	Planned outcomes and outputs	Impact measures
Draw up a list of criteria for what we want the ePortfolio to be able to do. This will later be used to evaluate the suitability of market-leading ePortfolio platforms.	*ePortfolio champion and information technologist. Verified by management.*	*01/09/2012*	*Time: An initial meeting with management to discuss requirements and goals. Research and development of criteria.*	*An ePortfolio criteria list.*	*Existence of criteria list and its success in informing the ePortfolio software selection process.*

Action	Who?	By when?	Resources required	Planned outcomes and outputs	Impact measures
Define market-leading ePortfolio solutions.	*ePortfolio champion and information technologist.*	*10/09/2012*	*Time: Researching market-leading solutions.*	*A list of market-leading ePortfolios.*	*Existence of market-leading ePortfolio list.*
Analyze ePortfolio solutions against the ePortfolio criteria list in order to decide which to implement.	*ePortfolio champion and information technologist.*	*15/09/2012*	*Time: Analyze ePortfolio solutions against criteria list.*	*ePortfolio recommendation and presentation to management*	*Efficiency of the decision making process in the management meeting to decide on the solution.*

Objective 2:

Action	Who?	By when?	Resources required	Planned outcomes and outputs	Impact measures

PHASE TWO: Planning, Design, and Implementation

Objective 1: *'Create a Buzz' about the new portfolio software*

Action	Who?	By when?	Resources required	Planned outcomes and outputs	Impact measures
Draw up and implement a communications plan that targets all different types of stakeholders (users, staff, leaders, trainers, assessors, parents, employers and so on).	*ePortfolio champion, a tutor and a member of management.*	*23/09/2012*	*Time: Meeting to decide communication approach for each stakeholder type.* *Booklet: communications plan to present to management.*	*ePortfolio communications plan*	*Effectiveness of communications plan in actioning marketing activities.*

Action	Who?	By when?	Resources required	Planned outcomes and outputs	Impact measures
Publicize real-life case studies via our website and newsletters.	*Website manager and ePortfolio champion.*	*28/09/2012*	*Time: Finding, creating, and publishing examples.*	*Case-study publications.*	*Reach of publications. Interest generated from marketing activity.*
Creation of online user guide and training video.	*Website manager, content producer.*	*28/09/2012*	*Software: Video editing program* *Time: Putting together training video and written user guide.*	*Video and written user guide produced.*	*Number of hits of the video and its impact on ePortfolio activity. Number of user guide downloads.*

Objective 2:

Action	Who?	By when?	Resources required	Planned outcomes and outputs	Impact measures

PHASE THREE: Evaluation and Continuation

Objective 1: *Evaluating impact and usage of ePortfolio solution*

Action	Who?	By when?	Resources required	Planned outcomes and outputs	Impact measures
Set general and quantifiable targets for site engagement.	*ePortfolio champion and information technologist.*	*01/12/2012*	*Time: Setting some useful, practical targets.*	*List of general and quantifiable targets of site engagement.*	*Usefulness of targets when coming to analyze actual site usage.*

Action	Who?	By when?	Resources required	Planned outcomes and outputs	Impact measures
Analyzing ePortfolio usage against targets.	*ePortfolio champion and information technologist.*	*20/12/2012*	*User data: Access to ePortfolio user data and feedback forms.* *Time:* *Putting together data results into easy to read charts and reports.*	*Usage reports and charts. Charts show usage versus targets and general metrics.*	*Statistical data showing how well targets have been met and where they haven't.*

Objective 2:

Action	Who?	By when?	Resources required	Planned outcomes and outputs	Impact measures

An `.odt` and also a `.doc` version of the preceding matrix is available for download from `http://maharaforbeginners.tdm.info`, in the links and resources menu. You will also find a version with the preceding examples included.

It is our hope that by getting you to think through the following sections, we will help you to ensure that your software implementation goes smoothly. Successful software implementations have more to do with cultural changes than they have to do with technological changes. Too many software implementations have gone astray; let's make sure that yours is not one of those. A classic failing software implementation runs like this:

1. One management member opts to adopt while others look skeptically on.

2. The manager brings in technicians to install, configure, and launch the software.

3. Staff and user time is not provided, neither is any further training, guidance, and development time planned or purchased.

4. The implementation quickly starts to lose direction and the project fails.

Let's be clear again, this Mahara Implementation Pre-Planner will only serve to guide your decision-making process, we cannot make your decisions for you, and we are leaving it up to you to form your formal implementation strategy for yourself.

Also, please bear in mind that as we write this Implementation Pre-Planner, we are catering for a wide readership, so some of the questions and suggestions we make in the following sections might sometimes be pitched at a larger, or smaller, or just different organizations to your own, and they may not all always seem relevant to your context. If this is the case, just skip that question or suggestion, and move onto the next one.

You need to start thinking about what you will need to do and what your staff will need to do if you are going to make it happen.

So, now that all the disclaimers are out of the way, please read on.

What's involved with a Mahara implementation?

Although real life is not always as neat and tidy as you would like it to be, a Mahara implementation will essentially pass through three broadly distinct stages:

- ◆ Analysis and Specification
- ◆ Planning, Design, and Implementation
- ◆ Evaluation and Continuation

To scaffold your Mahara implementation here, we have decided to take you through a sequence of opinions, questions, and suggestions. We have split those broader stages into some smaller phases as follows:

- ◆ **Analysis and Specification**
    - ❑ **Phase 1**: Decide if Mahara is right for you.
    - ❑ **Phase 2**: Understand your own specific needs and working conditions.
    - ❑ **Phase 3**: Choose between a Mahara-partner supported site and your own installation.
    - ❑ **Phase 4**: Scope out your implementation plan.

- ◆ **Planning, Design, and Implementation**
    - ❑ **Phase 5**: Create a buzz!
    - ❑ **Phase 6**: Get some quick wins in first!
    - ❑ **Phase 7**: Continuously involve the users in your planning and design process.
    - ❑ **Phase 8**: Keep going despite adversity!

- ◆ **Evaluation and Continuation**
    - ❑ **Phase 9**: Review and Re-evaluate.
    - ❑ **Phase 10**: Change and Embed.

Analysis and Specification

Certainly, the most important phase of all to get right is the Analysis and Specification phase. It is always best to try your absolute hardest to iron out as many difficulties as you can, before you unleash any new learning process upon your end users.

Deciding if Mahara is right for you

Before you do anything else, consider why you want a lifelong learning ePortfolio system such as Mahara and if you have the appropriate working conditions to make a success of it. There are, broadly speaking, two different types of ePortfolio system:

- The institutionally-owned Learning Management System
- The learner-owned Personal Learning Environment

As demonstrated in this book, Mahara is very much the latter. It is focused on offering learners a place to gather, store, and share their work with others as they progress along their personal and lifelong learning journeys.

Some other ePortfolio systems are focused, instead, on offering a facility to track learner-submitted work according to institutional—or accrediting body—needs. That is not what Mahara is about.

Mahara is a user-centered informal and reflective learning environment that also:

- Provides a platform from which a user can present his/her learning and competencies to others, for example a prospective employer, an application to a university, a promotion panel, or during a professional development review
- Provides a templating facility for ePortfolio pages
- Offers ease of use (no need to be a webhead!)
- Facilitates social networking in "Communities of Practice"

Digital habitats

You can read about stewarding digital communities in the book *Digital Habitats* by *Etienne Wenger*, *Nancy White*, and *John D. Smith*. It's well worth a read if you're thinking about setting up your own online communities of practice. You can find the book at http://technologyforcommunities.com/. Here, you can gain access to additional reading material.

- Allows for collaborative group pages
- Offers monitoring of other people's pages by means of a watchlist
- Provides a system for uploading and getting feedback on assessment items

- Allows you to feedback on other people's pages

- Supports a simple personal and professional development planning process, helping a learner with their action planning for their lifelong learning or career development processes

- Acts as a walled garden where you can control the user base

- Provides a very private individual storage space for learner's own artefacts

- Supports platform integration with an ever expanding range of Web 2.0 tools, such as YouTube and Picasa

- Offers the option to copy and move your portfolio to another location (including non-Mahara ePortfolio applications that support Leap2A)

- Allows you to limit and extend users' storage space

- Runs on a web server (making it available whenever and from wherever)

Mahara itself is not a Learning Management System. It, therefore, does not:

- Cross-reference against assessment/accreditation criteria set out by an accrediting body (such as formative and summative assessment trackers, or occupational standards for NVQs in the UK)

- Provide an audit trail of submitted and graded work

- Neatly archive and retain learner submitted work

Mahara, however, understands and responds to the fact that some institutions like to formally assess their learners' work, whilst still adopting a personalized learning approach as their driving paradigm. One option a learner may have in Mahara is to submit his/her work for assessment by tutors (see Chapter 6, *Course Groups and Other Roles in Mahara*). But the tracking of learner progress would then have to be facilitated by integrating Mahara with some other system such as:

- **A tutor maintained spreadsheet**: This could be stored and shared in a Mahara group files area or within a Google document, for example.

- **The Gradebook in Moodle** (`http://wiki.mahara.org/Roadmap/ Moodle_Mahara_Integration`): Mahara already supports Single Sign-On integration with Moodle, a system that can be used for assessment of achievements according to some criteria. This can be used to track progress against a time-tabled program of activity.

Mahara itself, then, is not trying to be a Learning Management System. It is a place where learners can reflect on their learning and showcase their work to others. As Mahara is pluggable, it's possible for development of further plugins that address this need for assessment.

The view of the Mahara project is that Moodle (and its competitors LMSs/VLEs) should do Moodle-like things and Mahara should do Mahara-like things. From Moodle v2.0 onwards, Moodle provides a portfolio API, which allows single click export of files, forums, and blog posts uploaded into Moodle across as artefacts in your own Mahara space.

For more information about transferring information to your Mahara ePortfolio from Moodle, see the Moodle documentation at `http://docs.moodle.org/en/Mahara_portfolio`.

There is also a fantastic extension for Mahara and Moodle that allows learners to submit their Mahara ePortfolio pages to their tutors in Moodle. It provides tutors with the ability to set an assignment where learners can submit their Mahara pages as assignments and have them graded as they would in an uploaded document or test.

All of this enables learners to use Moodle for taught and outcomes-driven assessment processes, and Mahara for their personalized, and ongoing, reflection/informal learning activities.

The plugin (plugins) can be found at `https://wiki.mahara.org/index.php/System_Administrator's_Guide/Moodle//Mahara_Integration/View_Submission` and there is a PDF documentation for System Administrators, discussing Moodle/Mahara integration, that can be found at `https://wiki.mahara.org/index.php/System_Administrator%27s_Guide/Moodle//Mahara_Integration`.

Recently, a new distribution of Moodle—TotaraLMS—has been developed. Totara adds a wrapper of **LMS (learning management system)** functionality on top of the Moodle vle's core code. Mahara can interact with TotaraLMS in exactly the same ways that it can interact with Moodle. TotaraLMS offers:

- A sophisticated heirarchy of competencies management tool
- Management of organizations and organizational roles
- Per user/per role learning plans
- user/role dashboards
- A sophisticated reporting tool

TotaraLMS for apprenticeships is a distribution of TotaraLMS, which adds a wrapper of functionality on top of the TotaraLMS core code in order to serve the more specific needs of apprenticeships programmes delivery in the UK. This codeline is managed by `OssServices.com`. The integration with Mahara is sophisticated and additional features include:

- An **evidence** tab on the learning plan that allows assessors to associate their own files as well as Mahara pages with QCF competencies
- A progress tracker on a learning plan, which tracks and displays progress against QCF (or similar) Awards, Certificates, and Diplomas—competencies can be achieved by assessor evidence and/or by Moodle course/activity completions

If you have decided that a lifelong learning ePortfolio such as Mahara is for you, it is now wise to decide whether Mahara is the platform that is best-suited for your organizational needs or not.

Danube University (Austria) researchers, Dr. Klaus Himpsl-Gutermann and Dr. Peter Baumgartner have published the document called *Evaluation of E-Portfolio Software* in February 2009 (download the PDF at `http://epac.pbworks.com/f/ijet_paper_himpsl_baumgartner.pdf`). Here is a link to Klaus Himpsl-Gutermann's Mahara profile for you to find out more information, `https://mahara.org/user/view.php?id=238`.

Dr. Himpsl-Gutermann and Dr. Baumgartner have evaluated and compared a range of lifelong learning ePortfolio solutions against the following criteria (and sub-criteria):

- **Essential criteria**
    - Input of keywords
    - Internal cross-references
    - External cross-references
    - Publication on the web
    - Pricing and license schemes
    - Simple data export
    - Support of all currently used A-grade browsers

- **Collecting, organizing, and selecting**
    - Simple data import
    - Comfortable data import
    - Searching, sequencing, and filtering
    - Annotations to files
    - Aggregating (integration of external data via feeds)
    - Version control of files

◆ **Reflecting, testing, verifying, and planning**

❑ Guidelines for reflection

❑ Guidelines for competences

❑ Guidelines for evaluation (self assessment and assessment by others)

❑ Guidelines for goals, personal development, and career management

❑ Guidelines for feedback (advice, tutoring, and mentoring)

◆ **Representing and publishing**

❑ Access control by users (owner, peers, authority, and public)

❑ Adaptation of the display—layout (flexible placing and boilerplates)

❑ Adaptation of the display—colors, fonts, and design

❑ Publishing of several portfolios, or alternatively, various views

◆ **Administrating, implementing, and adapting**

❑ Development potential of the provider and company profile

❑ Enabling technologies (programming language, operating system, and so on)

❑ Authentification and user administration (backed-up interfaces, and so on)

❑ e-learning standards

❑ Migration/storage/export

◆ **Usability**

❑ User interface

❑ Syndicating (choice of feeds for the individual portfolio)

❑ Availability and accessibility

❑ Navigation/initial training/help

❑ External and internal information function

❑ Interchangeable and adaptable user-defined boilerplates

❑ Personal storage, respective export function

As you can probably guess, Mahara does very well in this comparison. It comes out joint-top of the list alongside a proprietary (and equally excellent, if very different) alternative ePortfolio solution known as PebblePad (http://www.pebblepad.co.uk/).

Despite being good, PebblePad is not open source, although it allows the transfer of portfolio data via the Leap2A standard. The fact that Mahara is an open source and modular product means that:

- The code may be copyrighted by others (mostly by Catalyst IT), but it is under an open license (GNU General Public License—http://www.gnu.org/licenses/), meaning that it will always be available for you to use, and that it will always be cost-free for you to re-use.

- You can, therefore, switch your technical support agency at any point (there is no vendor lock-in).

- The product will always exist even if the current maintainers (currently Catalyst IT in New Zealand) choose to discontinue their support for it.

- Everybody can collaborate to develop what is needed (there is a modular/plugin architecture, and you can also contribute to the core code, if the core developers like what you have done!).

- There are no license fees for downloading and using the Mahara software—you can simply grab the code and start hosting it, if you have access to a web server. The software can also be hosted on a server within your organization without paying anything but the cost of server maintenance.

Understanding your own specific needs and working conditions

Never look for some place new to go until you completely understand and appreciate where you already are. Never try to make a change until you have a clear vision, and completely understand the benefits you will gain from making that change.

Here's how to start:

1. Clearly set out your overall aims:

   - What educational objectives do you want to achieve?

   - What business objectives do you want to achieve?

   - What organizational objectives do you want to achieve?

2. Understand your own working context. If you find yourself answering "no" to any of the following questions. You should start thinking, "Is it actually possible to turn this no into a yes?"

   - Do all those involved—your leaders, teachers/tutors, day-to-day administrators, IT support staff, and your future end users—have a common vision for your ePortfolio? (Even if you are working as a go-it-alone teacher, are you sure that enough of your students will buy in to this?)

❑ Is there a supportive external context for your ePortfolio implementation? Is there explicit support for this coming to you, for example, from central office, from government-funded agencies, or from accrediting bodies, trades guilds or worker's unions?

❑ Is there, and will there be, a consistent and reliable inflow of funding for your site's support?

❑ Will there be a dedicated steering group of visionaries and power-brokers who will work to make your implementation a success?

❑ Will you continuously invest to employ or skill-up the competent staff that you will need in order to disseminate knowledge to newer users?

3. Ensure you have sufficiently skilled and available (time/motivation to support) technical and pedagogical support infrastructures in place.

4. Ensure that your target end users have appropriate access to your Mahara system not only in terms of a reasonable internet supply, but also in terms of physical access to machines in both working and home-life contexts.

5. Understand that change affects emotions:

Successful change = Vision + Skills + Incentives + Resources + Action Plan

If you want to implement an ePortfolio solution successfully, you need to be able to develop and disseminate a shared vision. This vision optimistically encourages people to embrace changes in both technology-adoption and learning approaches. To succeed, this needs top-level support and needs to be a fully aligned part of a whole organizational approach. You will not only need to model the way for others to follow, but also need to enable and to motivate others to act.

You will need to know and to broadcast to your people where you are going, and why you are going that way. You will need to put the required training in place to make that vision happen. People will need incentives. Incentives can be financial, recognition-oriented, status-oriented, promotion-oriented, and so on. Adoption of your new ePortfolio system should become an expectation, part of a learner's assessment criteria, and part of a tutor's job description. You will also need a clearly structured action plan and appropriately designated responsibilities alongside sensible timescales.

The following table by Jacqueline Thousand and Richard Villa, neatly illustrates the negative emotional impact likely to arise (notice in particular the far right-hand column), if just one of these elements are not in place.

Vision	Skills	Incentives	Resources	Action Plan	Results in
✓	✓	✓	✓	✓	Change
-	✓	✓	✓	✓	Confusion
✓	-	✓	✓	✓	Anxiety
✓	✓	-	✓	✓	Opposition
✓	✓	✓	-	✓	Frustration
✓	✓	✓	✓	-	False starts

Adapted from *Knoster, T., Villa R., & Thousand, J. (2000), A framework for thinking about systems change*. In R. villa & J. Thousand (Eds.),Restructuring for caring and effective education: Piecing the puzzle together (pp. 93-128). Baltimore: Paul H. Brookes Publishing Co.

Prof. Gordon Joyes from the University of Nottingham first introduced "Threshold Concepts" and their importance when applied to an ePortfolio implementation. Joyes attributes the idea of "Threshold Concepts" to Jan Meyer and Ray Land (`http://www.etl.tla.ed.ac.uk//docs/ETLreport4.pdf`). Essentially, the point being made is that in order for somebody to perform a task effectively, he/she needs to go through some doorways of understanding. If these doorway thresholds are not traversed, the activity is not likely to be a success. For those of you implementing ePortfolios and encouraging their adoption, Joyes and his colleagues have so far come up with five important threshold concepts:

- **Concept 1—Purpose**: The purpose(s) for the ePortfolio must be aligned to the particular context. You need to make your ePortfolio genuinely work for you. It should help you to perform your learning and business functions effectively.

- **Concept 2—Learning Activity Design**: There must be a conscious design and support of a learning activity/activities suited to the purpose and the context. Mahara alone is nothing without a clear organizational sense of learning delivery structure. Your tutors need to be adopting a learner-driven, personalized learning delivery model, only then will Mahara be able to come into its own as a useful resource.

- **Concept 3—Processes**: The processes involved in the creation of the ePortfolio in this context must be understood, and both technical and pedagogic support needs to be provided. Both staff and learners need to be trained to understand how the platform works, and also how it can be made to work to best effect.

◆ **Concept 4—Ownership**: ePortfolio processes and outcomes need to be owned by the student. This not only leads to considering portability of their data, but also whether the tool allows use of their own phone camera, audio recorder, Web 2.0 applications, and so on. It also leads you to consider the learners' engagement with your Mahara platform. The learners need to see the Mahara environment as their own. They need to see it as a useful resource, which helps them to engage with your institution as they learn.

◆ **Concept 5—Disruptive Nature**: ePortfolios are disruptive from a pedagogic, technological, and organizational perspective. It is unlikely that Mahara will fit exactly within existing systems. Some changes will need to be made, and this will upset some people and disrupt some existing processes.

Unless you understand these five (and probably more) issues, you won't succeed in your action plan. By understand, we mean more than simply know that they are issues. You don't just need to be aware of these issues, you actually need to understand at your very core that these are centrally important—indeed key—to the success of your ePortfolio implementation. Unless you are practically oriented towards implementing your ePortfolios, while taking these issues into account, you must truly understand that you are likely to struggle.

Choosing between a Mahara-partner supported site or your own install

When choosing whether to use a Mahara partner supported site or to go it alone, the trade off is usually the extent and expertise of the support available (for example, from a Mahara partner) versus the amount of control you have over your own system (for example, total control over your own server). A compromise is usually possible and most Mahara partners are willing to serve to support your managers, educators, and IT experts to support themselves. You can view a full list of official Mahara partners at `https://mahara.org/partners`.

Scoping out your implementation plan

You are going to have to draw up some sort of implementation plan. We will leave you to determine for yourself how best to draw this up, but we will raise here some of the issues that we think you will need to address. Essentially, you are going to have to manage five actions:

◆ Decide on your implementation timeframe.

◆ Ensure you have staff commitment.

◆ Draft out your initial Mahara site plan, structure, and visual design.

◆ Draft out your Mahara-specific policies.

◆ Start to embed Mahara use into wider institutional and program priorities.

Deciding on your implementation timeframe

Your implementation timeframe may be longer or shorter depending upon factors such as:

- The size of your organization:
    - Are you going to implement at local level or at a large scale?
- The complexity of the Mahara platform you decide to implement
- The levels of digital literacy amongst your client group:
    - Do your action team or consultants have the expertise and motivation to develop quality content quickly?
    - Do you need to provide templates for your users to scaffold their entry into creating their own ePortfolio?
    - Do your end users suffer much from techno-fear?
    - Do you need to provide basic training in recording audio, video, image editing, and so on besides specific Mahara training?
- What staff resources you have available:
    - Are you directing staff or temporary consultants according to a project implementation plan?
    - Are you allowing these people the time they will really need?
    - Otherwise, are you happy for a much slower and more participative development process?

Ensuring you have staff commitment

In a large organizational implementation, if the ePortfolio idea does not have the support of 75 percent of an organization's senior management team, it is unlikely to be a success. Your leadership has to be dedicated to committing both financial and staffing resources to the implementation project! You will need to set up a steering group, if you really want the implementation to happen, and this steering group will have to include at least one major power-broker from your organization and at least one Mahara expert or visionary. Again, you may be wise to bring in a Mahara partner consultant as your expert/visionary.

In a smaller, more local implementation, the potential users really need to be telling you that they like the idea of using a digital ePortfolio before you throw yourself into it. Bear in mind that people often dislike anything they don't already know.

Drafting out your initial Mahara content, site structure, visual design, and staff roles

Make sure you have a good understanding of how Mahara works before you start. You have already made a good start by buying and reading this book. While it is wise to be aware of the fact that your Mahara content and structure may well change significantly as time goes by, it is even wiser to have a clear understanding of how your site is going to be essentially structured right from the outset. Let's get thinking:

◆ Who is going to install and set up your Mahara site? Are you giving them the time they need to do it?

◆ What are you going to do in terms of site theming?

◆ Are you going to reconfigure your Mahara site to work differently in any way? If so, you might have to buy in the right expertise to achieve this. One of the joys of open source software is precisely its configurability, but you will still need to buy in the skills to make these configurations happen. You may wish to integrate your Mahara look, feel, and functionality with your Moodle site for example, or with a website Content Management System such as Joomla!. Alternatively, you may wish to change aspects of the Mahara code to make it work in the particular way you want it to work. Some organizations, for example, like to change the word "Résumé" to "CV", and others like, for example, to close off the friends functionality within their site.

◆ Are there any integrations with other software that you will need to set up (such as Moodle)?

◆ Who will be the site administrator—controlling users, checking storage limits, monitoring acceptable use, and so on? If a staff member, will this be a dedicated element of their job description? Could you outsource this type of administrative support to, for example, a Mahara partner?

◆ Who will be responsible for monitoring external software developments, interoperability developments, and so on?

◆ Who is going to administer and report back on any end user surveys you conduct?

◆ Who is going to be your pedagogical visionary? How much time (and re-numeration) are they going to get to give presentations and enthuse about online reflective learning and knowledge transfer?

◆ Will you give any paid time to the tutors or managers you will be expecting to lead the way with your ePortfolio system? Will work on the ePortfolio platform become a paid element of their work, clearly articulated in their job description and properly timetabled into their working week?

◆ Will your IT support staff need Mahara training? Who will run this training?

- Who will provide first line technical support? (Basic help such as: "How do I log in?" "How do I upload my file?"). Would you prefer to outsource this support? Could you arrange and publish a timetable of offline and/or telephone and/or internet-live-support-based Mahara user "Support Surgeries" in which less confident users could approach competent ones for friendly and informal advice and support?

- Who will provide higher level technical support into the long-term? For example, bug fixing (which should be contributed back to the Mahara project), updating, upgrading, integrating (with other software), modifying, or extending your platform according to your needs. Would this be cheap and safe to outsource (an outsource supplier is often less likely to leave you in the lurch than an employee)?

- What Mahara user institutions are you going to set up, if any?

- What will be your core Mahara groups? Who should set these up?

- What will those groups actually exist to do? What will be their purpose?

 Tip! Start off by describing what already happens in a particular focus area offline and then apply that to what you hope will happen online.

- Who will be allocated responsibility for encouraging and moderating activity in those groups?

- What pages will need to be produced for your site?

- What other sites will need to link across to your Mahara site?

- What will be the main weblinks you will need to link to from your site?

- Who will set and monitor performance targets? Will this be a part of their job description?

Drafting out your Mahara-specific policies

You need to be clear as crystal about the rules of engagement! It is only fair on your end users and it is also fair on you. There is also, very often, an organizational need to draw up and adhere to formal policies. Here are some thoughts in this respect:

- What promises can you make in regards to the provision of Internet access? Will it be always available, freely available, and maintain a reasonable level of quality/stability?

- What terms and conditions of use will you need the users to agree to?

- What online responsibility/"netiquette" policies do you have in place?

- Is it important to set out an acceptable use policy?

- What privacy rights does the user have?

◆ Does the user leave the data with you when he/she completes his/her course/program/employment period? If so, for how long will they have access to the data when they leave?

◆ We advise you to leave intellectual property in the hands of the ePortfolio users themselves and not in the hands of your institution. ePortfolios should (in our view) be owned by the users themselves and remain their own responsibility until they contravene the institution's terms and conditions of acceptable use. This is often not possible, though. In the case of schools, colleges, and polytechnics, some countries make the institutions responsible by law to guarantee that no inappropriate content is hosted on their servers. If this is your case, you may decide to set up a procedure for regular spot-checks where an administrator masquerades as a random sample of learners (for instance, each month) to check up on users within your system.

◆ How effectively are you going to communicate policies such as these to your end users?

Starting to embed Mahara use into wider institutional and program priorities

If yours is a small-scale implementation, might you just be trailblazing the way for a large-scale implementation across your whole organization? If so, or if you are a larger organization already, here are some questions to get you thinking:

◆ Is Mahara usage a stated element of your curriculum delivery? Is the time to learn how to use Mahara explicitly allocated as part of a new user's workload?

◆ Is any requirement to engage with Mahara in a course, job role, or program clearly communicated and understood well in advance of any requirement to submit work?

◆ Is Mahara use referred to in your business development plan, organizational plan, and job descriptions?

◆ Is Mahara utilized in your quality improvement reviews and processes?

◆ Is Mahara adoption and use measured in your quality improvement reviews and processes?

◆ Are Mahara development workshops a fixed element of your staff's Induction and Continuing Professional Development Plans? Staff should be regularly discussing not only how to use the system technically, but also how to use the system for best learning and business impact and effect!

Planning, Design, and Implementation

Once you have thoughtfully made the decision, set up the guiding team, and scoped out the plan for a Mahara Implementation, you will need to get into the nitty-gritty of making it happen.

Creating a Buzz!

Whether you are running a large-scale implementation or a small-scale local implementation, you will have to motivate and enable your end users to engage. Here are some ideas that may help:

- Draw up and implement a communications plan that targets all different types of stakeholders, for example users, staff, leaders, trainers, assessors, parents, employers, external agencies, press and media, and so on.

- Publicize some real-life case studies and examples of Mahara in action. The quarterly online Mahara newsletter highlights such case studies (https://mahara.org/newsletter/).

- Make sure everyone gets a copy of your new user guide. You could use this book for your staff members and provide or adapt the online user guide provided by the Mahara Community at http://manual.mahara.org. This manual will always link to the latest version of Mahara. It is important to check which version of the manual you are using and that it matches your own Mahara version. Mahara docs are hosted at "Readthedocs" and you should see the **Read the Docs** button in the bottom right corner that allows you to switch to other branches of the documentation.

- Set the Expectations. You may wish to set explicit incentives and penalties connected to user adoption. For instance, if you do X, you get Y.... Hurrah! If you fail to complete X, Y is the consequence, booooo!

- Practically help people to overcome barriers.

- Offer support via telephone, face-to-face, live website support, or you could set up a Mahara group as a helpdesk for your users and make sure everyone knows how to access this sort of technical support and advice as and when they need it.

- Set up a User Suggestions facility, where users can come up with ideas and actively influence what gets done with your Mahara.

- Set the Standards. One idea is to award medals for implementing standards in pages and groups.

Getting some quick wins in first!

While it is crucial that you can see the big picture of what your ePortfolio platform will deliver before you start, it is important not to get bogged down with the big picture, and to focus in on some practical deliverables, which you can implement quickly. Either you, your platform designer, or your design team will need to quickly implement, and equally quickly and publicly celebrate some quick wins. Let's get you thinking:

◆ Can you identify some instant fixes where using Mahara would solve a real problem that you are facing?

◆ Alternatively, can you identify which of your own user groups would respond best to—and therefore quickly adopt—an ePortfolio as a media for learning delivery?

◆ If people need to migrate to Mahara from other means of gathering and presenting their portfolio evidence (paper-based work, another platform, a USB stick, a wiki, a website, and so on), how are you going to convince them that it will be worth the effort? (Don't forget they can always link back from their new Mahara pages to any previous websites they created, if the site is still available).

Continuously involving your users in the planning and design process

You are going to have to ask, listen to, and respond to whatever people want to do in their Mahara! To make your implementation work, you will need to:

◆ Conduct regular response analyses

◆ Get together for strategy reviews

◆ Do something in response to what you find out

You will need to get your users expressing and sharing their ideas, their reflections, and their learning (their pages) within groups who share similar interests. If you are going to get your Mahara site running, you are going to have to jump on any chance to ignite the fire that will turn it into a lively online community—always dealing with educationally and topically-burning issues of the day as they arise.

Response analyses can be, but need not be dull online or offline survey feedback routines. An equally good response analysis is a show of hands in a meeting, or a chat in a cafeteria.

Don't just ask questions such as:

◆ Have you used it? How often?

◆ Did you like it? How much?

Also ask more open, forward looking questions such as:

- How else could using a digital portfolio help you in your life or study?
- What other topics would you like to reflect upon with other people?

The most important thing, though, is that you get together to talk about the response and thereby, start to responsively and appropriately review your ongoing strategy.

 Remember, a proper Mahara site isn't a miracle of people, it is a miracle of community.

Keep going despite adversity!

Your Mahara implementation process will inevitably meet people who act as implementation resisters. It is a fact of life that many people react badly to change, even when it is good for them.

You will, therefore, need to apply some situational response tactics as your implementation progresses.

People can be implementation resistors:

The Pessimist might say, "We can't change! We're doomed!"

The Pragmatist might say, "We've done enough, let's not change too far!"

The Technophobe might say: "This is too difficult for me, it's not fair!"

The Traditionalist might say, "I'm just too busy for this, this is a nice to do, not a have-to-do!"

The Cynic may say, "This is just a passing fad, ignore it, it will go away!"

...and the implementation team's worst enemy, the Critic, might say, "Rise up and rebel! We cannot allow this to happen!"

Situational response tactics

How will you buy people in? You can apply two types of tactic when you need to subdue the implementation resistors out there—"Big Bombs" and "Sniper Fire".

Situational response tactic 1—Big Bombs

You use these tactics to try to affect the feelings of as many people as possible with the least amount of effort. Examples include:

- **Powerbroker support**: Get an institutional authority figure to express support in a public meeting or in a public newsletter.

- **Identify and provide missing information**: Is there something people need to know about Mahara's usefulness that you haven't told them? One example is that Mahara can serve as an online file storage area—a USB stick on the Internet. While this is not what Mahara is actually for, it is a useful utility that may start getting people to engage.

- **Visiting expert**: Bring in an external speaker, who can talk with expertise about Mahara and ePortfolios.

- **Generic questionnaires**: It is often a good idea to conduct a feedback survey, which picks up the mood of the crowd. The magic here lies in the public report-back stage in which you state how the crowd responded and go on to carefully and usefully explain where and why you agree and disagree.

- **User guide promotions**: Run events to promote your new user guides. Give user guides out at parties, in group meetings and events, in cafes, in induction programs, during training events, and so on.

- **Poster campaign**: Run posters all around your institution promoting use of your ePortfolio. For example, the Mahara logo with "Mahara means thinking" or "Mahara makes ME think!" written on it. (you may of course have a different institutional name for your own Mahara install and so will come up with better and more localized poster ideas).

- **Competitions and celebrations**: Best page awards, most medals awards, busiest user awards, most innovative online thought of the year, best online project and so on.

- **Mass e-mails, newsletters, SMS**, and **news forums**: Keep people up-to-date with the project. Give both the leaders and the users a clear and ongoing sense of project progress.

- **Formal training event**: Probably the best Big Bomb tactic of all? Bring in internal or external experts (for example, from a Mahara partner) to run a few day courses, which will really get cohorts of users confidently up and running with your platform.

Situational response tactic 2—Sniper Fire

Sometimes there will be particular people who you will need to influence in order to affect change. Some people will have more charisma and more interpersonal skills than others and it will be these people who you will need to win over, if you are going to encourage your people to adopt your platform. These people may not always be the people with the most important jobs, by the way! A secretary can often exert more influence than another manager, or a student in the class can often exert more influence over group behavior than the teacher:

- **Corridor conversations**: Identify an influential person and chat with him/her informally about the Mahara implementation (this can be a hugely useful tactic).

- **Mentor matching**: Get Mahara adopters into situations (you may have to do this subtly and covertly) where they can enthuse about their Mahara use with people who are Mahara-reticent.

- **Targeted e-mails, SMS messages, or phone calls**: Find your slow adopters and make them feel missed, make them feel identified, make them feel encouraged, and don't let up too quickly on encouraging them, there are all sorts of reasons why people may not feel involved.

- **Targeted feedback questionnaires and response strategy**: If you can identify the different types of change resistors in a survey (be careful not to be too crass about it!), you can conduct a more targeted communication response to these different types of needs and resistors.

Evaluation and Continuation

Once your platform is running, it's tempting to sit back, but you will need to think about what you are going to do next to ensure its continual development and sustainability.

Reviewing and re-evaluating

This is one of those things that is much easier said than done. It can be really hard to step back and take an honest, critical look at a platform that is in place.

Here are some questions you could be asking:

- Are the people you need to be recording or linking to their knowledge in Mahara actually recording and linking to their knowledge in Mahara? If not, why not? How can you make it happen?

- Is Mahara helping learners to achieve their qualifications? Is Mahara helping people to do their work?

- Can you offer targeted support for groups who have been slow to engage?

- Does everything really have to be digital?

- Are people actually identifying and meeting their learning, career, and personal goals?

- Is learning over Mahara ever being delivered more effectively through other online or offline approaches?

- Are there variations in success between different types of learners? Are there any good reasons for the variations? How should you respond to these variations?

- Do the groups, forums, or learning program briefs always match the aspirations and needs of the learners?

- Could you yourself set performance improvement targets based on metrics gathered from the sorts of questions that you have just asked?

- Are achievement targets set for all courses at all levels?

- Is Mahara participation a requirement? Should it be a requirement? Should you set participation targets or might that have a negative effect?

- If any targets are set, is everyone made aware of those targets? How? How effectively?

- Are staff or users themselves involved in the target setting?

- How do you communicate progress against targets? Simple graphical displays?

- How do you celebrate and reward individual successes and collective progress against targets?

- Are targets revised frequently enough? By whom? How ambitiously?

- Do you care about all these targets? Wouldn't it be best to leave the whole Mahara to grow ad hoc?

Changing and embedding

How are you going to make your Mahara ePortfolio site stick as one of the cornerstones of your learning delivery model? Or has it all been a flash in the pan?

A thriving site will often be in a constant state of flux, changing with the needs, and focuses of the organization and its people, embedding itself deeper and deeper as an element of the wider e-institution.

There are various ways in which you might have approached the change-management process required to implement Mahara usage in your organization.

Some organizations might take a very top-down, directive sort of approach. The wisest amongst those avoid horrific staff rebellion by putting their weight behind an expert who is brought in to make the change happen. This expert is often a consultant, sometimes a new staff member. The expert will follow a strict project plan and will have the authority to reward and rebuke as deemed appropriate by the implementation planners.

Other organizations might adopt a more bottom-up user-driven sort of approach. They implement the platform, publicize it, and then just wait to see what happens. The problem here is that it can result in pretty much nothing getting done. It is therefore best in this approach to encourage a knowledge-sharing culture. You could, for example, give the users dedicated time to show off their work and share their skills. This nudges progress along a bit without having to bring in an expert because the users are learning from each other.

In our view, an approach that sits in the middle of these two positions is a negotiated, circular approach, which clearly communicates the organizational drivers, but also gives ample space for the user community themselves to take the lead on what their learning content should cover. The Mahara platform itself, of course, allows nicely for this approach.

If you really want to change your learning and knowledge culture into a reflective, online ePortfolio supported learning and knowledge culture, you will probably have to continuously re-evaluate to what extent you wish to embed Mahara use into your organizational policies. Here are the key questions:

- Is Mahara usage going to be integral to your business development plan (this is the information age after all, and your country may even be a knowledge-based economy like the UK and USA)?
- Will Mahara usage be integral to your organizational policies and procedures?
- Will staff responsibilities for Mahara usage and management be a defined and renumerated element of their job description? Or would you prefer to leave Mahara to be a self-managing phenomenon?

Summary

In this appendix, you started thinking about an action plan for implementing Mahara in your organization.

You saw some of the reasons why a typical software implementation fails and thought about some of the things you can do to prevent this from happening.

You looked in detail at what is involved in implementing Mahara in your organization. You saw the stages that you will typically go through including Analysis and Specification, Planning, Design, and Implementation, and Evaluation and Continuation. You asked yourself many of the important questions that need to be asked at each step of the process and considered many of the challenges you will face.

You will have hopefully put together your own Implementation Action Plan listing all of your own objectives and actions necessary to meet them as well as some criteria for assessing their impact.

B
Installing Mahara

This book is aimed at Mahara users, rather than Mahara administrators. However, a new user may wish to install a Mahara instance in order to experiment. Also, lots of people like to install Mahara on their own Linux machines or on a web server of their own in order to organize their own personal learning data.

This section is for those of you who have some knowledge of web applications and servers or feel like you could have a good go at installing Mahara. We don't give full explanations of each technical term we use, as we assume some prior knowledge.

Many of the instructions in this chapter mirror the advice contained in the Mahara wiki on installing the software. See `http://wiki.Mahara.org/System_Administrator%27s_Guide/Installing_Mahara`. You can also see a shorter list of instructions on installing a development environment here at `https://wiki.mahara.org/index.php/Developer_Area/Developer_Environment`.

We recommend you have a read through these instructions as well as this chapter before attempting an install.

Don't worry, we will keep it as simple as possible...

What will you need?

Before you can install Mahara, you will need to have access to a Linux server. It may be that you run Linux on a laptop or desktop at home or that your company or institution has its own Linux servers, in which case, great! If not, there are many hosting services available on the internet, which will enable you to access a Linux server, and therefore, install and run Mahara.

It is important to choose a host that will allow you to set up the environment ready for Mahara—giving you, for example, the ability to manage your own PHP configuration and to add the required PHP extensions. It is really much better if you have access to your own virtual server or dedicated host—you have more control and are less likely to bump into issues later on.

It is important that you get a server to which you have root access. It is also important that you set your server up with the following features:

- **Database**: Mahara must have a database to work. The databases supported are PostgreSQL Version 8.3 or later and MySQL Version 5 or later. The Mahara developers recommend that you use PostgreSQL if possible but, for most installations, MySQL will work just as well.
- **PHP**: Mahara requires PHP Version 5.3 or later.
- **Web server**: The preferred web server is Apache - 2.0 or greater.
- **PHP extensions**:
    - **Compulsory extensions**: `gd`, `json`, `curl`, `libxml`, `SimpleXML`, `session`, `pgsql` or `mysqli`, `openssl` or `xmlrpc` (for networking support), `mbstring`, `mime_magic` or `fileinfo`, `zip`, and `unzip` utilities.
    - **Optional extension**: `imagick`
    - **Recommended extensions**: `zlib`, `zip`, and `bz2`

Again, ask your resident IT expert about the features listed above if you don't understand what they mean.

> A quick way to install some of the software listed in the preceding section is to use the `apt-get install` command, if you are using the Ubuntu/Debian Linux Systems. See `http://www.debian.org/doc/manuals/apt-howto/` to find out more.

Can I install Mahara on Windows?

At the moment, the Mahara developers offer no support for running Mahara on Windows Servers. It is designed to primarily work with Linux, Apache, PHP, and Open Source SQL databases.

This however doesn't mean that Mahara won't work on Windows. So, if you are feeling adventurous, why not give it a go and report back to Mahara on your experience? You can also visit `https://wiki.mahara.org/index.php/System_Administrator%27s_Guide/Installing_Mahara/Installing_Mahara_in_Wampserver` for some help with WAMP.

What about installation on other operating systems?

The Mahara developers clearly state that they don't test their system with any other operating systems, including Solaris, Mac, and BSD. Again, that isn't to say that Mahara won't work on these systems, it is just best if you play it safe and choose to run your Mahara on the system that it was built for—Linux.

Downloading Mahara

It's time for action. Let's start by seeing how easy it is for you to get a copy of Mahara for yourselves, and the best part is... it's free!

Time for action – downloading Mahara

You're going to start the installation process by downloading your own copy of the Mahara code:

> **1.** Go to the Mahara page on launchpad—`https://launchpad.net/mahara`. You will see a web page that lists the most recent series of Mahara. On the right of the screen is a box that shows the very latest stable version. Choose to download the code in a format you prefer. We recommend that you use the `.tar.gz` type as it is faster to download than `.zip`:

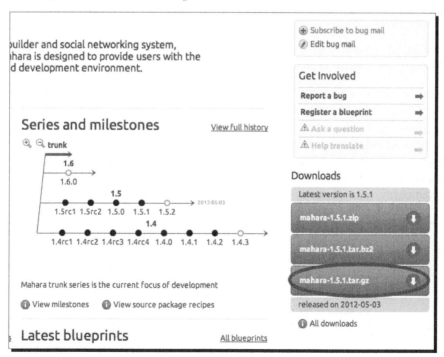

2. You may be asked if you would like to open or save the file. Select **Save File** and click on **OK**.

3. That's all there is to it. Go to the folder where you downloaded the package. In there, you should see your newly downloaded Mahara package.

What just happened?

You have just taken your first step on the road to installing Mahara. You have seen the website you have to go to for downloading the most recent version and learned how to download the package in a format you prefer.

Mahara code versioning

Mahara versioning works on a major/minor version system. Major versions represent a number of big changes to the code with the introduction of new features and sometimes reworking of existing ones. These are numbered 1.3.0, 1.4.0, 1.5.0, and so on. Minor versions are usually important bug fixes or security updates, and are numbered 1.5.1, 1.5.2, 1.5.3, and so on, in relation to the current major version. When a new version is ready for testing, there is usually an alpha, beta, and release candidate release—these aren't stable and shouldn't be used on a production site. You can find out more about Mahara releases here at `https://wiki.mahara.org/index.php/Developer_Area/Release_Policy`.

We always recommend that for a production site, you choose the latest stable release of any Mahara series as it will contain bug and security fixes.

Release candidates aren't production-ready, but they are useful for testing out a new version of Mahara on a test server. You could even try upgrading to a release candidate on a development server (make sure you have a backup of the database and Mahara data files first). Release candidates are specifically released to get feedback from users, so that as many bugs as possible can be found and fixed before the next stable version. If you find any problems with the release candidate or the upgrade, you should let the Mahara developers know about them.

Version support

Mahara only supports the two latest major software releases. So, for example, if the current version is 1.5, only 1.4 and 1.5 will be supported. If you are running a major version before this, you really should update to the next major version otherwise you won't be keeping up with the latest (crucial) security updates. Plus the fact—you're missing out on lots of exciting new features!

Using the command line

The best way of installing and administering your Mahara is to use the command line.

You will be doing a lot of the things in this area, assuming that you have Secure Shell Access to your server through the terminal command line.

If you have a Linux or a Mac computer, you can use the terminal on your machine to SSH into your Linux web server. Windows users can achieve the same functionality by downloading a free terminal client called PuTTY from `http://www.chiark.greenend.org.uk/~sgtatham/putty/download.html`.

Speak to your resident IT expert for more information on how to use the terminal or see `http://www.tuxfiles.org/Linuxhelp/cli.html` for an introduction to the Linux command line.

For now, let's just learn how to get the content of your downloaded package into the correct place on your server.

Time for action – creating your Mahara file structure

You're now going to extract the content of the code, which you downloaded in the preceding *Time for action – downloading Mahara* section, to the right place on your web server:

1. Copy the `mahara-1.5.1.tar.gz` (or whichever version you downloaded) package into your home directory on your web server. If you are copying the file to the server from your own computer, you can do this by using the `scp` command (on Linux or Mac):

    ```
    scp Mahara-1.5.1.tar.gz servername:pathtohomedirectory
    ```

2. Unpack the contents of the Mahara package on the Linux Server. On the terminal, you can do this using the `tar` command:

    ```
    tar xvzf Mahara-1.5.0.tar.gz
    ```

3. You will now see a new folder called `Mahara-1.5.1`, you will need to rename this to `public`. To do this on the terminal, you can use the `mv` command:

    ```
    mv Mahara-1.5.1 public
    ```

4. That's it! The Mahara code is now in place.

What Just Happened?

You just learned where to copy the Mahara package on your server and how to extract its contents.

Creating the database

A lot of the information created in your Mahara will be stored in a database. Mahara offers support for both PostgreSQL and MySQL databases. However, we prefer to use PostgreSQL. If you are interested, see `http://Mahara.org/interaction/forum/topic.php?id=302` for a discussion on why PostgreSQL is preferred to MySQL.

The way you create your database will depend on who you have chosen to host your Mahara. Sometimes, your web host will provide a graphical user interface to access your server database. Your web host may not even allow PostgreSQL, in which case MySQL is the way to go for you.

For smaller Mahara installations, we prefer to use something like phpPgAdmin, which is a software that allows you to manage PostgreSQL databases over the Internet. See `http://phppgadmin.sourceforge.net` for more information on setting up phpPgAdmin on your server.

Also, see, `http://www.phpmyadmin.net/` for phpMyAdmin, which works in a very similar way to phpPgAdmin, but operates on a MySQL database.

Time for action – creating the Mahara database

Let's get on with creating a PostgreSQL database, using your phpPgAdmin panel:

1. Open up your phpPgAdmin panel from your Internet browser and log in. The username is hopefully **postgres**. Contact your admin if you are unsure of the database password or how to locate the phyPgAdmin panel:

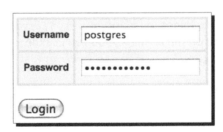

2. On the front page, there is a link that invites you to create a database, click on **Create database** there. On the resulting screen, give your database a relevant name such as **mysite_mahara**. It is important that you select the **UTF8** collation from the drop-down box. Finally, click on **Create**:

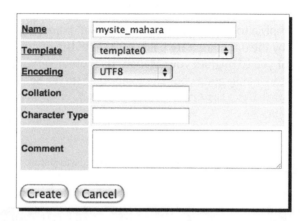

3. If you want to, you could also add a new user for your database. Use phpPgAdmin to create a new user and assign them permissions for the database you just created.

4. That's it, you're done!

What just happened?

You just created the database for your Mahara installation, using the Open Source phyPgAdmin tool available for Linux.

Another way to create the database on your server is to use the database command-line tool.

Have a go hero – using the command line to create your database

Using the command line is a much more elegant way to create the database, and quicker, once you get the hang of it. Why not have a go at creating the database by using the command line? For instructions on how to do this refer to the database section of the Mahara installation guide at `http://wiki.Mahara.org/System_Administrator%27s_Guide/Installing_Mahara`.

Setting up the data directory

Most of the data that is created in your Mahara is stored in the database. However, all the files that are uploaded by your users, such as their personal photos or documents, need to be stored at a separate place. This is where the data directory comes in.

The data directory is simply a folder that holds all of the stuff belonging to your users. Everything is kept safe by the data directory being outside of the home directory. This set up also makes it easy for you to migrate your Mahara to another server at some point in the future. If you're interested in migrating your site to another server, see `https://wiki.mahara.org/index.php/Developer_Area/Developer_Environment#Copying_a_local_install_to_another`.

 The data directory is often referred to as dataroot.

Time for action – setting up the data directory

Let's see how easy it is to set up your data directory:

1. Make the data directory outside of the public folder of your home directory. Create the directory using the `mkdir` command and call it `uploaddir`:

    ```
    mkdir uploaddir
    ```

     It doesn't really matter what you decide to call your `dataroot` directory, but try and choose a name that is relevant to what the directory is doing. The name suggested by Mahara and most commonly used is `uploaddir`, but other names such as `maharadata` would be just as good.

2. Set the permissions on this folder, using the `chmod` command:

    ```
    chmod -R 0777 uploaddir
    ```

3. Change the user of the new directory to be the same as your server, using the `chown` command. The user is usually `apache` or `www-data`:

    ```
    chown -R www-data:www-data uploaddir
    ```

4. And that's all there is to it, you now have a place where Mahara can put all of the stuff belonging to your users.

What just happened?

You just created your data directory and made sure that it was in a safe place in your home directory outside of the htdocs directory. Then you changed the permissions, users, and groups for the directory to make it easy for Mahara to put things in and to delete things.

Let's take a quick look at the file structure that you have just created for your Mahara installation:

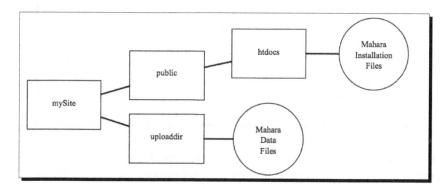

So far, you have downloaded and put the Mahara files into place on your server, and seen how to create the database and dataroot needed to store all the Mahara information.

Time for action – creating the config.php file

Now, you have to hold Mahara's hand by letting it know how it can access the database and how to find the dataroot. To do this, you use an important file called config.php:

1. In the htdocs folder of your Mahara site, you will find a file called config-dist.php. Use the nano command in your terminal to start editing the config-dist.php file:

    nano config-dist.php

> Other Linux people use much more sophisticated text editors such as Vim (http://www.vim.org/) and emacs (http://www.gnu.org/software/emacs/). We are simple folk and are perfectly happy with nano—http://www.nano-editor.org/.

2. Now, you will see the file open on the command line. Use the down arrow key on your keyboard to scroll down the page until you get to a section called **database connection details**. In the following example, the user is using MySQL5 rather than postgreSQL. Fill in the information so that it matches the details you used to set up your own database including your own database name (dbname), database user (dbuser), and database password (dbpass):

```
// database connection details
// valid values for dbtype are 'postgres8' and 'mysql5'
$cfg->dbtype   = 'mysql5';
$cfg->dbhost   = 'localhost';
$cfg->dbport   = null;
$cfg->dbname   = 'mysite_mahara';
$cfg->dbuser   = 'mysite';
$cfg->dbpass   = 'sharing';
```

3. Next, continue scrolling down the file until you reach a line that starts with **$cfg->dataroot**. Here, you must fill in the full path from the server root directory to the data directory that you created earlier in this chapter.

```
// This path must be writable by the webserver and outside document root (the
// place where the Mahara files like index.php have been installed).
// Mahara will NOT RUN if this is inside your document root, because
// this is a big security hole.
$cfg->dataroot = '/srv/mysite.tdm.info/public/uploaddir';
```

4. Now, have a look further down the file, you should see an option to add an e-mail contact. This e-mail address gets displayed if a form is suspected of being spam as a place of contact for those who stumble upon this. Fill in a relevant e-mail address.

5. Finally, you should add a password salt to your `config` file. This is a text string that helps to make user authentication more secure. Add a line similar to the following, but containing your own secret phrase:

```
$cfg->passwordsaltmain= 'your secret phrase here';
```

6. Congratulations, you've now finished editing the configuration file. Save it by pressing *Ctrl + X* on your keyboard (still within the nano editor). When asked, if you would like to rename the file, type *Y* for yes and name the file `config.php`. This will also save the file.

What just happened?

What you just did was very important. You let Mahara know where the database is and the user and password needed to access it. You also let it know the location of the `dataroot` directory as well as set a password salt.

Running the installer

Now that you've done all the hard work, it's time to let the Mahara installer do its magic. The main job that the installer does is to add new tables to the database that you created earlier.

Time for action – running the installer

Let's see how to start the installer:

1. The Mahara installer is started when you navigate to `wwwroot` (location where you have installed Mahara) in your Internet browser. For example, visit `http://mysite.tdm.info`.

2. The first page you see in the installer invites you to read the GNU General Public License. Click on **Install Mahara** at the bottom of the page to continue.

 If you don't see the GNU information screen, it is likely that you have done something wrong. Mahara will typically give you a message at this point explaining what the problem is. You can then have a look over at `mahara.org` for some help with fixing your problem.

3. The next page is where all the important work is being done. You will see each component being installed in the database. If everything goes well, the information section on the right-hand side should have a green tick for each component. When the installation has finished, click on continue at the bottom of the page.

4. And that's all there is to it! You will now see the home page of your very own Mahara.

What just happened?

You just ran the Mahara installer, which added all the necessary tables and data to your Mahara database.

The last step—setting up a cron process

Before you can be let loose on your Mahara, there is one last thing that you must remember to do to complete the installation—set up a cron job. If, like me, when I installed Mahara for the first time, you are thinking, "What on earth is a cron job?", don't worry, it is relatively simple.

The cron job is a process that simply enables a number of tasks to be performed regularly, typically every 10 minutes. This is useful for updating RSS feeds, among other things. The easiest way to add a cron process on a Debian or Ubuntu Linux Server is to add a new entry in a file called `crontab` by using the following command:

```
crontab -e
```

This will open up the default cron file for editing. Add a line similar to the following:

```
* * * * www-data php /path/to/Mahara/htdocs/lib/cron.php
```

Stars in the above example simply mean any value. If you are interested, see `http://www.adminschoice.com/crontab-quick-reference` for more information on `crontab` files. Also have a look at the Mahara information on using cron at `https://wiki.mahara.org/index.php/System_Administrator's_Guide/Cron_Job`. That's it, you're all done with the installation, so you can log in and start using your new software!

Mahara partners can help you with ongoing support, if you need that little bit of extra help.

What is a Mahara Partner and what can they do for me?

Most people using a tool like Mahara for the first time will shudder at the thought of doing an installation on a Linux server. In fact, "What is Linux?", is the most likely response. If this is you, there are people who can help you out!

Mahara Partners are specialists who know how to:

- Install Mahara on a Linux server
- Host your Mahara
- Offer support for developing your Mahara in the future
- Upgrade your Mahara when new versions come out
- Theme your Mahara
- Provide training
- Provide implementation consultancy support
- ....and more

Mahara Partners have a special relationship with the Mahara developer team and are very knowledgeable about how Mahara works. They can do all the things you don't feel comfortable doing, such as installing your Mahara, hosting it on the Internet and managing it. This will be at a cost and will depend on the individual partner.

Even if you have confidence that you could install Mahara on a Linux server, it is still very likely that a Mahara Partner has something to offer you. For example, you might want to brighten up the look of your Mahara to match your corporate branding, but have no knowledge of Internet technologies such as CSS and (X)HTML.

So, where can you find out more about Mahara Partners?

Finding a Mahara Partner

The easiest way to find a Mahara Partner is to visit the **Partners** section of the Mahara website. See `https://Mahara.org/partners`. This will open a page listing all the Mahara Partners. If you are thinking about using a Mahara Partner, have a look through the description of the services that each one offers and decide whether they are right for you or not. Each partner also has a website that you can visit to find out more information. The Mahara partners are based all over the world, so it is a good idea to find one that is close to wherever you are.

C
Pop Quiz Answers

Chapter 1

Learning about http://mahara.org

1	At mahara.org you can access help and support from community members and Mahara developers in community groups and forums.
2	By using the search member function in mahara.org groups.
3	To give help by answering questions, posing your own questions or to simply stay posted on latest goings-on in the Mahara world.
4	By visiting the partners page of mahara.org.

Chapter 2

Understanding your profile information

1	Five pictures.
2	Throughout the site, for example in the Online users side block or in a group.
3	Goals.

Chapter 3

Files, folders, and tagging

1	Tags.
2	You could structure your folder by file type, audience, topic, reference code, or any other structure that is useful for you.
3	Yes.
4	Your site administrator.

Writing a journal in Mahara

1	You can use your journal for both of these purposes, and more. You may also want to use it to record simple factual information at certain times. For example, you could bullet-point a few key learning points following each lesson in your journal. These can then be used as part of a revision program for an exam.
2	You can attach images and other files to your journal post.

Chapter 4

Creating a page

1	The Wall block.
2	The overriding time removes any individual access times that you have set.
3	This is a difficult to guess URL generated by Mahara that can be sent to people outside the Mahara site to give them access to your page.
4	You can set access to as many groups or individuals as you wish.
5	Yes, you can go back and edit your page access as many times as you wish.

Copying pages

1	Normally it will be called Copy of (page name), but the user who copied it may have renamed it.
2	The page access rights aren't copied when you copy a page. Also, depending on how the other user has set up permissions, not all artefacts are always copied, for example, you may find that some journals or files haven't been copied.

Export

1	Leap2A

Chapter 5

Creating Mahara groups

1	Anybody in the Mahara site can join an open membership group.
2	By making your group publicly viewable, you are allowing people outside of the Mahara to view and access materials in your group without being logged-in.
3	A group administrator can manage group members, create forums, edit and delete forum posts of other users, and edit group settings.

Group forums

1	Moderators can edit or delete topics/posts in your forum. They can also answer closed topics. They should be responsible for checking that users in the forum are following some standard guidelines for behavior and encourage effective discussions.
2	A sticky topic is one that stays at the top of a forum so that it is the first or one of the first that users see.
3	It is best to name your forums generally. Topics should relate to a more specific issue within the forum. It should be clear in a topic subject what is being discussed.

Chapter 6

Managing your institution

1	A CSV file. You could also consider getting your users to self register rather than manually adding them.
2	Any three from the following: They can respond to requests to join the institution, invite members to join the institution, add users, suspend users, turn users into institution staff members and make users into institution administrators.

Course groups, staff members, and tutors

1	Staff members have the ability to create and manage course roles as well as controlled membership groups. Staff members also have the power to create tutors in a group with course roles.
2	In a group with course roles enabled you are able to create tutor members.
3	Tutors are only present in course groups, not across the whole site. They are able to view work which has been submitted for assessment and to release it when it is ready to be returned to the user.

Index

Thank you for buying
Mahara ePortfolios Beginner's Guide

About Packt Publishing

Packt, pronounced 'packed', published its first book "*Mastering phpMyAdmin for Effective MySQL Management*" in April 2004 and subsequently continued to specialize in publishing highly focused books on specific technologies and solutions.

Our books and publications share the experiences of your fellow IT professionals in adapting and customizing today's systems, applications, and frameworks. Our solution based books give you the knowledge and power to customize the software and technologies you're using to get the job done. Packt books are more specific and less general than the IT books you have seen in the past. Our unique business model allows us to bring you more focused information, giving you more of what you need to know, and less of what you don't.

Packt is a modern, yet unique publishing company, which focuses on producing quality, cutting-edge books for communities of developers, administrators, and newbies alike. For more information, please visit our website: www.packtpub.com.

About Packt Open Source

In 2010, Packt launched two new brands, Packt Open Source and Packt Enterprise, in order to continue its focus on specialization. This book is part of the Packt Open Source brand, home to books published on software built around Open Source licences, and offering information to anybody from advanced developers to budding web designers. The Open Source brand also runs Packt's Open Source Royalty Scheme, by which Packt gives a royalty to each Open Source project about whose software a book is sold.

Writing for Packt

We welcome all inquiries from people who are interested in authoring. Book proposals should be sent to author@packtpub.com. If your book idea is still at an early stage and you would like to discuss it first before writing a formal book proposal, contact us; one of our commissioning editors will get in touch with you.

We're not just looking for published authors; if you have strong technical skills but no writing experience, our experienced editors can help you develop a writing career, or simply get some additional reward for your expertise.

Mahara 1.2 E-Portfoloios: Beginner's Guide

ISBN: 978-1-84719-906-5   Paperback: 264 pages

Create educational and professional ePorfolios and personalized learning communities

1. Create, customize, and maintain an impressive personal digital portfolio with a simple point-and-click interface

2. Set customized access to share your text files, images, and videos with your family, friends, and others

3. Create online learning communities and social networks through groups, blogs, and forums

Mahara 1.4 Cookbook

ISBN: 978-1-84951-506-1   Paperback: 308 pages

Over 50 recipes for using Mahara for training, personal, or educational purposes

1. Discover the flexibility of the Mahara system for portfolio use and web page development

2. Filled with tips and techniques for varied uses of features including HTML blocks, Journals, and Collections

3. Learn how to leverage the social networking components and groups features to build collaborative communities

Please check **www.PacktPub.com** for information on our titles

WordPress for Education

ISBN: 978-1-84951-820-8   Paperback: 144 pages

Create interactive and engaging e-learning websites with WordPress

1. Develop effective e-learning websites that will engage your students

2. Extend the potential of a classroom website with WordPress plugins

3. Create an interactive social network and course management system to enhance student and instructor communication

Moodle 2 Administration

ISBN: 978-1-84951-604-4   Paperback: 420 pages

An administrator's guide to configuring, securing, customizing, and extending Moodle.

1. Install and update Moodle on multiple platforms manually and using the CLI

2. Manage courses, cohorts, users, and roles

3. Get Moodle hooked up to repositories, portfolios, and plagiarism detection systems

Please check **www.PacktPub.com** for information on our titles

Lightning Source UK Ltd.
Milton Keynes UK
UKOW06f2021231013

219675UK00009B/646/P